JONAH

Brazos Theological Commentary on the Bible

JONAH

PHILLIP CARY

BrazosPress

a division of Baker Publishing Group
Grand Rapids, Michigan

©2008 by Phillip Cary

Published by Brazos Press
a division of Baker Publishing Group
P.O. Box 6287, Grand Rapids, MI 49516-6287
www.brazospress.com

Printed in the United States of America

Library of Congress Cataloging-in-Publication Data
Cary, Phillip, 1958–
    Jonah /Phillip Cary.
       p.   cm. — (Brazos theological commentary on the Bible)
    Includes bibliographical references and indexes.
    ISBN 978-1-58743-137-1 (cloth)
    1. Bible. O.T. Jonah—Commentaries. I. Title. II. Series.
BS1605.53.C37 2008
224′.92077—dc22   2008019716

For my mother and father:
where blessings begin
in the middle of things

CONTENTS

Series Preface   9
Abbreviations   15
Introduction: Christian Readers of a Jewish Book   *17*

Text   23

Jonah 1: **Jonah Goes Down and the Ship Is Saved**   *27*
   The Word of the Lord, *Jonah, and the Gentiles (1:1–3)*   27
   At Wit's End (1:4–6)   45
   Finding out Jonah (1:7–10)   54
   The Logic of Redemption (1:11–17)   64
   Excursus: The Sign of Jonah   78

Jonah 2: **Jonah's Psalm from the Depths**   *83*

Jonah 3: **The Repentance of Nineveh**   *105*
   Jonah Calls and Nineveh Believes (3:1–5)   105
   The King and God (3:6–10)   112

Jonah 4: **The Repentance of the** Lord   *127*
   Jonah Contends with the Lord *(4:1–4)*   127
   The Parable of the Gourd (4:5–11)   138

Epilogue: **Jonah, Jacob, and the Older Brother**   *163*

Subject Index   175
Scripture Index   181

SERIES PREFACE

Near the beginning of his treatise against Gnostic interpretations of the Bible, *Against the Heresies*, Irenaeus observes that Scripture is like a great mosaic depicting a handsome king. It is as if we were owners of a villa in Gaul who had ordered a mosaic from Rome. It arrives, and the beautifully colored tiles need to be taken out of their packaging and put into proper order according to the plan of the artist. The difficulty, of course, is that Scripture provides us with the individual pieces, but the order and sequence of various elements are not obvious. The Bible does not come with instructions that would allow interpreters to simply place verses, episodes, images, and parables in order as a worker might follow a schematic drawing in assembling the pieces to depict the handsome king. The mosaic must be puzzled out. This is precisely the work of scriptural interpretation.

Origen has his own image to express the difficulty of working out the proper approach to reading the Bible. When preparing to offer a commentary on the Psalms he tells of a tradition handed down to him by his Hebrew teacher:

> The Hebrew said that the whole divinely inspired Scripture may be likened, because of its obscurity, to many locked rooms in our house. By each room is placed a key, but not the one that corresponds to it, so that the keys are scattered about beside the rooms, none of them matching the room by which it is placed. It is a difficult task to find the keys and match them to the rooms that they can open. We therefore know the Scriptures that are obscure only by taking the points of departure for understanding them from another place because they have their interpretive principle scattered among them.[1]

As is the case for Irenaeus, scriptural interpretation is not purely local. The key in Genesis may best fit the door of Isaiah, which in turn opens up the meaning of Matthew. The mosaic must be put together with an eye toward the overall plan.

---

1. Fragment from the preface to *Commentary on Psalms 1–25*, preserved in the *Philokalia* (trans. Joseph W. Trigg; London: Routledge, 1998), 70–71.

Irenaeus, Origen, and the great cloud of premodern biblical interpreters assumed that puzzling out the mosaic of Scripture must be a communal project. The Bible is vast, heterogeneous, full of confusing passages and obscure words, and difficult to understand. Only a fool would imagine that he or she could work out solutions alone. The way forward must rely upon a tradition of reading that Irenaeus reports has been passed on as the rule or canon of truth that functions as a confession of faith. "Anyone," he says, "who keeps unchangeable in himself the rule of truth received through baptism will recognize the names and sayings and parables of the scriptures."[2] Modern scholars debate the content of the rule on which Irenaeus relies and commends, not the least because the terms and formulations Irenaeus himself uses shift and slide. Nonetheless, Irenaeus assumes that there is a body of apostolic doctrine sustained by a tradition of teaching in the church. This doctrine provides the clarifying principles that guide exegetical judgment toward a coherent overall reading of Scripture as a unified witness. Doctrine, then, is the schematic drawing that will allow the reader to organize the vast heterogeneity of the words, images, and stories of the Bible into a readable, coherent whole. It is the rule that guides us toward the proper matching of keys to doors.

If self-consciousness about the role of history in shaping human consciousness makes modern historical-critical study critical, then what makes modern study of the Bible modern is the consensus that classical Christian doctrine distorts interpretive understanding. Benjamin Jowett, the influential nineteenth-century English classical scholar, is representative. In his programmatic essay "On the Interpretation of Scripture," he exhorts the biblical reader to disengage from doctrine and break its hold over the interpretive imagination. "The simple words of that book," writes Jowett of the modern reader, "he tries to preserve absolutely pure from the refinements or distinctions of later times." The modern interpreter wishes to "clear away the remains of dogmas, systems, controversies, which are encrusted upon" the words of Scripture. The disciplines of close philological analysis "would enable us to separate the elements of doctrine and tradition with which the meaning of Scripture is encumbered in our own day."[3] The lens of understanding must be wiped clear of the hazy and distorting film of doctrine.

Postmodernity, in turn, has encouraged us to criticize the critics. Jowett imagined that when he wiped away doctrine he would encounter the biblical text in its purity and uncover what he called "the original spirit and intention of the authors."[4] We are not now so sanguine, and the postmodern mind thinks interpretive frameworks inevitable. Nonetheless, we tend to remain modern in at least one sense. We read Athanasius and think him stage-managing the diversity of Scripture to support his positions against the Arians. We read Bernard of Clairvaux and

2. *Against the Heresies* 9.4.

3. Benjamin Jowett, "On the Interpretation of Scripture," in *Essays and Reviews* (London: Parker, 1860), 338–39.

4. Ibid., 340.

assume that his monastic ideals structure his reading of the Song of Songs. In the wake of the Reformation, we can see how the doctrinal divisions of the time shaped biblical interpretation. Luther famously described the Epistle of James as a "strawy letter," for, as he said, "it has nothing of the nature of the Gospel about it."[5] In these and many other instances, often written in the heat of ecclesiastical controversy or out of the passion of ascetic commitment, we tend to think Jowett correct: doctrine is a distorting film on the lens of understanding.

However, is what we commonly think actually the case? Are readers naturally perceptive? Do we have an unblemished, reliable aptitude for the divine? Have we no need for disciplines of vision? Do our attention and judgment need to be trained, especially as we seek to read Scripture as the living word of God? According to Augustine, we all struggle to journey toward God, who is our rest and peace. Yet our vision is darkened and the fetters of worldly habit corrupt our judgment. We need training and instruction in order to cleanse our minds so that we might find our way toward God.[6] To this end, "the whole temporal dispensation was made by divine Providence for our salvation."[7] The covenant with Israel, the coming of Christ, the gathering of the nations into the church—all these things are gathered up into the rule of faith, and they guide the vision and form of the soul toward the end of fellowship with God. In Augustine's view, the reading of Scripture both contributes to and benefits from this divine pedagogy. With countless variations in both exegetical conclusions and theological frameworks, the same pedagogy of a doctrinally ruled reading of Scripture characterizes the broad sweep of the Christian tradition from Gregory the Great through Bernard and Bonaventure, continuing across Reformation differences in both John Calvin and Cornelius Lapide, Patrick Henry and Bishop Bossuet, and on to more recent figures such as Karl Barth and Hans Urs von Balthasar.

Is doctrine, then, not a moldering scrim of antique prejudice obscuring the Bible, but instead a clarifying agent, an enduring tradition of theological judgments that amplifies the living voice of Scripture? And what of the scholarly dispassion advocated by Jowett? Is a noncommitted reading, an interpretation unprejudiced, the way toward objectivity, or does it simply invite the languid intellectual apathy that stands aside to make room for the false truism and easy answers of the age?

This series of biblical commentaries was born out of the conviction that dogma clarifies rather than obscures. The Brazos Theological Commentary on the Bible advances upon the assumption that the Nicene tradition, in all its diversity and controversy, provides the proper basis for the interpretation of the Bible as Christian Scripture. God the Father Almighty, who sends his only begotten Son to die for us and for our salvation and who raises the crucified Son in the power of the Holy

---

5. *Luther's Works*, vol. 35 (ed. E. Theodore Bachmann; Philadelphia: Fortress, 1959), 362.
6. *On Christian Doctrine* 1.10.
7. *On Christian Doctrine* 1.35.

Spirit so that the baptized may be joined in one body—faith in *this* God with *this* vocation of love for the world is the lens through which to view the heterogeneity and particularity of the biblical texts. Doctrine, then, is not a moldering scrim of antique prejudice obscuring the meaning of the Bible. It is a crucial aspect of the divine pedagogy, a clarifying agent for our minds fogged by self-deceptions, a challenge to our languid intellectual apathy that will too often rest in false truisms and the easy spiritual nostrums of the present age rather than search more deeply and widely for the dispersed keys to the many doors of Scripture.

For this reason, the commentators in this series have not been chosen because of their historical or philological expertise. In the main, they are not biblical scholars in the conventional, modern sense of the term. Instead, the commentators were chosen because of their knowledge of and expertise in using the Christian doctrinal tradition. They are qualified by virtue of the doctrinal formation of their mental habits, for it is the conceit of this series of biblical commentaries that theological training in the Nicene tradition prepares one for biblical interpretation, and thus it is to theologians and not biblical scholars that we have turned. "War is too important," it has been said, "to leave to the generals."

We do hope, however, that readers do not draw the wrong impression. The Nicene tradition does not provide a set formula for the solution of exegetical problems. The great tradition of Christian doctrine was not transcribed, bound in folio, and issued in an official, critical edition. We have the Niceno-Constantinopolitan Creed, used for centuries in many traditions of Christian worship. We have ancient baptismal affirmations of faith. The Chalcedonian definition and the creeds and canons of other church councils have their places in official church documents. Yet the rule of faith cannot be limited to a specific set of words, sentences, and creeds. It is instead a pervasive habit of thought, the animating culture of the church in its intellectual aspect. As Augustine observed, commenting on Jeremiah 31:33, "The creed is learned by listening; it is written, not on stone tablets nor on any material, but on the heart."[8] This is why Irenaeus is able to appeal to the rule of faith more than a century before the first ecumenical council, and this is why we need not itemize the contents of the Nicene tradition in order to appeal to its potency and role in the work of interpretation.

Because doctrine is intrinsically fluid on the margins and most powerful as a habit of mind rather than a list of propositions, this commentary series cannot settle difficult questions of method and content at the outset. The editors of the series impose no particular method of doctrinal interpretation. We cannot say in advance how doctrine helps the Christian reader assemble the mosaic of Scripture. We have no clear answer to the question of whether exegesis guided by doctrine is antithetical to or compatible with the now-old modern methods of historical-critical inquiry. Truth—historical, mathematical, or doctrinal—knows no contradiction. But method is a discipline of vision and judgment, and we

---

8. *Sermon* 212.2.

cannot know in advance what aspects of historical-critical inquiry are functions of modernism that shape the soul to be at odds with Christian discipline. Still further, the editors do not hold the commentators to any particular hermeneutical theory that specifies how to define the plain sense of Scripture—or the role this plain sense should play in interpretation. Here the commentary series is tentative and exploratory.

Can we proceed in any other way? European and North American intellectual culture has been de-Christianized. The effect has not been a cessation of Christian activity. Theological work continues. Sermons are preached. Biblical scholars turn out monographs. Church leaders have meetings. But each dimension of a formerly unified Christian practice now tends to function independently. It is as if a weakened army had been fragmented, and various corps had retreated to isolated fortresses in order to survive. Theology has lost its competence in exegesis. Scripture scholars function with minimal theological training. Each decade finds new theories of preaching to cover the nakedness of seminary training that provides theology without exegesis and exegesis without theology.

Not the least of the causes of the fragmentation of Christian intellectual practice has been the divisions of the church. Since the Reformation, the role of the rule of faith in interpretation has been obscured by polemics and counterpolemics about *sola scriptura* and the necessity of a magisterial teaching authority. The Brazos Theological Commentary on the Bible series is deliberately ecumenical in scope, because the editors are convinced that early church fathers were correct: church doctrine does not compete with Scripture in a limited economy of epistemic authority. We wish to encourage unashamedly dogmatic interpretation of Scripture, confident that the concrete consequences of such a reading will cast far more light on the great divisive questions of the Reformation than either reengaging in old theological polemics or chasing the fantasy of a pure exegesis that will somehow adjudicate between competing theological positions. You shall know the truth of doctrine by its interpretive fruits, and therefore in hopes of contributing to the unity of the church, we have deliberately chosen a wide range of theologians whose commitment to doctrine will allow readers to see real interpretive consequences rather than the shadow boxing of theological concepts.

Brazos Theological Commentary on the Bible has no dog in the current translation fights, and we endorse a textual ecumenism that parallels our diversity of ecclesial backgrounds. We do not impose the thankfully modest inclusive-language agenda of the New Revised Standard Version, nor do we insist upon the glories of the Authorized Version, nor do we require our commentators to create a new translation. In our communal worship, in our private devotions, in our theological scholarship, we use a range of scriptural translations. Precisely as Scripture—a living, functioning text in the present life of faith—the Bible is not semantically fixed. Only a modernist, literalist hermeneutic could imagine that this modest fluidity is a liability. Philological precision and stability is a consequence of, not a basis for, exegesis. Judgments about the meaning of a text fix its literal sense, not the other way around. As a result, readers should expect an eclectic use of biblical translations, both across the different volumes of the series and within individual commentaries.

We cannot speak for contemporary biblical scholars, but as theologians we know that we have long been trained to defend our fortresses of theological concepts and formulations. And we have forgotten the skills of interpretation. Like stroke victims, we must rehabilitate our exegetical imaginations, and there are likely to be different strategies of recovery. Readers should expect this reconstructive—not reactionary—series to provide them with experiments in postcritical doctrinal interpretation, not commentaries written according to the settled principles of a well-functioning tradition. Some commentators will follow classical typological and allegorical readings from the premodern tradition; others will draw on contemporary historical study. Some will comment verse by verse; others will highlight passages, even single words that trigger theological analysis of Scripture. No reading strategies are proscribed, no interpretive methods foresworn. The central premise in this commentary series is that doctrine provides structure and cogency to scriptural interpretation. We trust in this premise with the hope that the Nicene tradition can guide us, however imperfectly, diversely, and haltingly, toward a reading of Scripture in which the right keys open the right doors.

R. R. Reno

ABBREVIATIONS

Acts	Acts	Jas.	James	Neh.	Nehemiah
Amos	Amos	Jer.	Jeremiah	Num.	Numbers
1 Chr.	1 Chronicles	Job	Job	Obad.	Obadiah
2 Chr.	2 Chronicles	Joel	Joel	1 Pet.	1 Peter
Col.	Colossians	John	John	2 Pet.	2 Peter
1 Cor.	1 Corinthians	1 John	1 John	Phil.	Philippians
2 Cor.	2 Corinthians	2 John	2 John	Phlm.	Philemon
Dan.	Daniel	3 John	3 John	Prov.	Proverbs
Deut.	Deuteronomy	Jonah	Jonah	Ps.	Psalms
Eccl.	Ecclesiastes	Josh.	Joshua	Rev.	Revelation
Eph.	Ephesians	Jude	Jude	Rom.	Romans
Esth.	Esther	Judg.	Judges	Ruth	Ruth
Exod.	Exodus	1 Kgs.	1 Kings	1 Sam.	1 Samuel
Ezek.	Ezekiel	2 Kgs.	2 Kings	2 Sam.	2 Samuel
Ezra	Ezra	Lam.	Lamentations	Song	Song of Songs
Gal.	Galatians	Lev.	Leviticus	1 Thess.	1 Thessalonians
Gen.	Genesis	Luke	Luke	2 Thess.	2 Thessalonians
Hab.	Habakkuk	Mal.	Malachi	1 Tim.	1 Timothy
Hag.	Haggai	Mark	Mark	2 Tim.	2 Timothy
Heb.	Hebrews	Matt.	Matthew	Titus	Titus
Hos.	Hosea	Mic.	Micah	Zech.	Zechariah
Isa.	Isaiah	Nah.	Nahum	Zeph.	Zephaniah

INTRODUCTION

Christian Readers of a Jewish Book

Preliminary matters about the context of the book of Jonah, its historical setting, the meaning of key terms, and the identity of its characters will be discussed in the comments on 1:1–2, but several features of the interpretive approach I take here are worth pointing out up front, as it were before we begin.

First of all, this is a Christian reading of the Scriptures of Israel, which Christians call the Old Testament because it contains the ancient covenant to be fulfilled by Jesus Christ. Like the whole Bible, the book of Jonah is about Christ and therefore about all those who find their life in him. It is also about the people of Israel, of whom Christ is king. He is not called Messiah, King of the Jews, for nothing. Christians can find themselves in this story only by identifying themselves with the Jews, his people, and thereby with the sole Israelite in it—the same person with whom Jesus identified when he described himself as "the sign of Jonah." So the point of the story will be found in these identifications: Christians have life only in Christ, who is the King of the Jews, who are the chosen people beloved of the LORD God, represented in this story by Jonah.

There are a great many things to be uncomfortable about in these identifications, and that is why it is good that this story is a comedy, as recent scholarship has often emphasized. Jonah is a comic figure: he does everything wrong, almost, yet through him the LORD God of Israel does everything right. All's well that ends well, as another great comedian once put it, but of course in the middle of the story things can get to be quite a mess. Jonah is a ridiculous excuse for a prophet—the holy man as screwup—and we are just like him. Why Jesus would want to identify with him is a deep mystery, as deep as his love for the rest of us. We will get to that point a little later, in the excursus on the sign of Jonah. But we

17

have to begin by being willing to identify with the ridiculous prophet ourselves. Otherwise we miss the point of the joke.

There is an ancient tradition of Christian reading called typology or figural reading that encourages such identifications, but also a strand of Christian moralism that resists them. How many sermons have you heard in which the scriptural screwup is taken as an object lesson in who *not* to be—as if the task of the Christian life is to do better than all those biblical characters who keep getting into so much trouble? It is as if the lesson were: the last thing we want in the world is to think of ourselves as sinners, as if we had anything in common with the stupid, disobedient, unbelieving wretches we see in the biblical story. We must be quite different from people like Peter (how could he *think* of denying Christ?) or Moses (if you're like *him*, you'll never get into the promised land!) or Sarah (don't you *dare* laugh at God!) or of course Jonah (how *could* he be so mean to those Ninevites?). You can do better than these people, the moralistic preacher would have you believe. Instead of identifying with them, your task is to be different from them and thus make yourself immune from the frightful things that happen when God starts to deal with people like that.

Such moralism, in its more scholarly forms, can be breathtakingly anti-Semitic. It is astonishing how regularly Christian commentators have warned other Christians against following in the footsteps of bigoted tribalistic Jews like Jonah. The lesson they would have us learn is to be better than these wrathful Old Testament prophets who do not know how to think merciful thoughts toward other people, the way we Christians do. Such lessons breathe the kind of self-righteousness for which the Bible invented the phrase "holier than thou" (Isa. 65:5 King James Version)—a phrase describing the spirituality of those who set themselves apart from their fellow Israelites by a religion that is better than God's. Any reader who wants to be above the prophetic animus directed against Nineveh is certainly playing at being holier than God, who has many words of wrath to say about Nineveh and the Assyrian Empire of which it is the capital.

How did we get to be so stupid? How did we become so convinced of our moral superiority that we must look down on Jonah as if he had failed to learn an elementary lesson about being nice to other people? An abundance of Sunday school material makes this the moral of the story—be nice to people, unlike Jonah the Jew—as if we are supposed to get our children to believe that God is the kind of dolt who is interested in teaching us such lessons in complacency. Thereby we display not only our self-righteousness but our aesthetic blindness, our thick inability to recognize a good story when it hits us between the eyes. For to perceive what this wonderful story is teaching us requires us to see that the joke's on us. Once we learn to read Bible stories in this way, identifying with the people who get it all wrong, we will be able to understand the real moral lesson about our moralistic misreadings, especially in their anti-Semitic form. There is a deep immorality in Christian moralism, which insofar as it presents itself as superior to Jewish self-righteousness, Pharisaism, and intolerance, is thoroughly self-righteous, "Pharisaical," and intolerant—murderous at heart (just ask the Jews), full of dishonesty and self-deception, not to mention wicked defiance of the God of Israel who loves his people.

And in case you didn't get it, now is the time to laugh. At the risk of explaining the joke (but what can I do? I'm a commentator) let me say: if you have already laughed at least once so far, then you're getting it. If not, then lighten up. These words about stupidity, self-righteousness, and wrath don't mean we can't have a good laugh—a laugh that's good for us. *Morally* good for us. For the joke really is on us, and it's about time that we learned to laugh at it.

What's more, you need to be able to laugh when you enter into situations of unbearable tension, which tend to arise when Gentiles talk about Jews. There is no getting around such talk when Christians read the Bible, especially when the Christians are Gentiles convinced, as I am, that an essential step to finding Christ in the Old Testament is what can be called an "Israelogical" reading of the text, one that sees figures like Jonah representing not only Christ, the church, and Christians, but also Israel and Judah. Indeed, I think we cannot see *how* Jonah represents Christ, the church, and Christians without seeing how he represents Israel and Judah. If I am right about this, then a good Christian reading of Jonah will necessarily have a great deal to say about the Jews.

The tension that it would help to be able to laugh about stems from the inescapable need of Gentile Christians to read the Scriptures of Israel as if they were *our* Scriptures too, as if all the good and bad things they had to say about God's chosen people were said also about us. This is rather tactless of us, and if it weren't for the resurrection of the Messiah of Israel, in whom Gentiles too are justified by believing, we would have no right to read Israel's story this way. The authorization of such reading can only be a gift, an utterly gratuitous blessing bestowed on Gentiles by the King of the Jews, in whom we believe. Yet now, because of what he has done, it does belongs to our obedience to this good and gracious King that we read Jewish stories as being about us, too.

This is not quite so strange as it seems, because the work of Christ is the culmination of God's gracious election, his choosing Israel to be a blessing for all nations. This is vitally important to understand: it is a good thing for Gentiles that the Jews are God's elect, his chosen people, just as it is a good thing for the whole world that one Jew, Jesus Christ, is God's chosen one, his beloved and only begotten Son. Let me say it again: it is good for all of us that the Jews are the chosen people. If we don't get this, then we will hang on to our anti-Semitic self-righteousness as if our salvation depended on it. Christians have in fact done exactly that for much, much too long, and we need to learn to read the Bible otherwise.

The book of Jonah is a good place to start. For as we learn to laugh at ourselves in the figure of Jonah, we may also notice how much it hurts, which is to say: how much it costs Israel to *be* the chosen people, a blessing for all nations. Just because it's a comedy doesn't mean Jonah doesn't go through hell. He says he does (in Jonah 2), and he's not kidding. Here we find not just comic suffering but profound comfort: Jonah does nearly everything wrong and gets into the deepest trouble imaginable, yet all the while he remains God's beloved and chosen one, not to mention one of the most successful prophets in the whole Bible. He is Israel, but he is also us. And we need his story.

It is a story about the relation of Jew and Gentile, whose particular message is embedded in a narrative strategy of parallelism, which it is good to be apprised of from the start. The book of Jonah is divided rather neatly into two halves, in both of which Jonah is a blessing to the Gentiles despite himself. He is indeed the only Israelite in the story, and because of him everybody else is saved from the wrath of God: a boatload of Gentiles in the first half, and the great city of Nineveh in the second half. But there are differences between the two halves, and a central premise of this commentary is that noticing these differences is key to understanding the point of the story.

The important differences to notice, I will suggest, have to do with all the things that do not go as well in the second half of the book as the first. At the end of the first half, Jonah has been saved from the depths of hell and all the Gentiles are sailing safely home, worshiping the LORD as they go. At the end of second half, the Gentiles are saved from destruction but they do not know the name of the LORD or even whether they are saved, and Jonah is in the middle of a confrontation with the LORD God in which it is apparently up to Jonah to decide whether to be reconciled with the mercy of God—which is not really good news, if you think about it. Still, the open-endedness of the book, concluding with a divine question that puts the ball in Jonah's court, is *so* wide open, leaving so much undecided, that we have to look well beyond Jonah himself to see where it is headed. Once we do, the same identifications as before come front and center, and we must ask how the people of Israel might have answered Jonah's question, how we ought to answer it, and (the good news) how Jesus Christ has answered it.

Two other features of the interpretation presented in this commentary are unusual enough to be worth drawing attention to before we start. First of all, I take it for granted that it is always important how the deity is referred to in the text: whether by the generic term *Elohim*, translated "God," or by the proper name of the God of Israel, translated "LORD." In the ancient world everybody knows about God, but very few people outside Israel know the name of the LORD. This is a big deal throughout the Bible, and you would think commentators would pay attention to it, but they don't. Commentaries on Jonah routinely proceed as if all ways of referring to the deity were equal, whereas they plainly are not. If you know about God but don't know the name of the LORD, then you don't really know who God is. This makes all the difference in the world for the fortunes of the sailors in the first half of the book as well as for the Ninevites in the second, and it explains a number of peculiar things in the narrative, such as the odd bit of retrospective information supplied by the narrator in 1:10, which has puzzled commentators so much that some of them have considered drastic measures like removing it from the text. But once we see that the pagan sailors do not automatically identify "LORD" and "God" as we do, this puzzling piece of the text begins to look like a brilliant and subtle literary device.

Another distinctive point of interpretation, where so far as I know this commentary is unique, is of critical importance for understanding the book's concluding question. The plant or gourd that protects Jonah in the final chapter and then withers away is, like several such plants in the Old Testament, an image of the lineage of David that seems to have died out. What is at issue in the open question at the end of the story is therefore not only God's pitying the Gentiles but his apparent abandonment of Israel, his allowing the messianic line to disappear like "a son of the night," as he himself so poignantly puts it. So as the book concludes, Jonah is a Jew without a Messiah, and he is not happy about it. His anger is not just about a dead plant but about the most important thing in the world, the future Son of David, which only he in the whole story is in a position to know about. The question he must answer concerns Israel's hope for the coming of a Son of David who is both the King of the Jews and the hidden desire of all nations. The absence of this beloved Son is almost too much to bear. The comedy of Jonah is likely to turn tragedy unless the Messiah himself comes to answer the question by becoming the sign of Jonah.

Several of my debts are worth pointing out, for those who wonder where my particular readings come from. I owe much to Karl Barth's theology of the word and election of God and to Kendall Soulen's exegesis of the biblical theme of Jew and Gentile. That Christ could be called the eternal repentance of the LORD (see comment on 4:2) is the sort of thought one has while reading Barth, whereas the importance for *Christian* theology of Israel's election as a blessing to all nations is something to be learned from Soulen's *God of Israel and Christian Theology*. In addition to these two prime theological inspirations, I am much indebted for my practical understanding of how biblical narrative works to Robert Alter's *Art of Biblical Narrative*. Meir Sternberg's *Poetics of Biblical Narrative* is also valuable, providing a theoretically weighty account of the kind of reading that Alter is so good at teaching you how to practice.

For assistance with Hebrew, which I do not read, I have used various interlinear Bibles, but have also found the appendix to Phyllis Trible's *Rhetorical Criticism* invaluable, with its painstakingly literal translation of the text, not exactly into English but into a kind of English X-ray of the verbal structure of the original. I am also much indebted to my colleagues and friends, especially Ray Van Leeuwen and Kent Sparks, who know their Hebrew and are willing to share. (I owe thanks to Ray for more insights than I could name, but one that comes especially to mind is his pointing out that Jacob insists on returning the blessing to Esau in the end, a point that unlocked for me much of the meaning of the biblical stories of jealous brothers.) Of course, all the mistakes I have made—I have not always followed their advice—are my own.

The English text of the book of Jonah on which this commentary based is my own modified amalgam of the King James Version, Revised Standard Version, New American Standard Version, and English Standard Version, all of which preserve some sense of the syntax and vocabulary of the original. (I understand there is also now a Christian Standard Version, which has the same aim. Other translations, which purport to give the meaning of the original rather than an approximation of its words, are useless for exegesis.) I have also made much use of the online version of Strong's Concordance (http://www.eliyah.com/lexicon .html), which lists not only the occurrence of words in the King James Version but also the corresponding Hebrew, so that one can learn, for instance, when a Hebrew word translated "evil" in one verse is the same as one translated "trouble" in another verse and when it is not. The text of the book of Jonah that follows is a product of these discoveries: wherever it has the word "evil," the same Hebrew word underlies it, and where it has the word "trouble," the Hebrew is different— and likewise with words like "call" and "cry," "spoke" and "said," "throw" and "hurl" and "cast," and many other sets of near synonyms. (An important exception is the word "people," which has to do duty for both the Hebrew word for ethnicity, *am*, and the Hebrew word for population, *enosh*, which used to be translated "men.") I have made similar modifications in other biblical passages quoted to illustrate the meaning of the book of Jonah.

Hearing the echoes between texts is one of the most important ways of perceiving the riches of the Scriptures, contributing to the wonderful experience I have had with this powerful little story, which always opened up new depths whenever I trusted an honest question or perplexity to lead me further in. Over and over again I found myself putting into practice the old hermeneutical rule that Scripture is the best interpreter of Scripture. There is a surprising number of discoveries to be made by following this rule to the best of one's ability. For example, the identification of the gourd with the lineage of David, which might be very surprising at first, follows quite naturally from well-established patterns of biblical imagery concerning growing and dying plants and the protection provided by their shade. It has been overlooked perhaps because Christian readers are not really accustomed to an Israelogical reading of Scripture, in which the meaning of obscure biblical parables and sayings is rooted in God's love for his people Israel. We are used to ecclesiological readings, discerning typological references to the church, the new people of God, in the Old Testament. But we neglect to situate them in the context of references to Israel, the ancient people of God, which is the rather obvious and primary meaning of much of the Bible including, as I suggest here, the parable of the gourd in the book of Jonah. Since the gourd represents the messianic hope fulfilled by Jesus Christ, the Israelogical reading of this text is key to unlocking its christological meaning. This is one more way in which Christians need to read more like Jews if we are to read the Bible well.

TEXT

¹:¹And the word of the LORD came to Jonah son of Amittai, saying, ²"Arise, go to Nineveh, that great city, and call against her, for their evil has come up before my face." ³And Jonah arose to flee from the face of the LORD to Tarshish. He went down to Joppa and found a ship going to Tarshish. And he paid the fare and went down into it, to go with them to Tarshish, away from the face of the LORD.

⁴But the LORD hurled a great wind onto the sea, and there was a great storm on the sea, so that the ship was about to break up. ⁵And the sailors feared, and each cried out to his god, and they hurled the wares that were in the ship into the sea, to lighten it for them. But Jonah had gone down into the furthest recesses of the boat, had lain down, and was fast asleep. ⁶And the captain came and said to him, "What's with you, sleeping? Arise, call upon your god! Perhaps the god will consider us and we won't perish."

⁷And each of them said to his neighbor, "Come on, let's cast lots, so we may know on whose account this evil has come to us." And they cast lots and the lot fell on Jonah. ⁸And they said to him, "Please tell us on whose account this evil has come to us. What is your occupation and from whence have you come? What is your land and from what people are you?" ⁹And he said to them, "A Hebrew am I, and the LORD, the God of heaven, I fear, who made the sea and the dry land." ¹⁰Then the people feared a great fear, and they said to him, "What is this you have done?" For the people knew that he was fleeing from the face of the LORD, for he had told them.

¹¹And they said to him, "What shall we do with you, so the sea will be calm for us?" For the sea was getting more and more stormy. ¹²And he said to them, "Pick me up and hurl me into the sea, and the sea will be calm for you. For I know that it is on account of me that this great storm is upon you." ¹³But the people dug in to turn to dry land but couldn't, because the sea was getting more and more stormy upon them. ¹⁴And they called to the LORD and said, "Please, LORD, please let us not perish for the soul of this man and do not lay upon us innocent blood. For

you, Lord, have done as you desired." ¹⁵And they picked Jonah up and hurled
him into the sea, and the sea ceased from its raging. ¹⁶And the people feared a
great fear of the Lord, and they offered sacrifice to the Lord and vowed vows.
¹⁷And the Lord prepared a great fish to swallow up Jonah. And Jonah was in the
guts of the fish three days and three nights.

²ʼ¹And Jonah prayed to the Lord his God from the guts of the fish:

> ²"I called from my trouble to the Lord,
>   and he answered me.
> From the belly of Sheol I shouted,
>   and you heard my voice.
> ³You threw me into the deep,
>   into the heart of the sea,
>   and the flood surrounded me.
> All your waves and breakers have passed over me.
> ⁴Then I said, 'I have been cast out from before your eyes,
>   yet I will look again to your holy temple.'
> ⁵The waters encompassed me, up to my soul.
> The depths surrounded me;
>   reeds were wrapped around my head.
> ⁶To the bases of the mountains I went down;
>   the earth with its bars was about me forever.
> But you brought my life up from the pit, O Lord, my God,
> ⁷when my soul was fainting within me.
> The Lord I remembered,
>   and my prayer came into you in your holy temple.
> ⁸Those who pay heed to vanities of deceit
>   forsake their loving-kindness.
> ⁹But I with a voice of thanksgiving will sacrifice to you;
>   I will pay what I have vowed.
> Salvation is the Lord's!"

¹⁰Then the Lord said to the fish, and it vomited Jonah out on dry land.

³ʼ¹And the word of the Lord came to Jonah a second time, saying, ²"Arise,
go to Nineveh, that great city, and call to her the call that I speak to you." ³And
Jonah arose and walked to Nineveh according to the word of the Lord. Now
Nineveh was a city great before God, a three days' walk. ⁴And Jonah started to
enter the city, one day's walk. And he called and said, "Forty days and Nineveh
shall be overturned!" ⁵And the people of Nineveh believed God, and they called
a fast and put on sackcloth from the greatest to the least of them.

⁶And the word reached the king of Nineveh, and he arose from his throne and
took off his mantle and covered himself with sackcloth and sat in ashes. ⁷And
he cried and said in Nineveh, by decree of the king and his great ones, saying,

"Let human and livestock, herd and flock, not taste anything, not feed or drink any water. [8]Let human and livestock be covered with sackcloth and let them call mightily to God; let them each turn from his evil way and from the violence in their hands. [9]Who knows? Perhaps God may turn and repent and turn from his burning anger and we won't perish." [10]And God saw what they did, how they turned from their evil way, and God repented of the evil he spoke of doing to them, and did it not.

[4:1]And it was grievous to Jonah, a great evil, and he was angry. [2]And he prayed to the LORD and said, "Please, LORD! Wasn't this what I said when I was in my own country? That is why I fled to Tarshish before. For I know you are 'a gracious and merciful God, slow to anger and abounding in loving-kindness,' and you 'repent of the evil.' [3]And now, LORD, please take my soul away from me, for it is better for me to die than live." [4]And the LORD said, "Is it good for you to be angry?"

[5]Then Jonah went out from the city and sat to the east of the city. There he made himself a booth and sat down under it in the shade until he should see what would become of the city. [6]And the LORD God prepared a gourd and made it come up over Jonah to be a shade upon his head, to deliver him from his evil. And Jonah rejoiced in the gourd with great joy. [7]And God prepared a worm when the morning came up the next day, and it struck the gourd and it withered. [8]And it came to pass that when the sun rose God prepared a strong east wind, and the sun struck Jonah's head and he fainted, and he asked his soul to die and said, "It is better for me to die than live." [9]And God said to Jonah, "Is it good for you to be angry about the gourd?" And he said, "It is good for me to be angry enough to die." [10]And the LORD said, "You pitied the gourd, for which you did not labor nor did you make it grow great, which was a son of the night and perished as a son of the night; [11]and should I not pity Nineveh, that great city, in which there are more than a hundred twenty thousand human beings who can't tell their right hand from their left—and also abounding in livestock?"

JONAH 1

Jonah Goes Down and the Ship Is Saved

The Word of the Lord, Jonah, and the Gentiles (1:1–3)

1:1 And the word of the Lord came

The book of Jonah does not begin with Jonah but with something better—the word of the Lord. It all begins with the word of him who began everything by saying, "Let there be light," and there was light. This is the same word that was with God in the beginning, as the gospel testifies (John 1:1). Of course the book of Jonah does not proceed like the gospel to speak of the word made flesh. Yet it does speak of the word made manifest, its intentions made clear, setting things in motion and bringing unexpected things to light. The same creative word that brought the world into being also governs history and makes its presence felt in human life, just as it quite visibly drives the events in this text.

This is a story originated, enfolded, and driven by God's address to his creatures. It begins with the word of the Lord, and in the end this same Lord has the last word. In the middle, his word moves events forward, telling the fish to vomit up Jonah, sending him on to Nineveh with a message, then arguing with the distraught prophet when Nineveh is spared. Jonah's flight itself is initiated by this word in a negative way—indeed the word often operates in a negative way—for what Jonah runs away from is the commission he has been given by this same word. And the sailors' throwing him overboard is occasioned by the revelation of the name of the God who sends this word, the name of the Lord. So the whole story is initiated and moved along and shaped by the word of the Lord, without which there would be no story, no movement, no tension, no flight, and no rescue. There is no meaning to the story, and the events of the story are inconceivable, without this word and without the particular deity whose word this is.

It is important to bear in mind that the LORD is the name of a particular deity, the God of Israel. As in most older Bible translations in English, the word "LORD" here, when printed with all capital letters, is not a title like the word "Lord" with only an initial capital letter. The LORD is not just any lord, nor is he merely "God" in general. He is altogether different from the gods of the nations, and "the LORD" is his name, not his title. When the God of Israel says, so often in the Scriptures, "I am the LORD," this is not an announcement that he is the boss but rather a proclamation of his name (Exod. 3:15; cf. Isa. 42:8: "I am the LORD; that is my name!").

The complication is that "LORD" is not actually his name, but represents a word used to avoid saying his name. The capital letters in the English text are a reminder that the underlying Hebrew word is the name for the God of Israel, transliterated *YHWH*. This name is, in Jewish reckoning, *the* name, *ha-shem*, the sacred name that is too holy to be spoken. When Jewish readers come upon the written name while reading Scripture aloud (for instance, in synagogue), they do not speak it but instead say *Adonai*, the Hebrew word for "Lord." This custom is reflected in older English translations of the Bible, where "Lord" stands for *Adonai* and "LORD" for *YHWH*. For English speakers to call God "the LORD" is thus to follow this Jewish practice of calling upon the name of the God of Israel without actually uttering it.

It is right, a good and joyful thing, for Gentile Christians especially to adopt this distinctively Jewish practice, because the name of the LORD is now given to Jesus Christ. Every Christian who confesses that Jesus Christ is Lord is proclaiming the name of Israel's God—without actually uttering it, just like the Jews—and saying this is the name given to Jesus, the name above every name at which every knee shall bow and every tongue confess (Phil. 2:9–11). The Gentiles' confession that Jesus is Lord fulfills the purpose of the repeated proclamation of this name in the Old Testament, the ancient witness to Israel's God: "So that all the peoples of the earth may know that the LORD is God and there is none other" (1 Kgs. 8:60). It is this same name that we hallow, keeping it holy and set apart precisely by not taking it upon our lips, when we pray as our Lord taught us: "Our Father, who art in heaven" (Matt. 6:9).

So the God whose word sets this story in motion is not just any God. He has a proper name, and it is not enough to describe him as God in general, as if he were nothing but the supreme Being, the first principle of all things, and the ultimate Good. He is indeed all these things, but we will miss the point of the story if we do not recognize from the beginning that he is first and foremost the LORD, the God of Israel. By virtue of the election of grace, in which he chooses Israel as his own people, the God who speaks in this story cannot be understood or identified apart from the history of Israel in which he is inextricably involved, just as we do not know Jesus if we do not recognize him as the Son of David, the King of the Jews. This is the LORD, the God of Israel, the God of Abraham, Isaac, and Jacob who revealed his name to Moses as I AM or (perhaps more accurately) I AM

WHO I AM or (perhaps more accurately yet) I WILL BE WHO I WILL BE (Exod. 3:14). Like Exodus, the book of Jonah is a story showing us who he will be, and thus at bottom it is about the proclamation of the name of the LORD. Through all the vicissitudes of the narrative, one thing is certain: he will be the God who has always already taken sides with Israel. It is precisely this God and no other— the LORD God of Israel—who sends Jonah to Nineveh, to the people who will eventually destroy Israel, so that even Nineveh might hear the word of the LORD and be saved. We will miss the surprise, the irony and offense of this story, if we do not reckon with the particular God who speaks here.

The word of the LORD *came*. We don't learn how it came: by dream or vision, by inner voice or the voice of another prophet instructing him. As usual, Scripture has little interest in the experience by which the word speaks to us. But insofar as it is experienced at all, it is experienced as an external word, as something that *comes* to Jonah, quite other than the thoughts of his own heart and in fact quite unwelcome. There is no quest for God here, no attempt to demonstrate how knowledge of God is possible, and certainly no desire to experience God's presence in our lives. The story proceeds as if the word of the LORD is unquestionably the most real thing in the world and that the rest of the universe can only catch up with its reality.

In that sense the book of Jonah is concerned with how we know God, but the question is asked from the opposite perspective from what is usual nowadays. We are invited, as it were, to ask the question from the word's own point of view. The world needs all the help it can get catching up with the reality of the word of the LORD—and in fact is doing all it can to run away. So what shall the word do about such hearers? What shall the word do about a prophet who flees from the LORD, sailors who call upon all kinds of gods but are terrified at the name of the LORD, a monster of the deep who swallows up the LORD's servant, an ignorant city that hears the word and repents, a prophet who hates the success of the word he is given to preach and talks back to the LORD? The problem of the book is not how we are to know God but how God is to deal with us and our more or less persistent efforts not to know him. Only a fool is capable of not knowing God—of hearing the word of the LORD and not believing it—and the LORD must deal with such fools somehow. From this book we learn how graciously the LORD deals with fools such as us.

Finally, before we proceed let us go back for a moment to the first word, that unobtrusive little particle "and" (often translated "now" or "but") whose force depends so much on drawing no attention to itself. It is over before we notice it, so that we can get on with thinking about weightier words such as "the word of the LORD." But now is the time to look back at the service it has performed. It got us into the story before we knew it, getting us thinking about the events to come as if they belonged to some larger series of events already under way, as if somehow we had just turned the page to begin a new chapter in a much larger book. And of course that is exactly what has happened. Not only does the book of Jonah belong to the much larger book called the Bible, the book of books, but the story of Jonah is a chapter in the much larger story of the dealings of the LORD God with Israel and the nations. So we begin by getting into the middle of things, *in medias res*, as classical literary theory puts it (Horace, *Ars poetica* 146). For this is how we always begin. Even our birth is always in the middle of an ongoing family history. Only the word of the LORD can begin at the very beginning. We follow.

to Jonah

Jonah's name means "dove." It is a name for someone you love. The beloved in the Song of Songs is called "my dove" (Song 2:14) and is praised for the loveliness of her "dove's eyes" (1:15). We must not forget that through all his troubles and failings, flight and disobedience, Jonah is the beloved of God. Like Israel herself, it can be said of him: "Whoever touches you touches the apple of God's eye" (Zech. 2:8).

Jonah is also a sign of peace, like the dove who comes back to Noah with an olive branch, signaling the end of God's wrath and the subsiding of the waters that for a time overcame the earth (Gen. 8:10–11). When the Holy Spirit descends upon the Lord Jesus coming up from the waters of baptism, it takes the form of a dove as a reminder of this Noachic sign of peace on earth to the one in whom God is well pleased (Matt. 3:16–17; Mark 1:10–11; Luke 3:21–22). Jonah the dove stands midway between these two signs, both of which signify a renewal of the earth protected from destructive waters: in the beginning stands a covenant with the earth itself, which will never again be flooded by waters that destroy all flesh (Gen. 9:13–17), and at the end a new covenant ushers in a new heaven and earth where there is no more sea (Rev. 21:1). Despite himself, Jonah becomes a sign of peace to those voyaging on dangerous waters and to those in the evil city who, one might have thought, had no prospect but destruction on the last day. Surrounded by chaos and evil, bearing a message that breathes condemnation, desiring only destruction, Jonah is nonetheless by God's appointment the dove of peace. Despite appearances, the book of Jonah—this book of the dove—is in the end a comedy of peace, like the history of the world.

son of Amittai,

The name "Amittai" is related to the word "amen" and means "truth." So Jonah is the dove of truth, sign of a love that is not just warm and soft like a dove but also faithful and reliable as a rock, founded on the truth. One could hardly choose a better name for a prophet of the LORD than "Jonah son of Amittai."

This name also locates Jonah in a particular place and time, providing us with the occasion to deal with some important preliminary matters. We know of Jonah son of Amittai from one other reference in the Old Testament: according to 2 Kgs. 14:25–27, he was a prophet active in Israel (i.e., the northern kingdom) during the reign of Jeroboam II. He is thus in a double sense a prophet of Israel, and for clarity's sake we must distinguish the two senses.

There is a broad and a narrow sense of the name "Israel." In the broad sense it refers to all the descendents of Jacob, renamed "Israel" after his struggle with God (Gen. 32:28). In the narrow sense, which is much less well known today, it refers to only ten of the twelve tribes descended from the twelve sons of Jacob. These are the ten tribes that broke away from the Davidic monarchy in Jerusalem after the death of Solomon, forming a separate kingdom in the north with its capital in Samaria under Jeroboam I (1 Kgs. 11:26–12:19). In the historical narratives of the books of Kings and Chronicles, the name "Israel" is typically used in this narrow, less familiar sense, referring to the northern kingdom. This is important for us to bear in mind as we discuss the story of Jonah, because things can be said about Israel in the narrow sense that are not true of Israel in the broad sense: for instance, that the nation of Israel was destroyed by the Assyrian Empire, whose capital city was Nineveh.

This feature of Jonah's identity as a prophet of Israel would no doubt have been uppermost in the minds of the original readers of the story, who were almost certainly not from the northern kingdom. They were Jews, also in a narrow and unfamiliar sense. They came from the southern kingdom, consisting of the tribes of Judah and Benjamin but named "Judah" (and later "Judea") after the larger of the two tribes. They were therefore called "Judeans," a name that eventually became the English word "Jews."

It is often helpful to remind ourselves of the English word's origin. For instance, when Jesus stays away from Judea because "the Jews" are seeking to kill him (John 7:1), the Greek term is *Ioudaioi*, which is more accurately translated "Judeans." The word "Jews" is inaccurate because it obscures the connection between Judeans and Judea that is obvious in the original, and thus makes it hard to see that one of the crucial sources of friction between Jesus and "the Jews" in the Gospels is geographical. Jesus is from the north and is in that sense not a Judean but belongs rather to Israel, the remnant of a nation that is no more. Hence Jesus is not a Jew in the narrow sense of the term, which explains why in the Gospels he sometimes addresses the Jews as if they were not his own people.

Of course in the broad sense with which we use the word today, in which "Jew" refers to any Israelite, Jesus is emphatically and unmistakably a Jew, and indeed everything in the Christian story of salvation depends on this: if Jesus is not a Jew, then Christianity is false. However, precisely because he is not a Jew in that earlier and narrow sense—not from Judea—the gospel teaching that he belongs to the house of David, the King of Judah, and therefore rightfully claims to be Messiah, the King of the Jews, was particularly stunning in its original context. For the distinction between Israelite and Jew, though unfamiliar to us, was surely not lost on the people who first followed Jesus or sought to kill him. Here was an Israelite, a successor to the northern prophets Elijah, Elisha, and Jonah, heading south to Judea and entering its capital like a triumphant king, as if he also were successor to David and Solomon. In him the lost northern kingdom lives, and in him also lives the lost royal lineage of the southern kingdom. In him indeed the two kingdoms are resurrected, reunited, and become together one kingdom of God. Such was the claim Jesus made by riding into Jerusalem on a donkey, like the Son of David riding in triumph and peace after defeating the enemy, putting aside his warhorse and chariot (Zech. 9:9–10).

The distinction between Israel and Judah was also very much on the minds of the original readers of the book of Jonah. Most scholars think the book is postexilic, which is to say it was written after the Babylonian exile of the Judeans. This means it was written long after the lifetime of Jonah son of Amittai, indeed long after the Assyrian exile of the Israelites and the subsequent destruction of the Assyrian Empire itself. It speaks of Nineveh in the past tense (3:3), as if it were already a thing of the past, which means that the people of Israel (in the narrow sense: the ten tribes) were already a thing of the past. Imagine reading this book, then, as a Judean at a time when your people are all that is left of Israel (in the broad sense: the twelve tribes). Your relatives to the north have been swallowed up by the empire of the Ninevites, which is now destroyed, and your own people were swallowed up by the empire of the Babylonians but have been vomited back out as if from the belly of the beast. And now in this story of a northern prophet swallowed up, vomited out, and sent to Nineveh, you see the story of both Israel and Judea, and you ponder the difference.

Assuming the book of Jonah is indeed postexilic, then its original readers were Jews, that is, Judeans, at about the earliest moment in history when that term could be used to refer to the whole surviving nation of Israel, the remnant of God's chosen people. Also, they were Jews at the earliest moment in history when one could begin to speak of a specifically Jewish religion rather than the religion of ancient Israel. It is the religion of a people who had lived for decades in exile without their own land, king, or temple but only the law of Moses—the *Jewish* law, as we can now call it—to govern them and keep them alive as a people. Having been kept alive by that law, they returned to find "the people of the land" (Ezra 4:4), the ignorant folk who had been left by their conquerors and did not know the law of the LORD (2 Kgs. 24:14). So the Judeans were required to teach them also to observe the law (Ezra 7:25). Eventually the teachers of the Jews came to use the term "people of the land" (*am ha'aretz*) to refer to all Israelites (in the broad sense) who refused to observe the law properly. From this Judean perspective, what seems to have been wrong with Jesus was that he was one of "the people of the land," a teacher who did not promote as strict an observance of Jewish law as the true Judeans.

In sum, then, the book of Jonah was addressed originally to the people of Judah, the returning exiles of the southern kingdom, but it tells a story about a prophet from Israel, the lost northern kingdom, in which the Judeans were no doubt meant to see themselves. Jonah's experience with Nineveh clearly derives its meaning from Israel's experience with the Assyrian Empire, whose capital city was

Nineveh, and just as clearly points toward Judah's experience with the Chaldean Empire, whose capital city was Babylon.

Jonah himself can be located a bit more precisely in the history of Israel. He is the successor of the great northern prophets Elijah and Elisha (in fact he is the next prophet named in 2 Kings after the death of Elisha) at a time that must count as the apogee of the northern kingdom's power. His one recorded act outside the book of Jonah is an oracle, described as "the word of the LORD, the God of Israel, which he spoke by his servant Jonah son of Amittai, the prophet, who was from Gath-hepher" (2 Kgs. 14:25). In accordance with this oracle, King Jeroboam II expanded the territory of Israel, restoring its ancient borders from Lebo-hamath (located near what is now the northern border of Lebanon) to the Sea of the Arabah (i.e., the Dead Sea), even capturing the city of Damascus, the capital of the Aramean kingdom, which had been the most pressing enemy of Israel in the time of Elisha (14:25, 28). At the same time, however, the prophet Amos was actively preaching against Jeroboam II (Amos 7:9–11) and prophesying that a nation would come to oppress Israel throughout the expanse of these newly restored borders, "from Lebo-hamath to the Brook of Arabah" (6:14). Doubtless he was prophesying the coming of the resurgent Assyrian Empire, which soon overshadowed Israel's brief moment in the sun.

In this one lone reference to Jonah outside the book of Jonah, we are not given the content or wording of the oracle he delivers. We can guess that his message had a very different tone from Amos's, less hostile to Jeroboam. But all that the biblical narrator tells us is that the reason behind the restoration of Israel's borders is not what Jeroboam might think. It is Israel's great national moment in the sun, but the biblical comment is poignantly bleak: "For the LORD saw that the affliction of Israel was very bitter, for there was none left, bond or free, and there was none to help Israel. But the LORD had not said that he would blot out the name of Israel from under heaven, so he saved them by the hand of Jeroboam" (2 Kgs. 14:26–27).

What history records as the greatest splendor of Israel, the Bible treats as a time of affliction and helplessness. When Israel had no one to help, the LORD stepped in and saved them by making use even of the wicked Jeroboam II, who followed in the ways of his namesake, Jeroboam I, the king who inaugurated the northern kingdom in a reign of idolatry, complete with golden calves (1 Kgs. 12:25–33). Things are going very badly in Israel at the height of its national glory, and it is only the mercy of the LORD that staves off disaster for a little while, because the LORD had not said he would blot out the name of Israel from under heaven.

The history of Israel goes downhill from there. After the forty-one prosperous years of the reign of Jeroboam II (2 Kgs. 14:23), the next two kings are assassinated in less than a year (15:8–15). But yet more ominous is the rise of the Assyrian Empire, which was perhaps already behind the waning of Israel's earlier enemy, the Aramean kingdom. From now on, the only successful kings of Israel are those who find ways of buying off Assyria. For instance, King Menahem rules ten years and escapes assassination, but must pay the king of Assyria to keep his throne (15:17–22). The next long-ruling king of Israel, Pekah, sees many of his people, especially from the area of Galilee, taken captive to Assyria (15:29). He is assassinated and replaced by Hoshea, Israel's last king, who proves to be a disloyal vassal to the king of Assyria and is therefore deposed (17:3–4). There follows an Assyrian invasion of the land of Israel and a three-year siege of its capital city, Samaria (17:5). When Samaria falls, the people of Israel are carried away to exile in the Assyrian Empire, never to return. It is to this empire that the LORD sends Jonah son of Amittai.

We do learn one more thing about Jonah from 2 Kings. He is from the town of Gath-hepher, which is in Galilee, only a few miles from Nazareth. When Jesus describes himself as "the sign of Jonah" (see Excursus) he is associating himself with a prophet whose hometown is within easy walking distance of his own. Of course, no prophet is honored in his own hometown, as Jesus reminds us, citing the examples of Elijah and Elisha (Luke 4:24–27). But this all the more identifies him with the tradition of northern prophets to which Jonah belongs. Jesus, who grew up just down the road from Jonah, succeeds him just as Jonah succeeded Elisha, who succeeded Elijah.

saying,

Now we are about done with preliminaries and ready to get started with the story, which is set in motion by the word of the LORD. But one further distinction is worth introducing before we plunge into the middle of things. It is obvious from the unfolding of this story that what the word of the LORD *says* is not always the same as what it *does*. The content of the word is hostile to Nineveh, and yet its actual effect is to save Nineveh. Since this is a Bible story, we must take this outcome to be providential, which is to say that the intention of the word is revealed by its effect, not just by its content. The content of the word is against Nineveh, but its intent and effect are otherwise. For to speak is to act, and the act of speech is not just the revelation of some content, but is itself a deed that changes things—especially when it is the LORD who speaks.

1:2 "Arise, go

The first thing the word of the LORD has to say to Jonah the Israelite, the prophet, the beloved dove of truth, is: get up and get going. It is as if nothing in this story moves until the LORD speaks. He often speaks like this to the prophets, as for instance to Elijah: "Arise, go to Zarephath" (1 Kgs. 17:9), and "Arise, go down to meet Ahab, king of Israel, who is in Samaria" (21:18), and "Arise, go meet the messengers of the king of Samaria" (2 Kgs. 1:3).

Behind this phrase is an obvious feature of the ancient world that is so unfamiliar to us that it is easily overlooked. They had no post offices, much less telephone and email. If you want to send a message, you must either go yourself or send a messenger. The latter option is available only to kings and other people of power and wealth, who can command the services of others. So to send a message in this ancient context, the LORD acts like a king commissioning a messenger and sending him on his way. This is the original sense of the term "mission," from the Latin *missio*, meaning "sending" (see also the Greek verb at the root of the word "apostle," *apostellō*, meaning "to send out").

Like all the prophets, Jonah is a man on a mission, just like the apostles sent out from God to speak his word, bearing a message from the great king of all kings. But unlike emails and other forms of communication made possible by modern technology and bureaucracy (the post office being, all in all, one of the most efficient bureaucracies we have), the messenger is a man with a mind of his own who may not only fail to arrive but try to start an entirely different story.

to Nineveh,

Nineveh would be instantly recognizable to the original readers of this story as the capital city of Assyria. Although a great and ancient empire, Assyria was relatively weak in the first half of the eighth century, when Jonah son of Amittai was active during the reign of Jeroboam II of Israel (786–746 BC). It underwent a resurgence under Tiglath-pileser III (744–727 BC), who began to reign over Assyria a year or so after Jeroboam's death. Within a quarter century Samaria had fallen to Assyria (722/721 BC), which carried off the people of Israel into exile, from which they never returned. It is after this, near the beginning of the next century, that Nineveh becomes the capital of Assyria under Sennacherib (705–681 BC). It remained the capital throughout the seventh century, until it was destroyed by the Medes and the Babylonians in 612 BC. It was never rebuilt. Its demise marks the beginning of the new Babylonian Empire, which becomes the nemesis of the southern kingdom, eventually conquering Jerusalem at the beginning of the sixth century (597 BC), assaulting it again and destroying it in 587 BC, and carrying off the Judeans into exile, from which they eventually returned about half a century later, beginning in 539 BC.[1]

The book of Jonah is almost certainly written with these returning exiles in mind, for whom the destruction of both Israel and Nineveh is old news but the future of Judah and Babylon is still an open question. Anachronistically, Nineveh is the city to which the prophet is sent in the book of Jonah, even though at the time of Jonah it is not yet the capital of Assyria. The important point is that it is the capital known to the book's original readers, who may have been hazy about which city was the capital of Assyria during the reign of Jeroboam II in the early eighth century but who knew all about Nineveh, the capital of the Assyrian Empire when it was destroyed for good near the end of the seventh century.

1. For details of this history, see *The Cambridge Ancient History*, vol. 3.2: *The Assyrian and Babylonian Empires and Other States of the Near East, from the Eighth to the Sixth Centuries B.C.* (ed. John Boardman et al.; 2nd ed.; Cambridge: Cambridge University Press, 1991).

Thus the book of Jonah is not a historical report about the activity of the prophet in the time of Jeroboam II but a parable written for returning Judean exiles about what might have been—and indeed about what could still happen, depending on how the original readers, the Judeans coming back to their homeland in the sixth century, handle their equivalent of Jonah's situation at the end of the book. To turn this story into a historical account of the prophet being sent to a city that is not yet the capital of Assyria would disrupt the parallel on which the whole book is based. For what the book of Jonah aims to get us thinking about is the situation faced by the Judeans with respect to Babylon, the capital of the empire that has swallowed up Judah, as it is illuminated by the situation of Jonah with respect to Nineveh, the capital of the empire that swallowed up Israel. It is a book about the suffering of the chosen people and what that has to do with the salvation of the Gentiles.

that great city,

The repeated epithet "great city" in the book of Jonah is always associated specifically with a God's-eye view of Nineveh. The epithet appears twice more in the LORD's speeches (3:2; 4:11), and the greatness of Nineveh before God is also mentioned in 3:3. Here, where it first appears in the story, it might be taken to mean nothing more than what we would now call "greater Nineveh" (see comment on 3:3). But the phrase will acquire more resonance as it recurs over the course of the book of Jonah. And of course we cannot forget its resonance with the eschatological lament over the evil city in the last book of the New Testament: "Fallen, fallen is Babylon the great! . . . Alas, alas for the great city!" (Rev. 18:2, 16). From what we have surmised of the original readers of the book of Jonah, they too could not but think of Babylon the great when they read of the great city of Nineveh.

and call against her,

The reference to Nineveh in the feminine is striking but hardly unusual. The capital of a mighty empire is called "she," just like a huge, well-armed battleship. All ships and cities and peoples, it seems, are "she," no matter their size and power, as if all had need of some tender lover and protector like the LORD, who is a husband for Israel, a people called "she" many times in the Bible despite bearing the name of a man.

Could the LORD possibly aim to take Nineveh as his beloved also? The prophets of Israel have said stranger things before. Witness Isaiah: "In that day Israel will be the third with Egypt and Assyria, a blessing in the midst of the earth, whom the LORD of hosts has blessed, saying, 'Blessed be Egypt my people, and Assyria the work of my hands, and Israel my inheritance'" (19:24–25). But such strange blessing does not yet appear at the beginning of the book of Jonah. In fact, as we begin, things are looking mighty ominous for Nineveh.

At this point we do not hear the content of what Jonah is to say to her, only its manner or (we could say) its communicative or rhetorical form. He is to *call*, the same verb used to describe a prayer of invocation: calling upon a god (1:6), calling to the LORD (1:14; 2:2), and calling mightily to God (3:8). It implies speaking up so as to get someone's attention. But instead of calling *to* her (as in 3:2, when Jonah's commission is renewed) the wording here would have him calling *against* her (more literally, "upon her"). It sounds like Jonah is not so much to address Nineveh or appeal to her as to make an announcement or even a cry for help, shouting Nineveh's evil aloud for all the world to hear, giving voice to the outcry of her victims.

Here is another unfamiliar feature of the ancient world to bear in mind: there is no such thing as a police force. Except for rulers and aristocrats who have their own soldiers or private guards, a person being attacked has no recourse but to call aloud and wait for the help of whatever people nearby are strong and just. Hence the original meaning of the English phrase "hue and cry": it is the shout that goes up in a peasant village calling everyone to drop their work in the fields and pursue some thief or murderer. The Bible speaks often of this kind of crying, as when the LORD hears the cry of his people enslaved in Egypt (Exod. 3:7, 9) or when the great outcry against Sodom and Gomorrah comes up to him (Gen. 18:20; 19:13), so that the LORD himself comes down "to see whether they have done altogether according to the outcry that has reached me" (18:21). For when the violent make up a whole city (and it is evident from Gen. 18–19 and Ezek. 16:49–50 that the sin of Sodom consists primarily of violence rather than sexual perversion), the outcry can do no good unless it comes to God in heaven, who is king and judge over the whole world.

for their evil has come up before my face."

The face of the LORD is his presence. To come before his face is like entering the presence of a great king, for he is indeed "the great king above all gods" (Ps. 95:3). Since it is the work of a king to render judgment, one of the things that comes before the face of the LORD is the evil of injustice. We shall see that the word "evil" designates the core of what is fearsome about the encounter between the LORD and human beings. Here at the beginning of the story, what comes before the face of the great king above all gods is human evil. The implication, to which the story does not yet give words, is that more evil is to come because of this evil, for the judge of the whole earth is one who does justice, rendering evil for evil.

The nature of Nineveh's evil is not mentioned, but it hardly needs to be. It is more infamous than the evil of Sodom and Gomorrah. As the prophet Nahum says at the end of his oracle against Nineveh, "Upon whom has not come your unceasing evil?" (Nah. 3:19). Nahum in fact provides just the background we need to understand Jonah's attitude toward Nineveh. "Woe to the city of blood," he says, "full of lies and plunder, never without victims" (3:1). He celebrates its destruction as good news, a confirmation of the goodness of the LORD:

> The LORD is good, a stronghold in a day of trouble.
> 　　He knows them who take refuge in him. . . .
> Behold! On the mountains the feet of one
> who brings good tidings,
> 　　who proclaims peace.
> Celebrate your festivals O Judah,
> 　　fulfill your vows,
> for never again shall the wicked invade you;
> 　　they are utterly cut off. (Nah. 1:7, 15)

The destruction of Nineveh means the salvation and peace of Judah, still threatened by the Assyrian Empire in the interval between Israel's exile and her own. So even the feet of those who bring the news of Nineveh's downfall are greeted with words of gladness (made familiar by the quotation from Nah. 1:15 found in Isa. 52:7 and set to music by Handel in *The Messiah*).

What the book of Nahum tells us about the book of Jonah is what it meant for Israelites or Judeans to rejoice in the goodness of God in the face of the evil of Nineveh: it meant expecting to hear the good news that Nineveh is no more, so it can never again invade their land and drench it with the blood of their children. So when we discover toward the end of the book how much Jonah hates Nineveh and desires its downfall, we must not imagine that it is because of some transient grudge or chauvinistic prejudice. This is the empire that would wipe his people off the face of the earth. Unless we do not care for our own children and do not desire to protect them from enemies coming to slaughter or enslave them, we are in no position to think our morality so superior to Jonah's as it is usually made out to be. The justice of the LORD in toppling empires and vindicating the oppressed is a thing to be celebrated. That is a given in the Bible. The deeper question is how much better the LORD's mercy is than his justice, how much farther it goes toward overthrowing evil and setting things ultimately to rights (see comment on 4:2).

1:3 And Jonah arose

We hear of no response that Jonah makes to the word of the LORD. Does he talk back? Does he say *anything*? If so, we do not learn what it is. Perhaps a secret here is withheld from us. Certainly his thoughts are withheld from us. All we see is how he gets moving.

The first move he makes is right. Just as the LORD commands, he gets up and gets going. "Arise," says the LORD in 1:2, and in 1:3 we read that "Jonah arose." When God speaks to you, you cannot sit still. But there Jonah's obedience ends.

to flee from the face of the LORD

We might well wonder what Jonah could be thinking. How can anyone flee from God, who is everywhere? The psalmist's prayer is surely not lost on Jonah:

"You know when I sit down and when I rise up; you discern my thoughts from afar" (Ps. 139:2). But what Jonah and his readers know—they practically feel it in their bones—is that there is more to the presence of the LORD than omnipresence and omniscience. There is a specific place where the God of Israel meets his people, hears their petitions, and judges their cause (1 Kgs. 8:27–40), a place, we could say, of the LORD's presence in person. When the original Judean audience of this story heard of Jonah fleeing from the face of the LORD, they would have thought immediately of the temple in Jerusalem. Scripture calls the temple "the house of the LORD": it is the place of his name, where his eyes and heart are always directed (9:3). It is in effect the palace of the LORD, the King of kings, and the sanctuary or holy of holies is his throne room, a place that is still called the "presence room" in palaces today, for it is where one comes into the presence of the king in person. The biblical idiom for this presence in person, as we have already noticed (see comment on 1:2), is "the face of the LORD." For to meet the king in person is to face him, to be confronted by him face to face. To be before his face is to be near enough to hear the word of his mouth.

All this imagery hovers in the background when the text speaks of fleeing from "the face of the LORD" (usually translated a bit more abstractly as "the presence of the LORD"). The imagery gives Jonah's flight a definite direction in sacred space: he is running away from the temple, the holy city, the holy land—away from all that signifies the presence of the LORD in person. It is as if he were doing his best to turn his back on the face of the great king and run out of the throne room, afraid to look him in the face and unwilling to hear the word of his mouth. His flight is not an attempt to escape divine omnipresence so much as an effort not to heed this word.

It is, of course, equally foolish and doomed. The point is that in fleeing the face of God Jonah is not making a mistake about the metaphysics of divine omnipresence, but committing the deeper error of disobedience. Jonah's literal, geographical movement away from the face of the LORD in Jerusalem gives a visible trajectory to his heart's refusal to hear the word of the LORD and obey it. But it also contains implicitly this good news: Jonah can no more escape obedience to this word than he can escape the omnipresence of God. That is what Jonah apparently does not yet know.

But aside from the sheer brazen foolishness of the thing, we need to consider more closely the motives of Jonah's flight. Everything in the story up to this point suggests that Jonah's mission represents the one and only opportunity for an Israelite to put an end to the Assyrian Empire. Going by what little we have heard so far of the word of the LORD concerning Nineveh, Jonah has every reason to hope that its future will be just like Sodom and Gomorrah's. Any Israelite who trusted in the LORD and had an ounce of fighting spirit would be eager to go and announce her doom. It has all the appearance of a mission to save his people, as if the LORD finally woke from his long slumber to keep covenant with Israel, to be faithful and righteous and execute judgment against the great ones of the earth who would swallow up his chosen people so that they are no more. But instead Jonah chooses to save his own skin.

Or so it appears. Later Jonah will offer a very different explanation for his flight: he wants to give the LORD no opportunity to have mercy on Nineveh (4:2)! Perhaps this counts as a nobler motive than sheer cowardice. But Jonah is quite an unreliable character, and we cannot really trust his account of things. Furthermore, there is no doubt that at this early stage in the telling of the story, we are meant to be lured into thinking that Jonah is running away because he is scared. We are supposed to think that he is driven by the same fear and unbelief that would drive any of us: faced with the prospect of calling out to the great city of Nineveh in the name of the LORD God of Israel, he does not believe the word of the LORD and does not trust that the LORD can deliver him from Nineveh's evil. So he runs in the other direction.

Let us, then, allow the story to lure us. Let us assume that Jonah flees the face of the LORD because he is afraid. It is a reasonable enough emotion under the circumstances. Sending an Israelite to preach to Nineveh in the eighth century BC is a little like sending a Jew to preach to Berlin in the 1930s. Short of a stupendous miracle, the prospect of success is not high, and a forlorn, gruesome death looks much more likely. Jonah flees because, in effect, he is not ready to be crucified just yet.

Hence it is all the more important that the great crucified prophet identified with him so explicitly (see Excursus). Jonah, like father Abraham and all Israel, is chosen by God for the blessing of all the families of the earth (Gen. 12:3; 22:18; 28:14; cf. Acts 3:25), but he is a chosen one who flees his election and the mission that comes with it, as chosen ones are wont to do in the Bible. The only absolute exception is the chosen one whose mission, it turns out, is to identify with Jonah. Jesus Christ, the chosen one who never for a moment turns in the opposite direction from where God sends him, has the mission of identifying with Jonah, the chosen one who flees his mission, and thereby redeeming all those who flee and exile themselves from the presence of God. To be the uniquely obedient chosen one, Jesus must stand in the place of the prophet Jonah, the disobedient fool, the elect one who tries his best to refuse the task of the elect but ultimately fails. One must suspect that Jonah ultimately fails to escape his election because the word of the LORD that comes to him is none other than the word that ultimately takes his place, taking upon himself the sin of Jonah, his flight and disobedience, and his three days in the abyss.

So let us follow where the story lures us. We will get to Jonah's own account of his motives soon enough.

to Tarshish.

Jonah heads toward Tarshish, in the opposite direction from Nineveh, in the Mediterranean instead of Mesopotamia. Unlike Nineveh it is a city famous for wealth not power, one that trades with Israel but poses no military threat. No doubt it is a cosmopolitan place where he can hope to find a few fellow exiles with whom to keep company, far from home but still able to get news through the famous ships of Tarshish, which carry goods from everywhere in the Mediterranean (1 Kgs. 22:48; 2 Chr. 9:21; Isa. 60:9).

Tarshish is not so well known today. Indeed, modern historians can only guess where it really was. The most favored guess is the Phoenician port in Spain known to the Greeks as Tartessos, which would be far away indeed. But the ancient Jewish historian Josephus, writing in Greek (*Jewish Antiquities* 1.6.1 §127), makes a different proposal and identifies Tarshish with the city of Tarsus, which is not far from Antioch on the eastern side of the Mediterranean, north of Israel. If that is so, then Jonah's destination has New Testament resonances: he is fleeing his inevitable mission by heading toward the city from which Paul the apostle, originally known as Saul of Tarsus, came to take up his unexpected mission.

And that is not the only New Testament resonance. On his way to Tarshish, Jonah passes through a city associated strongly with the memory of the apostle Peter, who is literally "the son of Jonah" (Matt. 16:17) as well as the successor of Jonah the prophet in the LORD's mission to the Gentiles.

He went down to Joppa

The LORD says "arise," and Jonah arises: he gets up in order to go down. He goes down not just in the sense of going down to sea level like all those who "go down to the sea in ships" (Ps. 107:23), but also in a striking movement on the map of sacred geography. From a Judean perspective, all travel away from Jerusalem means going *down* from the temple mount where God is present. This hint at the holy place from which Jonah descends is as much as we hear of Jerusalem, on which Jonah resolutely turns his back. Neither Jerusalem nor Israel is even named in the book of Jonah. Evidently Jonah is trying not just to leave them behind but to forget them. Yet they are always there behind his back, exerting an unseen but palpable pull on everything he does.

The action of the whole story takes place outside sacred space: first in the commercial, multicultural town of Joppa, then in the unhallowed waters of the sea, an abyss of death and destruction, and then in the great, wicked city of Nineveh and its environs. Yet as Jonah's flight is defined by what he flees from, so all the world outside sacred space is defined by the sacred space it is not, and the question of the story is whether that place of sacred presence is a good thing even for these other places. Can it be that an ethnic hodgepodge of people at sea, or even the greatest city of the world, might find its true blessing in the holy place from which Jonah descends and flees? Could Jonah's flight and self-imposed exile actually give them the emissary from this place that they have long needed?

This much is clear: for Jonah to head down to the coast is to head toward the Gentiles. It was along the seacoast just south of the Phoenician port of Sidon that Elijah, the great prophet of the northern kingdom, restored life to the son of the widow of Zarephath, who was not one of the people of Israel (1 Kgs. 17:8–24;

cf. Luke 4:25–26). Retracing Elijah's footsteps, the yet greater prophet of the north, Jesus of Nazareth, also went down to the coastland of Tyre and Sidon and healed the child of a Syrophoenician woman whom Matthew startlingly describes as a "Canaanite," using the name for a people whom the law of the LORD labels an abomination to be utterly destroyed (Deut. 7:1–5). This is the woman who, rebuffed by Jesus because "it is no good taking the children's bread and giving it to the dogs," won his admiration by replying, "Yes, Lord, but even the dogs under the table eat the children's crumbs" (Matt. 15:21–28; Mark 7:24–30). Evidently she was not the only one of her people who sought him out, for among the crowds following him around was a great multitude from Tyre and Sidon (Mark 3:8; Luke 6:17). Perhaps this is why, when Jesus warns the cities of Galilee about the day of judgment, he holds out Tyre and Sidon as examples: if they had seen the same works of Christ that were preformed in Chorazin and Bethsaida of Galilee, he says, they would have repented in sackcloth and ashes (Matt. 11:21–22; Luke 10:13–14). They would have responded like Nineveh, as we may put it—indeed as Jesus himself puts it (Luke 11:32; Matt. 12:41). Perhaps part of the reason he chooses to mention these two cities in particular is because so many people from that coastland actually did follow him, repent, and believe. At any rate, these are the kind of people that Jonah finds as companions on the boat into which he descends, the kind of Gentiles who seem to have a proclivity for believing the prophets of Israel and being healed by them.

Jonah finds his boat specifically at Joppa (now Jaffa, near Tel Aviv), which is the only Mediterranean port easily accessible to a Judean, situated on the only natural harbor on the eastern shore of the Mediterranean between Phoenicia and Egypt. It was the place to which the cedars of Lebanon were shipped for the building and rebuilding of the temple (2 Chr. 2:16; Ezra 3:7). Assigned to the tribe of Dan in the biblical apportionment of the land of Israel (Josh. 19:46), it was usually under Philistine control, as the tribe of Dan could not control the seacoast and migrated further north (19:47–48; cf. Judg. 18). It seems that the people of Israel were not sailors (when Solomon builds a fleet, it must be manned by sailors from Tyre; 1 Kgs. 9:26), and Jonah evidently meets none of his countrymen in Joppa. So we must imagine a city claimed by Israel but inhabited by Gentiles, important for what little contact Israel has with the sea, busy with commerce and occupied by many peoples, languages, and gods. It is not secular but pluralist, as multireligious as it is multiethnic, a microcosm of the known world, as port cities tend to be. Here no one god rules all and money talks.

Joppa figures in the New Testament as one of the first places the gospel spreads among the Gentiles. Many of its people believe in the Lord after Peter comes and raises a disciple named Tabitha from the dead (Acts 9:36–43), and it is in Joppa that Peter has the inspired dream that teaches him that even Gentiles can be clean (10:9–16, 28). We could think of it as the place on the borders of the Holy Land where the mercy of the Lord Jesus begins to overflow beyond Israel, pouring out to the whole world. In doing so it follows in Jonah's footsteps.

Of course Jonah has no intention of preaching good news to the Gentiles when he goes to Joppa, heading for Tarshish. But neither did Peter when he went to Joppa, nor Saul when he came from Tarsus. The prophet is precursor to the apostles precisely in the intensely ironic relation between his intention and God's sending. The mission that God has for his people is often quite different from the mission statements they write for themselves. But the LORD God of Israel has a way of getting his way with his people, for the blessing of the nations. Hence it is essential that Peter and Paul, like Jonah their precursor, did not choose their status as apostles or missionaries. As their Lord made clear, "You did not choose me, but I chose you" (John 15:16). This is his story, not theirs, which is why it is in the end not the story of something vain and unreliable like human religious experience but rather of something glorious and triumphant, the grace of God for all nations.

and found a ship going to Tarshish.

Jonah has moved from sacred to profane, from the presence of the LORD in the holy place of Israel to the world of commerce and technology, emphasized by the threefold repetition of the word "Tarshish," the name of Jonah's destination, in this one verse (1:3). In the ancient understanding of sacred space, "profane" does not mean obscene or wicked, but simply outside the sacred precincts, in an area not consecrated to a god but also not necessarily unclean. It is the sphere where humans go about their business not burdened by the immediate awareness of divine presence. It is the place where they build ships, which are perhaps the most advanced technological achievement of the ancient world—especially the ships of Tarshish, which were famous for carrying heavy cargos of precious metals over long distances, together with all kinds of luxury items: "gold and silver, ivory and apes, and peacocks" (1 Kgs. 10:22). So here at Joppa, Jonah finds some of the most impressive achievements of human craft, power, and wealth. He has a use for these things, though they prove to be not strong enough to save him.

And he paid the fare

We must remember that money itself is a relatively new and sophisticated element in the ancient economy. Not everybody has it, and much of the village economy of the Middle East operates without it, paying its debts in kind—for instance, when peasants pay rent by giving up much of their harvest to an overlord. The very fact that Jonah can pay a fare puts him on the high end of ancient society, an upscale customer. He has mobility and can belong, if he wishes, to a larger world than the holy land of Israel.

and went down into it,

In one sense, we could suppose that Jonah is moving up in the world, heading in the direction of wealth and power. But the text warns us against that supposition by repeating its description of Jonah's movement as a descent: he "goes down" into this ship of Tarshish, falling yet further away from the face of the LORD and thereby drawing that much closer to death, like those who, as the Bible often puts it, "go down to the pit" (Ps. 28:1; 30:3; 88:4; 143:7; Prov. 1:12).

Some memorable passages about the ships of Tarshish in the books of the prophets reinforce this warning. Isaiah, for instance, pictures the LORD bringing down everything the world looks up to, including the ships of Tarshish:

> For the LORD of hosts has a day
>   against all that is proud and lofty,
>   against all that is lifted up and high,
> against all the cedars of Lebanon,
>   lofty and lifted up,
>   and against all the oaks of Bashan,
> against all the high mountains
>   and against all the lofty hills,
> against every high tower
>   and against every fortified wall,
> against all the ships of Tarshish
>   and against all the beautiful craft;
> the loftiness of man shall be brought down,
>   and all the haughtiness of men shall be made low,
> and the LORD alone shall be exalted on that day. (Isa. 2:12–17)

And then there is a passage from the oracle Ezekiel addresses against Tyre, the Phoenician city on the Mediterranean seaboard north of Joppa. Also known for its wealth and splendor, Tyre will go down like a ship sinking on the high seas, carrying all its cargo to the bottom:

> The ships of Tarshish carried your wares;
>   you were filled up and heavy in the heart of the sea.
> Your rowers have brought you to the high seas;
>   the east wind has wrecked you in the heart of the sea.
> Your riches, your wares, your merchandise,
>   your sailors and your pilots,
>   your caulkers, your merchants,
>   and all your warriors within you,
> with all the company that is with you,
> sink into the heart of the sea on the day of your ruin. (Ezek. 27:25–27)

The prophet has his finger on the pulse of every rich person's nightmare. What if our cities, our civilizations with all their technology and power and wealth, go down like a ship foundering at sea? The whole infrastructure of our opulence is frailer than we like to imagine, buoyed up over the heart of the sea like a fragile wooden vessel that could easily be swallowed up by the abyss tomorrow. This is the nightmare evoked by the eschatological lament over Babylon the great in the last book of the Bible:

> And all shipmasters and seafaring men, sailors and all whose trade is on the sea,
> stood afar off and cried out when they saw the smoke of her burning:
>> "What city was like the great city? . . .
>>> Alas, alas for the great city,
>> where all who had ships at sea grew rich by her wealth!
>> In one hour she has been laid waste." (Rev. 18:17–19)

Fleeing in the opposite direction from Nineveh, Jonah is nonetheless descending into the heart of the nightmare that always threatens the wealth of the great city.

to go with them to Tarshish, away from the face of the Lord.

Jonah thinks he is going with these Gentile sailors to Tarshish, the land of profane wealth and success, far from the face of the Lord, but of course the Lord has other plans. This is a good point at which to consider the larger significance of Jonah's flight. Throughout this story Jonah represents Israel among the nations, Israel indeed alienated from Israel, the people separated from the land, going down to exile among the Gentiles. In Jonah 1 (Jonah 2 will be different) this exile is depicted as Israel's own movement, a flight from before the Lord in which the people of God turn their backs to his face, seeking respite in what turns out to be danger and chaos and destruction, putting their trust in the frail inventions of human craft, power, and wealth.

All the more striking, then, that the Lord Jesus, Israel's God in the flesh, chooses to identify with this fool of a prophet fleeing the face of the Lord. It is a choice of great humility, indeed humiliation. The church in her moments of greatest pride, which are far too many, would rather not follow her Lord in such choices, but separates herself in her own estimation from wayward, disobedient, and unbelieving Israel. Precisely in this separation from God's chosen people, which her Lord did not will, she finds herself among Gentiles, almost wholly Gentile herself. She thus finds herself willy-nilly in exile with Jonah. There is no escaping this path of exile in history—not for God's chosen people. And so also individual Christians may follow Jonah's story, knowing that they have often enough followed Jonah's path downward, away from the face of the Lord.

At Wit's End (1:4–6)

1:4 But the Lord hurled a great wind onto the sea, and there was a great storm on the sea,

The second round of the Lord's altercation with Jonah begins. We have heard the word of the Lord to Jonah and Jonah's response (or rather nonresponse) of fleeing from the face of the LORD. Now it is the LORD's turn to do something about what Jonah has done. Whereas in the first round he spoke, now he acts.

It is about the most active intervention imaginable, short of destroying the world. Indeed it is a reminder of the flood in Noah's time by which he did destroy the inhabited world. But the language here is more violent than in the Noah story. The biblical narrative has at its disposal many ways of describing the LORD's sovereignty over all the events in the universe. Later in this story, for instance, the LORD is said to prepare or appoint a fish (1:17), a gourd (4:6), a worm (4:7), and a strong east wind (4:8). But the wind here is different: he *hurls* it as if it were a weapon, a spear or a stone meant to smash the little human vessel to bits.

Both the wind and the storm are "great," a recurrent word in the book of Jonah. Not only Nineveh (1:2; 3:2, 3; 4:11), the wind, and the storm, but also the fear of the sailors (1:10, 16), the fish that swallows Jonah (1:17), the aristocracy of Nineveh (3:5, 7), the evil that Jonah finds in the salvation of Nineveh (4:1), and his delight in the gourd that protects him (4:6) are described as "great." It is as if to remind us that this is a story about great things. One might think at this point that it is just a story about a few people on a boat, but it is far bigger than that. The greatest forces in the world are in play here, and great things are at stake. And the poor sailors are in the middle of it, threatened by a power far too great for them.

"Great is the LORD, and abundantly to be praised; his greatness is unsearchable," sings the psalmist (145:3). An unsearchable greatness is necessarily a transcendent greatness, greatness beyond all greatness. It is greatness that, unlike the size of a great city or the extent of the sea, cannot be measured. Behind the great wind and the great storm, hurling them at the little boat, is something great beyond all greatness. Yet it is the greatness of unfathomable loving-kindness, as the psalmist proceeds to teach us:

> The LORD is gracious and merciful,
>   slow to anger and *great in loving-kindness*.
> The LORD is good to all,
>   and his mercies are over all that he has made. (Ps. 145:8–9)

This teaching echoes the founding proclamation of the name of the LORD in Israel's history (Exod. 34:6–7), which as we shall see is the crucial bone of contention between the LORD and Jonah (see comment on 4:2). Jonah is angry with the LORD's slowness to anger, the greatness of his mercy and loving-kindness, and the crucial issue to be resolved between them is whether the LORD should indeed extend his mercies over all that he has made. Jonah says he knew about this greatness of divine mercy from the beginning and that is why he fled.

So it is the greatness of God's mercy and loving-kindness that pursues Jonah on the high seas and will not let him escape. Of course the sailors don't know this, so they must fight against the greatness of the wind and storm without benefit of any glimpse of the unfathomable mercy that hurls these things at them. To them the great mercy of the LORD looks like cruel disaster and the end of the world.

so that the ship was about to break up.

It is as if the world itself is about to break up. The orderly little human world of a ship at sea, so carefully constructed and maintained, is overwhelmed by the vast unruly waters surrounding it on every side. No work of human hand or mind, no technology or skill, is a match for the huge inhuman power of the waters, a power of disorder that resolves all things back to their elements, shattered wood and dismembered flesh. It is like Noah's flood inside out: back then it was the whole created order drowned in a watery chaos except for the one ship of safety carrying the remnant of creation, but now it is the one ship about to be broken and swallowed up, returned to as good as nothing while the rest of creation goes on as before. At this point, all the world Jonah has is this fragile wooden structure borne up by hostile waters and populated by terrified seamen.

1:5 And the sailors feared,

The book of Jonah began with a dialogue, faulty as it was, between a man and his God. Now the interaction between them widens to take in a new set of characters, a crew of sailors from all over, representing many nations, as we can infer from their worshiping many gods (1:5). As the second round of action proceeds, it is not Jonah who responds to the LORD's fearsome activity but these poor terrified sailors, who have no idea what's hit them. It is as if Jonah ducked the LORD's punch and it hit the boat instead, and now the sailors have to figure out what's happening to them and what to do about it.

It is not exactly fair, of course, but the LORD has better things than fairness in mind. By the end of the chapter these people will not only be safe under his protection but they will know the LORD by name. This is no accident; it is what is supposed to happen when Gentiles get in the way of the altercation between the LORD and his beloved. At the end of the book it is precisely this message that the LORD impresses upon an angry, suffering Jonah. Should not the LORD have compassion on all these poor ignorant Gentiles (4:11)? Indeed, what do you think you are for, Jonah—you prophet, God's chosen one, dove of truth? Your troubles all along have been for the blessing of the nations. This is the deeper sense in which Jonah cannot succeed in his project of fleeing before the face of the LORD. Despite initial appearances, the LORD has sent him for the good of the Gentiles, and for the good of the Gentiles he goes, even when he flees.

But in the middle of the story there are moments of terror and confusion for Jonah and everyone else. Let us return to the poor sailors, caught in the middle of this. No doubt they have seen wind and storms before, but as the previous verse hinted, there is something outsized about this particular wind and storm, which (as we learn next) promptly causes everyone to get religion. Evidently these people recognize right away that there is a meaning in this great storm—if only they can find out what that is before it's too late.

Their fear has a definite shape, which we can see portrayed in the psalm:

> Those who go down to the sea in ships,
>   who do business in great waters,
> they see the works of the LORD,
>   and his wonders in the deep.
> For he commands
>   and raises the stormy wind,
>   which lifts up the waves of the sea:
> they mount up to the heavens
>   and *go down to the depths*.
> Their soul is melted *because of the evil*.
> They reel to and fro
>   and stagger like a drunkard
>   and are *at their wit's end*. (Ps. 107:23–27)

That wonderful concluding phrase, taken from the King James Version, is a point to which we shall frequently return. The sailors are at wit's end in that they have come to the limit of all their resources, even the prodigious intelligence of the creature made in God's image. Their coming to this limit is shown by the way they reel and stagger like drunkards, incapable and bewildered even though they have drunk no wine but are simply being slapped about by the force of the sea. That same force overwhelms them inwardly, as the soul within each of them loses all its strength and melts away because of "the evil"—a word that resonates throughout the book of Jonah as a name for everything that human beings need to avoid.

They are of course quite literally overwhelmed, with the waves coming up over their heads, mounting up to heaven, but also—interesting that we forget this side of it—with the trough of the wave reaching down to the depths, exposing as it were the bottom of the world. (This is how the great tsunami of December 2004 announced itself to many people along the coast of Indonesia. Boats far off from shore rested for a few moments on the bottom of the sea, surrounded by rocks and starfish.) When the LORD commands and lifts the waves of the sea, the heavens above and the depths beneath can no longer be counted on; they seem to tremble and shake as if the world itself is about to be shattered. It is very much like the undoing of creation, as the prophet says, remembering Noah's flood:

> For the windows of heaven are opened,
>   and the foundations of the earth tremble.
> The earth is utterly broken,
>   the earth is torn asunder,
>   the earth is violently shaken,
> the earth staggers like a drunkard. (Isa. 24:18–19)

It is as if the earth itself is being cut out from under their feet, staggering with them in terror. The anguish of these poor sailors reveals to them the great and mighty works of the LORD, his wonders in the deep, showing them the ultimate fragility of all that is not God, even heaven above and earth beneath. In these great waters to which they have gone down, they see not just the prospect of certain death but the dissolution of the world, the breaking up of what little ground is under their feet, the smashing of every wall and boundary that keeps chaos at bay. There is just a little wooden contrivance between them and the pathless abyss of destruction. To be on a boat in the middle of a great storm is to know what it is like for the world to near its end. For these sailors, the Day of the LORD is at hand.

and each cried out to his god,

Terrified, at their wit's end, they cry out. Their prayer begins as a cry of distress, an outcry like the inarticulate voice that comes from us when we slip and fall or meet some enemy, stronger than we are, who attacks and beats us. We cry out for help, not knowing what to say, saying anything. So these people, all in the same boat, do their best to cry out to their gods, each in their own way. None of them minds that their neighbors call upon different gods, using different names and different rituals. They know that each nation and people has its own gods, and they are willing to believe that each religion is equally meaningful and valid. This is clearly a diverse, multicultural crew, displaying a vibrant religious pluralism. Fat lot of good it does them.

The sociologists tell us that the function of religion is to maintain the meaning of the world, to bless its structures with a story and a hope. Most of the time this appears to work, and it is as if the gods were keeping things together and preserving cosmic order. That is why we invent religions in the first place. But there are times when the whole structure of things is under threat, when *everything* is about to fall apart, and we cry out to our gods in vain. So these sailors are at wit's end, trying every god they can think of, knowing none that can help.

and they hurled the wares that were in the ship into the sea, to lighten it for them.

There are of course practical things the sailors can do, and they do not neglect to do them. They respond to the hurling of the wind and the storm as best they can by hurling away the cargo—which is the whole point of their voyage. It is a matter of priorities. When your ship is about to go down, your values get clarified.

Mammon is a great god whose grandeur overspreads the human world, yet his power has severe limits in some directions. The closer you come to death the less help he is. He is one god the sailors can afford to displease at the moment. It is a striking religious choice, for of course it is Mammon, the god of commerce and profit, who set this ship of Tarshish in motion to begin with, Mammon who got it built, Mammon who established its goals and objectives, Mammon who is the *raison d'être* of the voyage for most of those aboard. But when a great wind is hurled at you on the sea, all that is sacred to Mammon goes overboard—it is too heavy to carry, not worth keeping. This is ordinary human wisdom, and it is often enough to save the ship. Not in this case, of course. For these sailors have not yet discovered which deity they are really dealing with.

The futility of their efforts, which will become more and more apparent, is perhaps already signaled by the word "lighten," which in other usages can mean that something has become "a light thing" (as the King James Version translates it in, e.g., 1 Sam. 18:23; 1 Kgs. 16:31; 2 Kgs. 3:18; Isa. 49:6), which is to say something negligible, even despicable, as when a pregnant Hagar despises her barren mistress, Sarah, taking her very lightly (Gen. 16:4). So perhaps the ship also is lightened in this sense, becoming practically negligible in the middle of the great storm, a light thing easily blown about by the great wind.

But Jonah had gone down into the furthest recesses of the boat, had lain down, and was fast asleep.

The scene shifts now to Jonah, in a different place from the sailors laboring to save the ship. It is time to hear more of Jonah's descent. He has gone down so far that he has missed all the excitement. Descending to the furthest recesses of the ship, perhaps down in the cargo hold, he has laid himself down and then fallen down even deeper in sleep. There at the bottom of the boat he becomes as it were the unknown secret at its core, the hidden meaning of its disaster—like Israel among the nations, the chosen ones who give meaning to the world and its history. Unknown to the terrified Gentiles on deck, the Israelite unconscious in the inner part of the ship is the clue to the real story of their lives. Even the violence of the sea is determined by his hidden presence. It is no comfort to them now, but it all means something.

And it may be, despite all appearances, that they are not really in danger so long as Jonah is with them. Would the LORD really sink the vessel that contains the apple of his eye? Jonah is the representative of Israel among the nations, God's beloved among the peoples. Of course we are reminded of a yet more representative Israelite who also slept in a boat threatened by a great storm that terrified everyone else aboard—who were all nonetheless quite safe because he was with them (Matt. 8:23–27; Mark 4:35–41; Luke 8:22–25). We must wonder if in this episode too Jesus deliberately identifies with Jonah, the obedient prophet identifying with the disobedient. Of course Jonah is unlike Jesus in that he has no power of his own to still the waves. Yet when push comes to shove he does still the waves. He accomplishes this by giving himself up to death, satisfying the wrath of God and freeing everyone else from threat of harm. We would all be doing well if we were as effective as Jonah, this prophet who in spite of himself anticipates Christ in so many ways.

And of course in many ways we do resemble disobedient Jonah without really noticing, being quite capable of sleeping through disasters and unconscious of the ruin we bring upon our neighbors. The church should consider identifying with Jonah, but with less innocent confidence than our Lord Jesus. The number of ways we have run away from the word of our Lord, descended among the nations, and fallen asleep among the disasters for which we are responsible are no doubt beyond counting. But perhaps we could consider first of all the great disaster of the dissolution of Christendom, which leaves the West full of wealth and contrivance, commerce and technology, pleasures of all sorts to be bought and consumed, but no meaning of life worth living for. It would be worth hurling it all overboard if we could find who slumbers at the bottom of it all.

Individual believers might also consider if the shoe fits. Dante speaks of being "so full of sleep at the point where I abandoned the true way" (*Inferno* 1.11–12) that he never consciously realized how he came to be lost in the dark wood of his own sin. What he does not add, though it is implicit in much of his poem, is that this kind of sleep can cause the ruin of the social world, not just of one person's moral character. None of us has a right to be unconscious of the terror and ruin around us, and none of us should presume that we bear no responsibility for it.

So it is a very good thing when Jonah is revealed in the inner depths of the boat. From Jonah's perspective, it is not just some sailors who have found him, but the same LORD from whom he is fleeing. As the psalmist reminds us: "You search out my path and my lying down, and are acquainted with all my ways" (Ps. 139:3). This depth of divine knowledge is for the comfort of the obedient and the discomfiture of the disobedient, but in both cases for our good.

1:6 And the captain came and said to him,

The altercation between Jonah and the LORD continues. The LORD is not about to leave the sailors to struggle with the storm alone. Using the ordinary virtues of a good captain, the LORD has a new way to get at Jonah and call him back to himself.

The captain of the boat is obviously a man of integrity. He is unquestionably a better man than Jonah—and perhaps the most righteous human being in the whole book. But he is a man at wit's end. The representative of ordinary human responsibility coping with problems too big to manage, he wakes up the man of God to remind him that he too has responsibilities. All honor to mere human responsibility! By waking the irresponsible and disobedient prophet, the captain does the most any human being can do to save the lives of all aboard.

"What's with you, sleeping?

This is like when we ask someone, incredulously, "What were you *thinking*?" Or in the inimitable words of the King James Version, "What meanest thou, O sleeper?" Of course Jonah is not thinking at all. He is unconscious, doing his best to mean nothing at all, like someone too depressed to get out of bed. What else is there to do when you are fleeing the God who made heaven and earth and even your very self? You hide as far down in the depths of your own obliviousness as possible. Others get drunk or take drugs or commit suicide. Jonah descends as deep into darkness as he can, away from the light of day and far from any kind of awareness. He dwells in darkness of heart and soul and mind and strength, all that is within him which by right belongs to the Lord his God.

But God does not leave him there. "Who can hide in secret places so that I cannot see them?" says the Lord to his disobedient people (Jer. 23:24), adding, "Do I not fill heaven and earth?" Not even in your dreams can you hide from the Lord of all. But God is gentle with the runaway prophet, sending him an honest captain who calls him out of his unconsciousness and nescience. The blessing of disobedient Jonah begins here.

It is not insignificant that it begins with a merely human word. It is the first merely human word in the story, and it is a good one. Indeed, except for Jonah's speeches, every human word in this story is responsible and intelligent, grounded in the fear of God. Things are not all wrong with the world when people who do not know the Lord by name can speak such good words.

Arise,

Unbeknownst to himself, the captain repeats the Lord's first word to Jonah, calling him back to his duty, his responsibility to that initial word. Of course "arise" here means, "Sleeper, awake!" It is a reminder that we all shall arise not just from sleep but from death in the resurrection.

To be awake is to pray. Now and for eternity, the heart that is not dead or asleep calls out the name of its God. Hence the persistent association in Scripture and tradition between watching and praying, vigil and supplication. Jonah's captain is part of this tradition, as if he were telling us all: "Wake up! Stop playing dead! Get up and pray!" When human responsibility is at wit's end, it is long past time for the heart that is holy, set apart for the service of the Lord, to get up and call upon the name of its God.

The scriptural connection between wakefulness and prayer is of course clearest at Gethsemane, when the founding members of the church play Jonah and fall asleep precisely when their Lord has most need of their prayers. "Watch and pray!" is his word to them (Matt. 26:41; Mark 14:38), and in Luke 22:46 it is even "Arise and pray!" (very much like the captain's word here), but they do not obey because, though the spirit is willing, the flesh is weak. So their Lord must go on without them. Only what is about to happen to Christ's flesh—the human flesh of the divine word—is sufficient to wake these sleepers from death forever. Were it not for the word made flesh, surely none of us would ever wake up:

> Sleeper, awake!
>   Rise from the dead,
> and Christ will give you light. (Eph. 5:15)

That is perhaps the deepest reason why the captain's word echoes the word of the
LORD at the beginning: Jonah is raised out of his dead sleep by a reminder of the
only word that can really waken any of us.

call upon your god!

Everyone aboard is crying to his god except Jonah, and now the captain orders
him to join them. But he uses the verb for invocation, indicating something more
definite and articulate than the verb for crying in 1:5. You can cry in wordless
distress like any hurt animal (and human beings are so often hurt animals), but
to call upon your god you must speak his name. To call to a person is to try to
get his attention and to get him to come nearer. To call upon a god is to utter his
name and ask for his presence and help. That is why services of worship begin
with an invocation, a word of prayer that calls upon God to be present in and
with the congregation.

In the case we are considering now, as often in the Bible, to call upon the name
of the LORD, who is "a very present help in trouble" (Ps. 46:1), is like calling upon
a friend or ally to come help you in battle (the most common use of the verb
"to help" when its subject is not God but human beings; e.g., Josh. 1:14; 10:4;
2 Sam. 10:11; 1 Chr. 12:22). The sailors in their battle with the sea have been
calling upon their gods, who seem to be too far away to hear or help. The gods
of the nations typically need some place in the midst of their land, some shrine
or temple, in which to dwell; they are not really available on the open sea. Only
the LORD, the God of heaven who made the sea and the dry land (Jonah 1:9), is
in a position to hear a motley crew from all over the world when they cry out in
distress from the midst of the waters.

It is all the more instructive, then, that in 1:6 a pagan calls Jonah to prayer. A
peculiar form of self-righteousness is widespread among Christian theologians,
who often talk as if only Christians have any concept of the grace of God. This is
a bizarre belief, refuted nearly every time a pagan prays. If we want a proof text,
then here it is: the pagans are praying for divine grace and they call the monotheist
to wake up and join them. We are not told of any works-righteousness here (it
is the essence of Christian self-righteousness to think that everyone else is self-
righteous). We do not hear of the sailors claiming to have earned divine favor,
performing rituals to cleanse themselves or take control of divine power (sacrifices
of thanksgiving will come later, in 1:16). It seems that the pagans know all about
the concept of grace. You don't have to be a Christian to believe in a gracious god
and pray for help, and unlike Christian theologians the Bible never entertains
the bizarre belief that pagans do not believe in unearned divine mercy. The only
problem with these pagans is that they don't know which god to call upon. For
that, they need to learn the name of the LORD, but the one who can teach them
this has been lying oblivious in the bottom of the boat, insensate in his disobedience, a parable for self-righteous Christians.

Perhaps the god will consider us and we won't perish."

The captain does not yet know enough to accuse Jonah of being the source of their problems. All he can do is hope that somebody's god, of all the gods whose worshipers are aboard this boat, might be willing and able to help. "Perhaps . . ."—or, as the king of Nineveh later puts it, "Who knows?" (3:9)—there may yet be a god who can keep them from perishing. Here at wit's end, anything is worth a try, and they all have an obligation to try with their own god—even this idiot sleeping at the bottom of the boat.

Perhaps . . . who knows? It may seem like the captain is whistling in the dark, but he has it right—more than he knows. It turns out that the great, unknown, and terrifying God he is trying to reckon with has already considered them and does not intend for them to perish. Things are better than they seem, as usual in a comedy. The only real problem is Jonah, and the LORD is dealing with him right now, through the captain himself.

Notice that the captain speaks quite naturally in the plural. He wants Jonah's God, whoever it is, to consider *us*, not just *me*—so that we, all of us, may not perish. The captain speaks as one who bears responsibility for everyone on board. How natural human responsibility looks when we see it in a good man—so natural we hardly notice it. *Of course* a good captain speaks like this! But not everyone is such a good man. Jonah, by contrast, must hide from his neighbors precisely because he is fleeing from his God. So he can speak only for himself, in the first person singular.

Yet apparently he does not even do that. We might think he would make some response to the captain's urgent and intelligent plea, but we do not hear any such thing. The story gives us no word of Jonah replying to the captain or calling upon the name of the LORD at this point. It appears that Jonah has no word to say, no response to make to God or man. As a prophet his whole calling is to speak, yet so far in this story he has been silent. This is not only disobedience to his LORD; it leaves everyone else in the lurch.

Finding out Jonah (1:7–10)

1:7 And each of them said to his neighbor,

Round three begins. It is no longer direct interaction between the LORD and Jonah but rather an intricate dialogue (the most complex dramatic scene of the story) between the sailors and Jonah, which culminates when the sailors eventually turn from Jonah to address a word to Jonah's God, so that by the end of Jonah 1 the dialogue between the LORD and Jonah with which the book began has transformed itself into a dialogue between the worshiping sailors and the LORD.

But as round three begins, Jonah appears as just one of a whole boatload of people talking to each other. They are described as "neighbors," which means creatures who should love one another, not bear false witness against one another, not covet one another's goods, and so on. "Neighbor" is the key term used in the legislation of the Torah, the word of God given to Israel, to indicate those who are bound together in the ethical bonds of community and mutual obligation ("love your neighbor as yourself" [Lev. 19:18], "you shall not bear false witness against your neighbor" [Exod. 20:16], and so on, in many other pieces of legislation). To this the book of Jonah now prompts us to add—we can scarcely avoid putting it this way—that our neighbor means everyone who is in the same boat with us, threatened by the same storms, and fighting against the same sea. All of us mortals need one another, and that is why Scripture calls us neighbors and puts us under obligation to one another.

"Come on, let's cast lots,

In the ancient world there are many ways of casting lots. Here the lots probably consist of some kind of marked stones that could be thrown or rolled like dice in order to indicate who is chosen and who is not. Casting lots of this kind is like tossing a coin and calling heads or tails. Cast repeatedly, lots could be used to pick one person out of a whole group through a gradual process of elimination, by asking a series of questions like this: "Is it my family or yours? Mine. Then is it male or female? Male. Then is it my son or me?" The rulers of ancient Israel used lots that functioned this way to inquire of the LORD about who was guilty (1 Sam. 14:40–42) or who was to be king (10:19–21). Like many other ancient cultures, Israel thus considers what looks like a game of chance to be a form of divination, understanding the outcome to be under divine control. Jonah's neighbors on the boat do likewise.

It's a smart move. At wit's end, they can do no better than try something that will take the next move out of their own hands. Having done all that human intelligence and courage can do, they give up their own efforts and seek the unknown god who threatens them. They try to put themselves at his disposal by using the most religiously neutral (and therefore least idolatrous) form of divination possible— one that, unknown to them, is remarkably similar to the kind of divination used by the chosen people themselves. Here a practice that in other contexts could easily become superstition is the deepest form of religion available.

What is more: the unknown God who threatens them is full of mercy—despite all appearances—and he mercifully answers their desperate inquiries.

so we may know on whose account this evil has come to us."

This is the second occurrence of the word "evil" (cf. 1:2), and now it points toward Jonah, not Nineveh! Of course the sailors don't know this yet, but we do.

The sailors know they don't know what they need to know, so they do the intelligent thing: they try to find out. Much of their speech in the book is in the mode of inquiry. They are ignorant Gentiles but they do not want to stay that way.

And they cast lots and the lot fell on Jonah.

The LORD is setting up Jonah as the fall guy, the scapegoat. The parallels are extensive, as we shall see. First of all, the law of God requires that lots be used to choose the scapegoat on Yom Kippur, the Day of Atonement. The priest is to cast lots over two goats, "one lot for the LORD and the other lot for *azazel*" (Lev. 16:8). Azazel, many scholars now think, may be the name of an erstwhile demon or hobgoblin, which had by the time of the writing of the Torah become the name of the waste places, the habitation of demons, to which the goat is sent. Hence recent translations give this Hebrew word as a name, "for Azazel," rather than the term used in older translations, "for a scapegoat." Yet Scripture elsewhere seems to know nothing of such a demon, and it would surely be a mistake to see some half-forgotten hobgoblin as parallel to the LORD in ownership of these two goats. The waste places, on the other hand, are of the essence. The difference between the two goats is the difference between clean and unclean, and therefore between a creature fit to be offered to the LORD in the temple and a creature fit only to be thrown away, out into the waste places, like Jonah thrown out into the sea. The unique English term "scapegoat," a shortened form of "escape-goat," is still preferable because of how it reminds us that the animal is let loose to escape in the wilderness.

Choosing the scapegoat is a striking example of divine election, which is to say, of God's way of choosing. At first there is nothing to distinguish the two goats, both of which must be pure and unblemished in order to be presented to the LORD at the beginning of the rite. But after the lots are cast one of them becomes a holy sacrifice well pleasing to the LORD, while the other becomes unclean, unfit for the temple or the presence of God. It looks arbitrary, a matter of mere chance, but in fact the lots are the authorized means by which the LORD chooses which creature shall be the sacrificial victim and which shall be the unclean thing cast into outer darkness. Divine election often looks this arbitrary, as the LORD himself would have us notice (Deut. 7:7–9).

One point is very important for those of us who are unfamiliar with the Old Testament sacrifices to understand: the scapegoat is the animal that is *not* sacrificed, not offered to the LORD, because it is unclean. To be chosen as the scapegoat is to be rejected as unworthy of God, an abomination rather than an offering. Hence the scapegoat is not sacrificed but simply thrown away—again, like Jonah thrown into the sea.

All the more striking, then, that Jonah represents the chosen people, the apple of God's eye, and that Jesus Christ chooses to identify with Jonah. This is the very logic of redemption: the vocation of the chosen is to be the rejected, thrown out from the presence of the LORD. This is the mystery, the hidden meaning behind the apparent arbitrariness of God's choices. Why choose Jacob rather than Esau, when both are still in the womb and neither has done anything good or evil to make a moral difference between them (Rom. 9:11–12)? Why choose Israel (i.e.,

Jacob) out of all nations, when she is no greater or better than the rest of the human race, all made in God's image (Deut. 7:7)? It seems as arbitrary as taking a lump of perfectly homogenous clay and using one part of it to make a vessel for sacred use in the temple and another part to make a chamber pot, a vessel for filth and dishonor to be thrown out with the garbage (Rom. 9:21). It is just like choosing one goat as holy and the other as unclean, simply by a roll of the dice.

To get past the impression of unfairness, we have to notice the reversals contained in the logic of redemption: first and foremost, the chosen one, our Lord Jesus Christ, becomes unclean—the true scapegoat—so that the rest of us may be made clean, an acceptable offering to the LORD. This is not a sudden change in the divine plan but the fulfillment of the LORD's promise that Jacob and his seed, the chosen people, will be a blessing for all the families of the earth (Gen. 28:14; cf. 12:3). And the same logic of redemption is visible in Jonah, the descendent of Jacob who is thrown away so that a whole boatload of Gentiles might not perish (Jonah 1:15). The election of God is, as the older translations aptly put it, "the election of grace" (Rom. 11:5). It is good news even for those not chosen, because the elect are chosen for the blessing of others.

None of this explains away the deep mystery of election. Why is Jacob chosen rather than Esau? Why is Israel the chosen people among all nations? Why is the one man Jesus Christ the chosen one, the eternal Son of God? We have no explanation for any of these choices, but they are glorious, and in retrospect we can see something of the depth of wisdom from which they come, and thereby join in Paul's doxology:

> Oh, the depth of the riches and wisdom and knowledge of God!
> How inscrutable are his judgments,
> how unsearchable his ways! (Rom. 11:33)

The lots tell the sailors that Jonah is the guilty one. But they are soon to realize as well that he is the LORD's chosen one. This will cause them great fear but will also be for their salvation. They too can join in Paul's doxology.

1:8 And they said to him,

The whole boatload now talks to Jonah together, as if all nations were addressing Israel: "What's with you?" We need not imagine them all speaking literally in one voice. It may be that the captain speaks for them, as a king speaks for his people. But in any case, they're all in this together, and evidently they're of one mind.

"Please tell us

They won't let Jonah be silent any longer. They are polite and careful about it—they say "please"—but they know they have to make him speak or they die. So it is time for Jonah to be responsible—to give a response.

on whose account this evil has come to us.

That is, "Tell us about yourself." The sailors don't come right out and say it—they are too wary for that just yet—but they invite him to identify himself as the source of their troubles. It is as if to say: "If the shoe fits, Jonah, please wear it." There is in fact no mistaking that the word "evil" has now definitively migrated from Nineveh to Jonah (cf. 1:2, 7). The evil in which they find themselves originates right here, in the man to whom they are speaking. The secret meaning of their disaster, about which they were stumped earlier, is now visibly present in the flesh in front of them. Yet they are remarkably patient and fair with Jonah, wary and circumspect: there is a dreadful power associated with this man, and they don't want to get in the way of it. So they beat around the bush.

What is your occupation and from whence have you come? What is your land and from what people are you?"

The sailors pose a long series of questions, none of which is quite to the point. Normally, the first question asked of someone who has been picked out by lot as guilty is, "Tell me what you have done" (1 Sam. 14:43; cf. Josh. 7:19 and Jonah 1:10). But instead of demanding that he confess his crime, the people on the boat give Jonah a chance to explain himself. They ask not about what he has done but about who he is, hoping perhaps that somewhere in the facts of his identity—his ethnicity, homeland, and occupation—there is an explanation of what is happening to them that will reassure them that this isn't as bad as it looks.

1:9 And he said to them, "A Hebrew am I,

Jonah speaks now for the first time in the story, identifying himself at last—not that he is very forthcoming about it. He does not give his name. He answers the last question first and never gets to the others—never mentioning, for instance, that he is a prophet from Israel. And the answer he does give is rather evasive. Replying to the question about his ethnicity ("from what people are you?"), he describes himself as a Hebrew, which is a very vague term, far less specific than "Israelite," a word that is never used in this story. It is in fact a rather peculiar term, in that unlike other terms for ethnicity, it does not locate him as belonging to any particular place (like "Assyrian" or "Ninevite") or clearly identify his lineage (like "Israelite," literally "son of Israel," or "Jew," literally "son of Judah"). It seems to refer to a loose group of peoples, not necessarily speaking the same language (in the Old Testament, "Hebrew" is not yet a term for a language), some of whom may have claimed an ancestry going back to a man named Eber, many generations before Abraham (Gen. 11:16–27). Insofar as this term refers to ethnicity at all, it could include any number of peoples outside Israel.

It may be, in fact, that the primary meaning of the term has to do not with ethnicity but with social status. In scriptural usage, and in other ancient documents that use what seems to be an Egyptian version of the term, "Habiru," Hebrews are typically homeless, often refugees, sometimes mercenary soldiers or deserters, always in some sense outsiders and foreigners. In Genesis, when the sons of Israel are not yet a nation but only one man's family, the Egyptians treat the Hebrews as a whole class of dirty scum (39:14) who are too disgusting to eat with in the same room (43:32). In Exodus, the word "Hebrew" occurring in the mouth of an Egyptian can easily mean something like "foreigner" (1:15–16; 2:6–7, 11–13). Later the Philistines call the Israelites "Hebrews," especially when they notice them serving as mercenaries in the Philistine army or deserting (1 Sam. 14:11, 21; 29:3). It is not a term the Israelites typically used among themselves. So when they describe their God to Pharaoh as "the LORD, the God of the Hebrews" (Exod. 3:18; 5:3; 7:16; 10:3), perhaps the sense is that he is the God of a people that to the Egyptians are nothing but dirty, homeless foreigners.

Evidently this is how Jonah is presenting himself to the people on the boat. What he conveys to them, in effect, is this: "I'm just a foreigner, having no real home, worshiping at no temple, serving no God but the one up in heaven." But perhaps precisely this rootless anonymity is cause for greater uneasiness. If any god at all bothers with such a man, it must be the one who surveys the whole wide earth from up in heaven, the God above all gods.

and the LORD, the God of heaven, I fear, who made the sea and the dry land."

After identifying himself (sort of), Jonah identifies his God. Once again he avoids revealing his own ethnicity. He does not describe the LORD as God of Israel. Nonetheless, he must give away the really crucial point. Now, for the first time in this story, we hear a human being speaking the name of the LORD, the holy name that is so sacred to the Jews that they no longer speak it. To take this name upon one's lips, even in the era when it was still permitted, is inevitably a solemn confession of faith. Evidently this faith was not forthcoming except in response to the urgent questions and dire need of Gentiles.

This will not be the last time that Israel comes to faith in response to the Gentiles. For Paul, indeed, this is the secret key to the history of the world, the mystery that opens out upon the consummation of all things: not only do Gentiles believe the good news of a Jewish Messiah, but their belief provokes the Jews to jealousy and therefore to faith (Rom. 11:14). The story of Jonah has this Pauline dynamic, and like Paul it can in conclusion only look forward to Israel's faith as a future miracle of God that must be awaited in hope. Meanwhile, the story gets on with the business of describing how Jonah's confession of faith saves the Gentiles.

The designation "God of heaven" was used by Jews in the Babylonian exile and afterward to describe their God in discussions with Gentiles (2 Chr. 36:23; Ezra 1:2; 5:11–12; 6:9–10; 7:12, 21, 23; Neh. 1:4–5; 2:20). Jonah's use of the term here is consistent with exilic and postexilic Jewish usage: it is a way for Israelites to talk with non-Israelites about the God of Israel. It is of course a title of majesty, immediately evoking the picture of one who sits enthroned in heaven and surveys the whole earth, seeing all there is to see and not being particularly impressed:

> He sits enthroned above the circle of the earth,
>   and its people are like grasshoppers.
> He stretches out the heavens like a canopy
>   and spreads them out like a tent to live in.
> He brings princes to naught
>   and reduces the rulers of this world to nothing. (Isa. 40:22–23)

"Fear" here is the standard term for religion, reverence for a god. It is not simple fear for one's life, as in Jonah 1:5 when the sailors are afraid of the storm, but it does not exclude such feelings either. It refers to all the activities by which one serves a god in reverence and submission, the way the servants of a great king serve him—in this case, one who brings princes to naught and reduces the rulers of this world to nothing—and it therefore includes the feelings you have when you are called to come before the face of the great king who is your judge and you realize you are not worthy to stand in his presence. It is quite a reasonable thing to fear the God of heaven from the depths of your heart.

But this is a good king, rich in mercy and long-suffering, who repents of evil (cf. 4:2). Anyone who knows him will know this, and before the end of the chapter we will see the natural fear of coming into his presence being tempered by thanksgiving and gladness for his mercy and loving-kindness. The fear of the LORD opens out onto such feelings, which go far beyond fear. For of course in the end perfect love casts out fear (1 John 4:18). But we do start out with the fear of the LORD, which is the beginning of wisdom (Prov. 9:10). What is happening at this point in the story is that a new sense of the word "fear," meaning not the sheer terror of destruction but reverence for the LORD, has come into view. As Jonah 1 works toward its conclusion, which is a happy ending for the sailors, this new sense gradually takes over and become the emotional tone of the whole story so far.

But at this stage there is still quite a bit of sheer terror. The God of heaven is not too far away to track them down and take hold of them, for his arm reaches as far as his sight. To say he made "the sea and the dry land" is to locate his creative power everywhere under heaven. As the psalmist says, calling Israel to worship: "The sea is his, for he made it, and his hands prepared the dry land" (Ps. 95:5). The upshot is that both vertically (heaven and earth) and horizontally (sea and dry land) God possesses the whole universe that he has made. Even the heaven itself, with its stars and angels, is his creation:

> By the word of the LORD were the heavens made,
>   and all the host of them by the breath of his mouth.
> He gathers the waters of the sea together in a heap;
>   he lays up the deep in storehouses.

Let all the earth fear the LORD;
  let all the inhabitants of the world stand in awe of him. (Ps. 33:6–8)

The movement of the psalmist's verse could well trace the movement of the sailors' thoughts: from God in heaven to the depths of the sea that are in his hand to the inhabitants of the earth who had better fear him.

But we have not yet seen why the sailors believe what Jonah has to say about this. Why should they think that Jonah's word is true—that the LORD, Jonah's God, is actually the God of heaven, who created the sea and the dry land?

1:10 Then the people feared a great fear,

The word "people" here is different from the word for ethnicity translated "people" in 1:8. It is the same word used for the population of Nineveh in 3:5, thus emphasizing the parallels between what happens with the people of Nineveh in Jonah 3 and what happens with the people on the boat in Jonah 1.

The people on the boat have come to the crucial turning point of their lives, which is also the turning point of Jonah 1. It is indicated by the unobtrusive little word "great," which marks the difference between their newfound fear and their previous fear of the great wind and the great storm (1:5). From now on, they fear a great fear (cf. 1:16), for they fear the great God of heaven, who hurled the wind at them and caused the storm. That is, they fear the LORD, who is "a great God, the great king above all gods" (Ps. 95:3). Salvation has come upon these people, and from this moment all is well with them, for they believe the word of the prophet Jonah confessing the greatness of the LORD, and therefore they fear a great fear.

To see how they come to this faith and fear requires that we give careful attention to the extraordinarily subtle movement of the narrative in this verse. Jonah has just spoken for the first time in the story, largely evading the question about his own identity but confessing the name of the LORD. Why should the sailors believe him? What is it in Jonah that gives them this confidence in his word and this recognition of the greatness of his God? The answer of the narrative is clear: Jonah's guilt.

and they said to him, "What is this you have done?"

It's not as if they don't know. They are now perfectly aware of what Jonah has done, as the narrative goes on to inform us, and that is why their fear is so great. Their words here are a cliché, an immediately recognizable formula of accusation. "What have you done?" is the question that God asks Eve after the first sin (Gen. 3:13) and Cain after the first murder (4:10), that Jacob asks Laban when Laban cheats him (29:25), and that Laban asks Jacob when Jacob sneaks away (31:26). The people of Judah ask, "What have you done to us?" when Samson gets them in trouble with their overlords (Judg. 15:11), and Samuel asks Saul, "What have you done?" when he finds that Saul has committed sacrilege (1 Sam. 13:11). In asking this question, the people on the boat are done beating around the bush. This is not a polite inquiry but an announcement of Jonah's guilt, together with a demand that he offer what explanation of his actions he can. It turns out that he has no explanation to give. He resumes his silence, just like when the captain asked him, "What's with you, sleeping?" (1:6). He cannot justify or even excuse what he is doing.

But no matter: they know now what they need to know. These are smart people, and they get the point right away. They put two and two together, and suddenly they understand the whole thing.

For the people knew that he was fleeing from the face of the Lord, for he had told them.

This is what we did not know they knew. The narrator has withheld this piece of information until now, so that we might have the missing piece of the puzzle just at this point, at the moment when the people on the boat "get it," so that we can "get it" with them. But this will take a moment. We need to stop and figure it out: exactly how does this piece fit into the puzzle?

Think about how the narrator's sudden intrusion into the story at this point disrupts our expectations. Shouldn't this information about Jonah fleeing from the Lord be precisely what the sailors' inquiry uncovers? But it turns out, they already know. So what have they learned by casting lots and uncovering Jonah's guilt? And what new piece of information has Jonah given them, to make them suddenly fear so great a fear? If they already know that Jonah is running away from God, then why did they need to cast lots to find out that he is the one on whose account this evil has come to them?

Let us try to put two and two together. Our aim is to see why, at the culmination of their desperate inquiries, Jonah's confession that the Lord is the God of heaven is the key piece of information they need—and why they believe it when they hear it.

The crucial thing to bear in mind is that up to this point, the people on the boat do not know the Lord. They have heard his name, of course, when Jonah told them he was fleeing—that's *our* new piece of information as readers—but they obviously did not know who this particular God is, from whom Jonah is fleeing. Our puzzlement is caused by a false assumption lying behind the question, "If they already know Jonah is running away from God, then why . . . ?" No one on the boat has our generic concept of God: they know only particular gods, each with his or her own name. So when Jonah said he was fleeing from the Lord, they did not jump to the conclusion that this was the one God who made heaven and earth, the ruler of all things, and they surely would not have believed it even if he told them. Why should they believe that Jonah's God is such a big deal? They evidently assumed, as was perfectly natural, that this was just one more of the many gods of the nations worshiped on board the boat, local deities who cannot really be of much harm or help out on the open sea.

That is why when the storm comes upon them, even though they all know Jonah is fleeing from the LORD, it does not occur to them that he is at fault for anything other than his failure to call upon his god (1:6). For them a man's relationship to his god is his own private affair, as it is in every well-behaved religion in a pluralistic society. The adherents of various religions ought to contribute to civic life, praying for the common good in times of trouble, but Jonah's disobedience against his own god is not their business—not until the unknown God who hurled the great wind against them reveals that he is none other Jonah's God.

That is what is revealed by the lots and sealed by Jonah's confession. The two and two that the sailors now put together are the name of the LORD and the identity of the great, fearsome God who is threatening to kill them all. Now they realize for the first time *which* God they are dealing with: the God of Jonah, whose name is the LORD. And now they have every reason to believe that Jonah is telling the truth when he says that the LORD, his God, is no less than the God of heaven, who made the sea and the dry land. Some such God, high and mighty and great beyond their ken, must be behind this great storm and their mortal danger.

The key connection is their wholly correct assumption that the same God who hurls the storm at them is in control of the lots. So it is clear from the moment the lots fall on Jonah that the God they are dealing with is Jonah's God. And they already knew that his name is the LORD and that Jonah is fleeing from him, because Jonah told them. What they need from Jonah at this point is an explanation of how his flight could have gotten all of them into so much trouble. His confession of faith is exactly the explanation they need, the only possible explanation of the disaster he has brought upon them: that the LORD, the God from whom Jonah is fleeing, is none other than the God of heaven, who made the sea and the dry land. Jonah is trying to flee from the one God from whom no one can escape, the God who looks down from heaven to survey the whole surface of the sea and the earth and all who dwell therein.

When they understand this, they are terrified. It is worth noticing that the most important insight of your life can come to you in a moment of great fear. This is not the usual philosophic sort of proof for the existence of God. Yet it is a moment of deep understanding and genuine intelligence, in which they come to lasting insight about the nature of existence and the God who made it all.

Another point worth noticing is the role that Jonah's guilt plays in all this. The sailors believe Jonah's word precisely because of the magnitude of his guilt. If he were simply bragging about the greatness of his God, they could dismiss him with the kind of tolerance that makes religious pluralism work: you have your god, we have ours; you think your god is great, we think the same of ours; and we can leave it at that. But this situation is different: Jonah is not bragging but confessing the name of the God against whom he has sinned. With the great storm giving them every reason to believe in the greatness of Jonah's guilt, the sailors now have every reason to believe in the greatness of his God. This is more than religious toler-ance; in fact, it is where all tolerance reaches its limit. They have to intervene in

Jonah's religion, because getting things right between him and his God is now a matter of life and death for them all. The God of this disobedient prophet is too unmistakably real for them to have any trouble believing in him.

This may be one of the deeper reasons why this book must be a comedy: the only reason why the word of Jonah the prophet is convincing is because he is such a screwup. There may be a lesson here for the people of God, who usually prefer to think that their witness to him is convincing because they are such good people. (Where I come from, we talk about how "the LORD is working in my life" to much the same effect, and we usually don't mean he is working the way he does in *this* chapter of the Bible.) There are important ways that our failures make our confession of faith credible. Consider the penitent Judeans, for instance, who returned from Babylon to hard times in their own land, confessing that the LORD God of Israel punished his people for their sin against him, yet because of his great mercies they were not consumed, for he is a gracious and merciful God who keeps covenant and loving-kindness (Neh. 9:31–32). Any Babylonian or any of the people of the land to which they were returning who was impressed by such a confession and believed it would be putting two and two together just like the sailors. Think of it: what nation has ever survived such an exile? Yet what kind of nation would deserve such an exile? Surely they must have sinned greatly, becoming an unholy abomination, yet just as surely they must have a great God, who is God of heaven as well as God of Israel, and who is gracious and merciful, abounding in loving-kindness. For to survive such an exile and return home is like being swallowed up by the sea and yet coming back alive.

The Logic of Redemption (1:11–17)

1:11 And they said to him, "What shall we do with you, so the sea will be calm for us?"

The discussion enters a new stage. No more inquiry about who is at fault for the evil that has come to them. That is settled. Time now to turn to the future, what is to be done about the storm. Knowing what's what, they can consider their own agency and its possibilities. Leaving behind the unanswered question "What have you done?" they turn to the deliberation: "What shall we do?"

Grammatically, the people on the boat have turned from object ("this evil that has come *to us*") to subjects ("what shall *we* do?"). And in the process, Jonah has turned from subject ("what have *you* done?") to object ("what shall we do *with you*?"). He's the source of their troubles, so he's what they have to do something about. But unlike the cargo they hurled overboard, Jonah is an object that is also a subject who thinks and acts, someone who might have something to say about his own future. So they ask him.

What they are expecting is a word from the LORD, who they have learned is the God hurling this great storm at them. He is Jonah's God, which means that

Jonah is not only the cause of the evil that has come to them but also their lifeline to the terrifying power behind it all. So Jonah's words hold the key to their future as well as his own. He must tell them what to do.

For the sea was getting more and more stormy.

Another remark from the narrator (cf. 1:10) is designed to elucidate the sailors' thinking. But this time it is a bit more obvious. The sea is getting insistent, driving their inquiries forward with some urgency. If they don't get things right with Jonah—and soon—they die.

The storm is the LORD's way of impressing upon them their utter dependence on the word of the LORD. It forces them to turn to Jonah, as the prophet of the LORD, for instruction about how to propitiate this great and angry God. Like Jonah's guilt (see comment on 1:10), it teaches them to believe in the LORD.

1:12 And he said to them, "Pick me up and hurl me into the sea,

The prophet tells them that they should treat him not like a prophet but like cargo. They hurled the ship's cargo into the sea when they had to (1:5); now they should hurl Jonah in the same way. At this point, that's all he's good for.

Jonah speaks here both as a prophet, instructing them what to do to propitiate the wrath of God, and as a man who is just ready to give up (not for the last time, as we shall see in Jonah 4). It seems that he is already looking forward to being dead—everything he has done so far points in that direction, his many descents that keep bringing him closer to the depths, to the realm of nonbeing, fulfilling the common biblical phrase about going down to the pit (see comment on 1:3). There was never much space between his sleep down at the bottom of the boat and the endless tracts of water that are for him a place to sleep forever.

This time Jonah will not even need to make the descent under his own power. The suicidal notion of throwing himself overboard is something he does not even consider—the whole logic of the story goes against it, as we shall see. It will all be done for him, as the strong arms of the sailors pick him up and throw him overboard. All he has to do is hand himself over, give himself up. He can finally give up *being* entirely, which is surely easier than continuing his flight from the God of heaven, from whom nothing is hidden.

Who can so much as draw breath when the LORD is his pursuer? Better to be drowned where there is no breath of life at all. That is the sort of thing Job wished for in his first long speech, that heartrending lament when he cursed the day of his birth and wished it had never been, concluding:

> The thing that I have feared has come upon me,
>   what I have dreaded now befalls me;
> I have no peace or quiet,
>   no rest but only trouble. (Job 3:25–26)

So now the LORD, who is "the thing that I have feared," has come upon Jonah, caught up with him at last, and, unlike Job, Jonah seems to have found it something of a relief: it means that he finally gets to stop fleeing, stop fearing, stop breathing, stop being. He is like a Job who comes as close as possible to getting his wish—to become like one who has never been born.

And yet in handing himself over to God in this way, Jonah is also at his most Christlike. He gives up his life so that others might live. He propitiates the wrath of God by submitting to it himself so that others may be freed. We would all be doing well if we were as much like Christ as Jonah is. Though Jonah may give himself up in despair, he does have his priorities straight: he treats the lives of these good sailors as more valuable than his own. There is enough real love in this to be the beginning of good things, including Jonah's own obedience. In Jonah 2 he turns to God in heartfelt prayer and trust—but only *after* he has given himself up to death for the sake of these people he hardly knows. Greater love has no man (John 15:13).

and the sea will be calm for you.

The prophet instructs the sailors how to propitiate the wrath of God: you do it by getting rid of the prophet who instructs you. This would not be the first time people killed the messenger, even a messenger from God. Jesus tells a parable about this just a few days before his crucifixion (Matt. 21:33–46). This turns out to be the fundamental shape of redemption: we kill the ultimate messenger—God's own Son—and that is the propitiation to end all propitiations.

But the people on the boat are understandably reluctant to give it a try. So Jonah tries to convince them, by reminding them of what by this time they already know.

For I know that it is on account of me that this great storm is upon you."

At last we get an admission of guilt from Jonah, an explicit answer to their repeated inquiries about the cause of all their troubles (1:7–8). It comes as an act of generosity. It does not inform them of anything new but rather reminds them of what they already know, with the aim of convincing them that they're not going to get out of this alive so long as Jonah is with them. Jonah is like a ticking time bomb, or more precisely a homing device planted on their ship, attracting a guided missile that is rapidly closing in on them. They need to throw this dangerous thing overboard.

This is the last time they ask Jonah for anything. He has presented them with a very unwelcome option, which they would do anything to avoid.

1:13 But the people dug in to turn to dry land

The people on the boat are trying to *return*, to *turn back* to the dry land. This is the same verb later used for the Ninevites turning from their evil ways (3:8) and God turning from his fierce wrath (3:9). Here of course it is merely a change of physical direction, but it provides a visible image for what repentance of heart is like: turning away from the way of death and turning back to the land of the living. But their own efforts at turning the boat back to the land of the living won't be enough.

The queer metaphor of digging explains why. They dig their oars into the sea as if it were dry land. But the sea is not dry land. Land gives you purchase, a place to stand, the wherewithal to move in whatever direction you choose—all things that the pathless sea denies you. That is why human beings cannot live on the sea without technological contrivance, without the art of shipbuilding, which constructs a little world of wood where a person can set foot, with sails that grab the air and oars that dig in the water. But now that little world is about to be broken (1:4), and the great storm on the sea makes such an upheaval all around them that it is no good trying to dig into it. It is as if they are playing make-believe on the surface of the deep, pretending water is earth. On a good day—even on a not so very bad day—the sea will let you get away with this kind of thing. But not today.

but couldn't, because the sea was getting more and more stormy upon them.

They *couldn't*. The clause poses human ability against the strength of the great storm, and the humans lose. They have no power to save themselves.

The sea that made them afraid by getting more and more stormy (1:11) is now getting more and more stormy *upon them,* as if to drive home Jonah's point that "it is on account of me that this great storm is *upon you*" (1:12) and to underline his unwelcome answer to their question about what to do so that the storm may be (to translate very literally) "calm from *upon us*" (1:11–12).

Still, the people on the boat don't like what Jonah and the sea are both telling them. They would much rather just get back to dry land and throw Jonah safely off the boat. It shows how afraid they are that they actually try to do this, despite the growing storminess of the sea against them. For the thought of doing what Jonah says is even more terrifying than the raging waves.

So what are they so afraid of? That is where the story starts to turn into good news. It turns out that their great fear (1:10) is the fear of the LORD (1:16). What their awful experience on the heart of the sea is teaching them—what the LORD himself is teaching by hurling this great storm at them—is the fear of the LORD, which is the beginning of knowledge and wisdom (Prov. 1:7; 9:10). Once again, things are going much better than they seem.

1:14 And they called to the LORD and said, "Please, LORD,

The first prayer to the LORD in this story comes from the mouth of Gentiles. Now they are not simply crying out in terror to all their various gods but calling upon the God of heaven by his proper name. Something very good indeed is taking place out here on the stormy sea.

It takes a lot to get Gentiles to call upon the name of the LORD, but using Jonah, the LORD has done it. The storm itself would not have been sufficient. Disaster would not have converted anybody on board unless there was a prophet to tell them what it means and who is behind it. Jonah, alone and miserable, cowering under the wrath of God and waiting to die, has begun to fulfill his calling as a prophet.

This is one of the great surprises of this wonderful book, which we must not miss. The people on the boat are not just incidental to the story, instruments that the LORD uses to deal with Jonah. On the contrary, Jonah is the instrument that the LORD uses to deal with them, bringing them to a knowledge of the living God. Their coming to the LORD in humility and need, followed in short order by thanksgiving and worship, is one of the reasons that God made Jonah a prophet in the first place. So all is well, and Jonah truly is a prophet, an instrument of the LORD's peace and salvation. Such is the way of the LORD with his beloved, his chosen one, his dove of truth. Such is the way of Israel, the way that Christ will follow, and we after him.

please let us not perish for the soul of this man

The sailors echo the captain's earlier words to Jonah: "Perhaps the god will consider us and we won't perish" (1:6). But now that they're sure they've got the god's attention, they are worried that what they're about to do will make things worse. The repetition of "please" ("we beseech thee" in the King James Version) indicates their sense of trespass in even addressing the great God of heaven, like peasants coming into the presence of a great king with something outrageous to ask him. And they do have something outrageous to ask, in effect: "Let us dispose of this man who belongs to you, in order to save our own lives." That the LORD's own prophet told them to do this doesn't make it any less terrifying.

They speak of Jonah's *nephesh*, which means both life and soul. Similarly, *psychē* in the New Testament means both life and soul, as when our Lord speaks of gaining the whole world and losing one's *psychē* (Matt. 16:26), where the key word has been translated both "life" and "soul" because in fact it means both. Throughout the ancient world "soul" simply meant life. In Old Testament usage everything with the breath of life has a soul, and in Aristotle (*On the Soul* 2.3) even plants have souls—vegetative souls, the later philosophical tradition calls them—for, after all, they have life.

But the human soul is special. The covenant with Noah, which is binding on the whole human race, makes clear that the LORD will demand the life of any human being who takes another human life—soul paying for soul, lifeblood for lifeblood (Gen. 9:3–6). This universalizes a principle familiar to everyone in Jonah's world, which the sailors have very clearly in view when they pray to the God of heaven not to kill them for taking Jonah's life. The individual soul does not belong to itself. You belong to your god, just as you belong to your family, tribe, and nation. To take the life or soul of someone who belongs to a powerful deity is to take away what is sacred to that deity, and this is likely to get you in trouble. Think of how killing a member of a powerful family in Sicily might once have gotten you in trouble with the Mafia, or how U.S. citizens are safe from being mistreated by governments in Latin America or the Middle East, which torture their own people but don't want to jeopardize their support from the United States. When you belong to a powerful god, family, or nation, there are consequences for messing with you. And the more powerful is that to which you belong, the more serious are the consequences and the more far-reaching the protection under which you live.

The sailors know all this—and at a gut level—so they are afraid of what will happen if they mess with the LORD's anointed. But they see they have no choice—the raging of the storm and their own inability has convinced them of that. Whether they like it or not, they must deal with the LORD, the God of heaven, who is dealing with them. They have to take Jonah's life into their hands.

and do not lay upon us innocent blood.

Worse than the storm *upon* them (1:12–13) is the prospect of innocent blood *upon* them. That is why they braved the storm rather than get rid of Jonah (1:13). These are people of courage and integrity pushed past their limits. So they have to cave in and let the LORD have his way.

They speak like Pilate washing his hands of innocent blood (Matt. 27:24) but theirs is a deeper and more genuine fear. They are intimidated not by a noisy crowd but by the God of heaven himself (Jonah 1:9). They speak in the fear of the LORD, and therefore they are heard. For all that they throw Jonah overboard, they do not in fact shed his blood and indeed do him no harm at all. And, by the will of the LORD, Jonah becomes the propitiation that saves them from death. They are what Pilate would have looked like if his deeds had been done in obedience.

For you, LORD, have done as you desired."

The sailors acknowledge not only that the sea is his to do with as he desires (Ps. 95:5), but that Jonah is his prophet, so that the word of Jonah is the word of the LORD: in doing what Jonah tells them, they are doing what the LORD wants. Yet it is not a comforting thought, for they are still pagan enough to worry that they are stuck in the kind of story you find in Greek tragedy. The gods they know are perfectly capable of putting people in a situation where every choice they could make is shameful and guilty, like Agamemnon who has the choice of either sacrificing his daughter Iphigenia or else defying the command of Zeus and thus stranding the whole fleet and failing in his duty as commander-in-chief of the Greeks (Aeschylus, *Agamemnon* 205–37). A man in that situation has no option that leaves him blameless.

The sailors are afraid that such is their own situation. But what can they do? ("Who knows?" as the pagan king of Nineveh later says in 3:9.) The best thing to say is that this is all the god's doing—he is great and has done as he desired; therefore let not his displeasure come upon them for the blood of Jonah. Still, it must seem to them a very dicey proposition. For they do not know that what this God desires is their salvation, not their destruction.

1:15 And they picked Jonah up and hurled him into the sea,

This is obedience to the word of the LORD spoken through the prophet (1:12), an act of faith for which they are justified—the same justification by faith that we shall see in the Ninevites (3:5).

Jonah is not killed but thrown away, like garbage thrown overboard, a chamber pot emptied out, or the scapegoat sent into the waste places of the wilderness. This is what you do with dirt and refuse: you take it from the ordered place of human habitation and toss it aimlessly out into the place of disorder, where everything belongs that has no place. Cleanliness and order mean keeping things in their place, like stowing things on a boat where they belong. The things that have no place are thrown overboard because they belong nowhere in the ordered little world of the ship. They are swallowed up by the open sea, which is pathless and placeless, without landmark or location or home.

This has always been the logic of cleanliness, which is to say the logic of getting rid of the unclean. When you throw something into the garbage, it is still someplace, yet the exact place doesn't matter. The whole point is that you lose track of it, forget it, consign it to the unmarked and disordered realm where places have no meaning. That is why it is a matter of distress or of comedy when you throw something out that has a place in your home: when the wedding ring goes down the drain or the winning lottery ticket gets thrown out with the trash and everybody has to jump into the dumpster to look for it. That is supposed to be the place where you don't look for anything, where all is forgotten because nothing really has a place. And going there gets you filthy, as you become part of the garbage.

To be a scapegoat is to be part of the garbage, bearing all the moral uncleanness of God's people out into the waste places, where it no longer has a place in their lives (Lev. 16:21–22). But now we have the deep reversal that belongs to the logic of redemption (see comment on 1:7): Jonah is one of the holy people, chosen because "the LORD set his heart on" him (Deut. 7:7) and given a special place among all the nations. Yet for the sake of a boatload of unclean Gentiles he is thrown overboard, taking with him every uncleanness that would make them offensive to the LORD his God. The sign of this is not only that the storm immediately ceases to rage, but that the boat promptly becomes a temple, a holy place in which are offered sacrifices well pleasing to the LORD.

Jesus Christ is of course the true scapegoat, but he is also the true sacrifice: he corresponds to both goats on the Day of Atonement, the one that is sacrificed in the temple and the one that is sent out into the waste places. On the cross he is the sacrifice whose blood is shed to make atonement for the sins of the whole world, and in his burial he becomes unclean, a corpse to be laid in the depths of the earth. For this is another point of the sacrificial system that we need to understand: an acceptable sacrifice must be clean, pure and unblemished—and there is nothing more unclean than a human corpse, nothing that must be kept further from the holy grounds of the temple. (To get the gut-level sense of this, imagine embracing a corpse that is a few days old, or better yet preparing a corpse for burial and then going immediately to supper without washing your hands. The sacrifice is, among other things, a holy meal, a supper to which one must come only after being purified.)

So Jonah thrown overboard is less like Christ on the cross than like Christ buried and descending into hell. Augustine sees here a sequence, comparing the wood of the ship to the wood of the cross, then picking up on the biblical comparison between Jonah's burial in the sea and Christ's three days of death: "As, therefore, Jonah passed from the ship to the belly of the whale, so Christ passed from the cross to the sepulcher, or into the abyss of death. And as Jonah suffered this for the sake of those who were endangered by the storm, so Christ suffered for the sake of those who are tossed on the waves of this world" (*Letter* 102.34).

But then a funny thing happens, as in all good stories about lost wedding rings or lottery tickets in the dumpster. Once you find the precious thing and know where it is, you can only laugh. As the Christian tradition tells the story, there in the underworld is father Abraham with Lazarus in his bosom, waiting for the coming of the Lord, who goes to hell not as its victim but as its conqueror. He alone walks free among the dead, untouched by the dangers of death and damnation, like Israel walking dry-shod through the sea with waters heaped up on every side. And even hell then is not the same. Like every other time he touches the unclean—bleeding women, lepers, corpses—he does not get dirty but makes them clean, even if it requires giving life to the dead. Jonah too, like every believer, is buried with Christ so as to be raised to newness of life with him. But first he has to spend some time in an unusual dumpster.

We all know what's coming, but first let us get back to the boat, where the happy ending comes for the sailors.

and the sea ceased from its raging.

It is just as Jonah promised. In this regard at least, he is as good as his word. While the sea closes over his head and sucks him to the bottom, above him it calms down like a great angry beast suddenly tamed, turning from ravenous anger to gentleness and peace. Jonah, in his own way, has stilled the storm like Christ. For all his disobedience and foolishness, Jonah has by the grace of God accomplished the sort of things that Christ accomplishes: calming the sea, converting the Gentiles, and teaching them the name of the LORD. His prophetic mission is already, astonishingly, a great success. Through him the LORD has triumphed not only over the sea (that part is easy for the maker of heaven and earth) but even over human hearts. All is going well.

Not that Jonah is in a position to see any of this as the sea closes over his head, but the fact is that the story is now well on its way toward its happy ending. So it is in every comedy: things look crazy, not to mention dangerous, in the middle of the story—but all's well that ends well. As Jonah sinks into the depths, we might think of Shakespeare's four lovers getting lost in the depth of the woods, bewildered by a midsummer night's dream which to them must have seemed more like a nightmare: lost love, lost identities, terrifying transformations. But all is well, and no one is hurt, and the goodness of their end was never really in doubt. They see all this when they wake up and take their troubles for a dream. It is as if, over this comedy as well as over the whole history of the world, sweet Jesus speaks the words he spoke to Julian of Norwich: "All things shall be well." "You shall see yourself that all manner of thing shall be well. . . . What is impossible for you is not impossible for me. I shall keep my word in all things and I shall make all things well" (*Revelations of Divine Love* 32).

1:16 And the people feared a great fear of the LORD,

For the second time the sailors fear a great fear (cf. 1:10), but this time it is explicitly described as the fear of the LORD, and it clearly means the reverent fear that is the ground of worship, thanksgiving, and praise. All is well, and they know all is well, and indeed they are ready to celebrate.

and they offered sacrifice to the LORD

Jonah 1 draws to a close by giving us an astonishing picture. While the son of Israel sinks into the depths of the sea, above him people from all nations join in thanksgiving and praise, worshiping in the name of the LORD, the God of Israel, and offering him sacrifice. This inverts the picture of Noah's flood, which drowns all nations in the depths while the chosen one, the beloved who finds grace in the eyes of the LORD (Gen. 6:8), rides safely above the waves.

What is not often noticed is that this picture from the book of Jonah is actually the normative biblical picture. After the flood God declares that he is not going to do things that way anymore (Gen. 9:11). He will not destroy the world while saving only a few. The picture of Jonah sinking into the depths shows what comes of this divine declaration: the chosen one, the prophet who represents Israel and therefore the whole chosen people, precious in the LORD's sight and beloved like a dove, sinks into the depths of destruction after bestowing upon the Gentile sailors an inestimable blessing. The Gentiles know the LORD and are saved from death precisely because of the suffering and death of God's chosen.

This is why Jesus, the Savior of the whole world, identifies with Jonah, not with Noah. He does not come to save himself or even his own people. He thus fulfills the calling of Israel, which is chosen not for its own salvation but for the blessing of all the families of the earth. Yet as we are about to see, even in the depths of the sea the LORD does not abandon his chosen one. In that way too Jesus identifies with Jonah, being the fulfillment of his work.

and vowed vows.

Vows of sacrifice and praise are the typical fruit of gratitude borne by those whom the LORD rescues:

> I will come into your house with burnt offerings,
>   and I will fulfill my vows to you—
> what my lips uttered
>   and my mouth promised when I was in trouble.
> I will offer to you burnt offerings of fatlings;
>   with the smoke of the sacrifice of rams
> I will make an offering of bulls and goats.
> Come and hear, all you who fear God,
>   and I will tell what he has done for me. (Ps. 66:13–16)

The vows also serve to show that the sailors' conversion to the LORD will last beyond the time they get off the boat. If they are like the vows we find in the psalms, they will require these Gentiles to give testimony to the mercy and loving-kindness of the LORD in the presence of the congregation of Israel in the temple at Jerusalem:

> What shall I render to the LORD
>   for all his goodness to me? . . .
> I will offer to you the sacrifice of thanksgiving
>   and call upon the name of the LORD.
> I will pay my vows to the LORD
>   in the presence of all his people,
> in the courts of the house of the LORD,
>   in your midst, O Jerusalem. (Ps. 116:12, 17–19)

Such a gathering of the nations in Jerusalem is how the Bible envisions the culmination of redemption in an eschatological banquet joining Jew and Gentile (Isa. 25:6–8; 60:4–9; 66:19–21; Zech. 14:16; Matt. 8:11; Luke 13:29). As we near the end of Jonah 1, therefore, we are already getting a hint of the glorious fulfillment of all things.

It is of course only a hint, and there are all sorts of reasons why it cannot yet be the promised consummation. The original Judean readers, seeing this picture of Gentiles worshiping in the name of the LORD while an Israelite is consigned to his exile in the sea, would no doubt have thought of a striking example they had right in front of them of long-lasting Gentile worship in the name of the LORD within the boundaries of Israel itself, which could hardly be seen as a harbinger of redemption. After the destruction of the northern kingdom, the Assyrians resettled an ethnically diverse group of people (including Babylonians!) in their place, who subsequently came to worship the God of this land, the LORD, for protection from wild beasts, under the instruction of an Israelite priest who was sent back from the exile for this purpose (2 Kgs. 17:24–41). So the exiles returning from Babylon found Gentiles worshiping the LORD in the holy land alongside all their own gods and offering sacrifices to him outside the covenant with Israel (Ezra 4:1–4). After centuries of interbreeding with the remnants of the children of Israel who still dwelled there, these people came to be known as Samaritans—a people who were particularly offensive to the Judeans but whom our Lord in an especially emphatic way made their neighbors (Luke 10:29–37). All sorts of problems arise for Jews when Gentiles believe in a Jewish prophet. But the Samaritans are the first stage of the spread of the name of the LORD God of Israel—which is the name of the Lord Jesus Christ (Phil. 2:9–11)—beyond Judea to the ends of the earth (Acts 1:8).

1:17 And the LORD prepared a great fish

Of course the picture of Gentiles worshiping the LORD while the LORD's prophet sinks into the deep cannot be the end of the story. For even the waste places of the deep hide nothing from the God of Israel. Just as Jonah confessed, he is the God of heaven, who made the sea as well as the dry land (1:9). Thus one of the great psalms of praise, after calling upon the hosts of heaven and urging, "Let them praise the name of the LORD, for he commanded and they were created" (Ps. 148:5), turns to the praises that rise from the earth, beginning with the great things of the deep: "Praise the LORD from the earth, sea monsters and all deeps" (148:7).

So the LORD prepares a great beast from the deep to do his work. The word "prepared" can also be translated "appointed." It is a verb for governing, arranging, and ordering rather than creating, but its use here presupposes that the LORD is the sovereign creator of all things, even of the denizens of the deep. As Israel sings in her worship: "The sea is his, for he made it" (95:5). Likewise the psalm of creation testifies that even Leviathan, the great sea monster, was made by the LORD, apparently just for the fun of it:

> O LORD, how manifold are your works!
>   In wisdom have you made them all:
>   the earth is full of your creatures.
> Yonder is the sea, great and wide,
>   which teems with things innumerable,
>   living things both small and great.
> There go the ships,
>   and Leviathan that you formed to play in it. (Ps. 104:24–26)

We no longer feel in our gut how astonishing this confession of the sovereignty of God the creator is, though perhaps the sailors at sea still know.

The great fish is a comic version of an ancient nightmare, the great monster of the deep that represents chaos and destruction, the flooding and undoing of the world. I saw the origins of this nightmare once when I stood with a very small child at the seashore and watched the waves roll in, and he was frightened because he did not see what could keep them from rolling on and on and swallowing him up. For all who can feel the roots of that child's fear, the LORD God brings assurance and order to the world, saying to the sea: "Thus far you may come and no farther, and here shall your proud waves be stayed" (Job 38:11). The same setting of boundaries to the sea is pictured on the third day of creation, when God separates land from water, making a place where human beings can dwell. After this, the first of the creatures that God makes to live and move under heaven are "the great sea monsters" (Gen. 1:21). This is a reversal of the view of ancient Near Eastern mythology, which bases the ordering of the world on a primal battle between a god like Baal and the monsters of the watery chaos. God does not first slay the monster of the deep and then order the inhabited world, but first orders the world in peace, then creates great and marvelous things even in the deep.

Yet in bearing witness to the power of the God of Israel, Scripture often reckons with the nightmares of ancient Near Eastern mythology and puts them to its own uses. The crossing of the Red Sea is frequently described in poetry that evokes the picture of divine victory over the monsters of the sea, one of which was called Rahab:

> Was it not you who cut Rahab in pieces
> and pierced the dragon?
> Was it not you who dried up the sea,
> the waters of the great depths;
> who made the depth of the sea a way
> for the redeemed to pass over? (Isa. 51:9–10)

And again, the more familiar name of Leviathan:

> You divided the sea by your might;
> you broke the heads of the dragons in the waters.
> You crushed the heads of Leviathan. (Ps. 74:13–14)

So in completing the trajectory of descent that he began by going down to Joppa in Jonah 1:3, descending now to the bottom of the sea, Jonah ends up testing the limits of the power of the LORD his God, the God of heaven who made the sea and the dry land. Is the LORD really master even over the hidden depths of darkness, the bottoms of the mountains, the foundations of earth and sea? Do the monsters of chaos, those great nightmares of the destruction of all order and habitation, obey his word? Do the dragons of the deep praise him? Jonah will find out in his own flesh.

It is indeed nightmare turned into comedy. The creature that swallows Jonah up is not one of the terrible monsters of the deep, not Rahab or Leviathan, but just a great big fish. After the great wind and the great storm and the sailors' great fear, the word "great" has attached itself to something rather homely, a great big hunk of comic deflation. It is like being swallowed up by the greatest empire the world has ever known and discovering that is it, well, rather ordinary, a place where one can build a house, plant a garden, and raise children (Jer. 29:5–6). It's just a fish. And oddly, inside the belly of this beast Jonah can live.

The lesson is that there is a deep beyond deep, beyond the furthest limits of the world. Look beneath the waves to the very bottom of the sea, and all you find is rocks and fish. Call the latter a sea monster if you wish, it is no big deal. Wherever you go in the world, the LORD who created it is there before you and can prepare a way for you, even if the way is just a great big fish. For what is deeper than the depths and before the beginning of the world and beyond its end is the word of the LORD who created them and you, who keeps faith with the people of his covenant.

> For thus says the LORD who created you, O Jacob,
>   and he who formed you, O Israel:
> "Fear not, for I have redeemed you,
>   I have called you by name,
>   you are mine.
> When you pass through the waters, I will be with you." (Isa. 43:1–2)

Jonah is Israel, and Israel has passed through the waters before unharmed and dry-shod, for the LORD was with her. That has not changed and will not change forever.

to swallow up Jonah.

As he sinks, Jonah is swallowed up twice: first when the waters close over his head (2:5) and then when the great fish takes him in. Yet it turns out that the latter is rescue, prepared by the LORD for Jonah's salvation. So after all, Jonah is perfectly safe in the heart of the sea, far from home and in exile from any land in which a man can live.

This has happened before. The original readers of the text would have seen it right away: long ago Israel passed safely through the sea in their exodus from Egypt, and much more recently Judah was swallowed up by the greatest beast of them all, Babylon the great, under the rule of Nebuchadnezzar who, the prophet says in the name of Israel, "has swallowed me up like a sea monster" (Jer. 51:34). Indeed, swallowing up is a recurrent biblical image for the enemy overcoming Israel (Isa. 49:19; Lam. 2:16; Hos. 8:8). And yet after being swallowed up by Babylon, the remnant of Israel is kept safe. Jonah swallowed up by a sea monster is an image of the Jewish people in exile, still alive and still having a future, singing the songs of Zion even in the belly of the beast:

> If the LORD had not been on our side—
>   let Israel now say—
> if the LORD had not been on our side
>   when man rose up against us,
> then they would have swallowed us up alive
>   when their anger burned against us;
> then the flood would have overwhelmed us;
>   the waves would have gone over our soul;
> the raging waters would have gone over our soul. (Ps. 124:1–5)

To meditate on Jonah swallowed up in the depths is therefore to think of the Jewish people alive in exile. We must not overlook how astounding this is. Just as a man does not live in the depths of the sea, nations do not survive in exile. To be in exile is to be not only far from home but far from one's god, far from the land and the temple that give the life of the nation its meaning. So when other nations go into exile, their temples destroyed and their gods defeated, they do not return. Israel itself never returned from Nineveh to worship its golden calves, which Jeroboam taught them to say had brought them out of Egypt.

But Judah returns. Lacking temple and land, the Judeans still have a future, a meaning, and an identity as the beloved people, chosen and precious. For their God has not been defeated. Their exile is not the failure of the LORD their God but his punishment for their sin, rebellion, and faithlessness. Because they believe this, they will live. It is indeed an implausible story: because Judah is unlike all the other nations, its military defeat is not the defeat of its God but his loving discipline. Because he lives, all is well with them, even when they are in exile and the temple of the LORD is in ruins. Like Jonah, they still have a future even when they are swallowed up by the great monster of the deep. The meaning of their exile is not destruction but penitence. It is hard to believe. But it is also what actually happened.

Christians are initiated into the same faith when they too are buried in the water and drawn out of it for a new life. Jonah in the depths of the sea is therefore also an image of baptism and especially of that moment when the water has closed over the head of the believer, who is now buried with Christ. Perhaps the ancient Christians had this in mind when they devised the anagram of Christ as fish. You have to put it in Greek: *ichthus*, *Iēsous **Christos** Theos Uios Sōtēr*—Jesus Christ, Son of God, Savior—the one who meets you at the bottom when it seems you have been swallowed up by some monstrous evil, even by death itself. Baptism assures you: you have already died with Christ, already been crucified with him. Now you will suffer with him, but you have already found him in the depths, and there is no deeper place you can go where he is not there before you to sustain and keep you, even unto eternal life. You have already been with Jonah in the heart of the sea, and you have returned. Now you will live.

And Jonah was in the guts of the fish three days and three nights.

Jonah has completed his long descent from before the face of the LORD, which is the basic arc of the story in Jonah 1. Now he has hit bottom. He's as far down as you can get. And there God is with him and he is saved.

He is there three days and three nights. This number, so important in biblical narrative, reminds us of many things. Turn a page in the Bible, and you can find that it takes a three days' walk to get from one end of Nineveh to the other (3:3). Go not so far back in history, and you find that Samaria, the capital city of Israel, had to endure a siege of three years (2 Kgs. 17:5). Israel was to go out three days into the desert to worship the LORD, according to the initial proposal submitted to Pharaoh (Exod. 5:3). Their three days in the desert turned into forty years and then into a new life in the Promised Land.

Finally, of course, the great one who identified with Jonah spent three days in the tomb and called this the sign of Jonah. Since so much of our reading of this book depends on identifying Jonah with Israel and Judah and therefore with Christ, the King of the Jews, we need to give some detailed attention to the New Testament passages where our Lord makes his identification with Jonah explicit, for these are also the passages where his identification with Israel seems most severely strained.

Excursus: The Sign of Jonah

And the Pharisees came and began to argue with him, seeking from him a sign from heaven, testing him. And he groaned in his spirit and said, "Why does this generation seek a sign? Amen I say to you, if this generation will be given a sign." (Mark 8:11–12)

And there came the Pharisees and Sadducees testing, and asked him to show them a sign from heaven. And he answered and said to them, "When evening comes, you say, 'Fair weather, for heaven is fiery red.' And in the morning, 'Foul weather today, because heaven is fiery red and threatening.' The face of heaven you know how to discern, but the signs of the times you cannot! An evil and adulterous generation seeks after a sign, and a sign will not be given to it except *the sign of Jonah*." And leaving them, he went away. (Matt. 16:1–4)

And when the crowd was gathered, he began to say, "This generation is an evil generation. It seeks a sign, and a sign shall not be given to it except *the sign of Jonah*. For just as Jonah became a sign for the Ninevites, so will the Son of Man be for this generation. The Queen of the South will rise in the judgment with the men of this generation and condemn them. For she came from the ends of the earth to hear the wisdom of Solomon, and behold a greater than Solomon is here. The men of Nineveh will be resurrected in the judgment with this generation and condemn it, for they repented at the preaching of Jonah, and behold a greater than Jonah is here." (Luke 11:29–32)

Then certain of the scribes and the Pharisees replied, saying, "Teacher, we wish to see a sign from you." And he answered and said to them, "An evil and adulterous generation seeks after a sign, and a sign shall not be given to it except *the sign of Jonah* the prophet. For as Jonah was in the belly of the sea monster three days and three nights, so shall the Son of Man be in the heart of the earth three days and three nights. The men of Nineveh shall be resurrected in the judgment with this generation and condemn it. For they repented at the preaching of Jonah, and behold a greater than Jonah is here. The Queen of the South shall arise in the judgment with this generation and condemn it, for she came from the ends of the earth to hear the wisdom of Solomon, and behold a greater than Solomon is here." (Matt. 12:38–42)

The New Testament passages about the sign of Jonah can be arranged in order of increasing explicitness, beginning with Mark 8:11–12, which does not mention Jonah at all. The context of all these passages is Jesus's refusal to give a sign upon demand—even after having given many signs to the people, such as the miraculous feeding of the multitude, which immediately precedes the first two passages (Mark 8:11–12; Matt. 16:1–4). The two longer versions (Luke 11:29–32; Matt. 12:38–42) are placed in the context of the accusation that he casts out demons by the power of Beelzebub. Luke's version adds an explanation of the meaning of the phrase "the sign of Jonah," where Jonah is a sign to the Ninevites, and the longer passage from Matthew adds the comparison of Jesus's three days of death and burial to Jonah's three days in the belly of the sea monster. The two longer versions then contrast the unbelief of this "evil and adulterous generation" with the faith of Gentiles—the Ninevites responding to Jonah's preaching and the Queen of the South coming to Jerusalem in a foretaste of the eschatological banquet to feast on the wisdom of Solomon, the anointed Son of David. And now one greater than Solomon or Jonah is here, and this generation refuses to believe but wants him to give signs!

What all the passages have in common is that Jesus immediately diagnoses this generation's demand for a sign as a form of unbelief. In each of the passages we should imagine him groaning in spirit as he refuses to play their game. Matthew 16:1–4 especially highlights this diagnosis. His enemies want him to give them "a sign from heaven." Evidently healing and feeding the multitude, which took place in the immediately preceding chapter, are miracles too earthly to convince them! So Jesus looks up at the face of heaven and observes that they all know how to read the signs there. When it turns fiery red in the evening it is a sign of good weather, whereas the same color at morning is a sign of bad weather. Anyone can read these signs; it does not take the erudition of a scribe or a Pharisee. But one does need to discern—to know the difference between evening and morning—to know what time it is. And that is what the Pharisees and their ilk do not know. They have not discerned "the time of their visitation" (Luke 19:44) because they do not believe and therefore do not know the man whose word they are hearing. The very fact that they're asking for a sign shows that they have no idea who this is or, worse yet, that they have a very good idea (for who cannot discern when it is evening?) and are doing their best not to believe him.

Therefore all of us who say we believe and yet deny Christ—which is to say, all of us who follow in the footsteps of the apostle Peter—are the evil and adulterous generation of which Christ speaks. To recognize this is to discern what time it is, the time when Christ visits us and speaks his word in our hearing, calling us to repentance and faith. To believe this is to recognize ourselves as those to whom Christ speaks and therefore those to whom the sign of Jonah is given. And this is very good news indeed.

Jesus is the sign of Jonah, given to an evil and adulterous generation. For others he will perform all manner of miraculous signs, healing the sick and feeding the hungry and casting out demons, displaying the glory and righteousness of the kingdom of heaven. But for an evil and adulterous generation—determined not to be poor and afflicted, doing its best to lack a broken and contrite heart, seeking every glory and righteousness besides that of the kingdom where Christ is king—no other sign is given. No other sign is good enough, great enough, or powerful enough. For the point is that Jesus himself is the sign of Jonah. This is the point that unbelief refuses to see, the point without which all other signs signify nothing.

In calling himself the sign of Jonah, Jesus makes himself the sign to end all signs. All other signs signify this sign, which signifies nothing but himself. If we don't get this, it is because we think there is some greater or better sign he could give us. That is precisely what makes us evil and adulterous: we are to forsake all others and cleave to this one, yet we would rather he give us something else, some miracle or maybe some dramatic change in our lives as a testimony that he is present among us. We do not want to be stuck with nothing to show for ourselves but Jesus Christ. So we are like scholars commenting on a text that we do not recognize is about ourselves, and therefore we do not discern that this is the time of our visitation.

To call Jesus "the sign of Jonah" does not mean that he signifies Jonah. The reverse is closer to the truth: Jonah—like Solomon, like the heavenly figure of the Son of Man in Dan. 7, like all signs in the Old Testament—points toward Christ, the sign to end all signs, which is to say, the sign that all signs are about. But why then is he specifically the sign *of Jonah*?

Jesus is the sign of Jonah because he is a sign the same way Jonah is a sign. Jonah offered Nineveh no sign but himself. He did no miracles and had little to say, and that little was ironic and enigmatic, like a parable about not knowing what time it is. The mystery, the hidden meaning, is right there on the surface, as if to say: Don't you know whose word you're hearing? That's what time it is, the time when your LORD visits you and speaks to you. And *now* you want a sign? The Ninevites knew better, and when Jonah came as a sign among them they believed his word and repented.

Yet the sign of Jonah is good news, for the Ninevites did believe, and therefore it must be that we can too. Of course this also leaves us with no excuse for our unbelief. Indeed the great, evil city Nineveh has every right to rise up at the last day and condemn all of us who follow in Peter's footsteps, but that is only because (and here again is good news, the gospel) a greater than Jonah is indeed among us, and he is stubbornly persistent in being nothing less than the sign of Jonah, given to an unbelieving generation so that we may believe.

Need it be said that we should not be so foolish as to think ourselves worse off than those who first heard Jesus preach? If we are paying attention at all, we will realize it is not easier to believe him just because he is visibly present. We have indeed not been put to the test like that earlier generation, who took his visibly present flesh, hung it on a cross, and then buried it in the heart of the earth. Yet we, more than they, are that evil and adulterous generation of whom Jesus speaks, for like the Ninevites we are those to whom came one who had already been buried three days. Those who first heard Jesus preach did not have that advantage, because he had not yet died.

Jonah is a sign in his own person because he had been as if three days dead, and yet there he is in the heart of Nineveh proclaiming the word of the LORD. So Jesus is to us the sign of Jonah, three days dead yet there he is in the heart of us, present among us in word and sacrament, preaching and mystery, as enigmatic as a parable whose meaning is hidden right on the surface and therefore impossible for an evil and adulterous generation to understand—unless like the Ninevites we believe in him.

JONAH 2

Jonah's Psalm from the Depths

2:1 And Jonah prayed to the LORD his God from the guts of the fish:

From the fish to his God! Such is the direction of Jonah's prayer at the nadir of his helplessness, when he has no other recourse. He is still a comic figure, though no doubt he feels miserable enough. This is a moment of comedy like that indicated in the wonderful title of the Flannery O'Connor story, "You Can't Be Any Poorer Than Dead." Jonah indeed prays as one who is dead and buried in the heart of the sea, from which no one has power to return. He is as poor as you can get, with no resources and no plausible hope of rescue. Escape from this utmost poverty is a miracle reserved for the end of days when the sea gives up the dead that are in it, and death and hell deliver up the dead that are in them (Rev. 20:13).

And yet Jonah prays, even from the fish to his God. There is nothing else to do. Like Abraham, his father in faith, he awaits the resurrection of the dead (Heb. 11:19). That is the kind of faith that lies at the root of biblical prayer. This also explains why, even when it stares death in the face, the Bible is a comedy.

2:2 "I called from my trouble to the LORD, and he answered me.

Jonah's prayer begins by describing itself in the past tense, in a kind of prefatory summary. From its inception this prayer is way ahead of itself, describing both itself and the LORD's answer as if they had already happened. For indeed the whole prayer speaks of itself as having already been prayed, narrating the process of its coming to be as well as its being answered. Here in the depths of his helplessness Jonah looks at the mercy he begs for as an accomplished fact. Thus he speaks as a prophet, one who confidently tells us of the ways of the LORD. We could say: he speaks eschatologically, looking at the whole story from the standpoint of its end and fulfillment. To use another technical term, he speaks proleptically, which is to say, he narrates the end of the story as if it had already happened, speaking of his future redemption as a thing accomplished in the present.

This startling proleptic or eschatological perspective is reinforced in the opening sentence by the use of the third person to describe the LORD, as if this discourse were more narrative than petition. It is as if the prophet's prayer were far-seeing enough to stand outside itself like an omniscient observer viewing the whole interaction between man and God, between human prayer and divine response. Indeed Jonah prays this psalm as if it were the word of the LORD itself—which of course it is, being Holy Scripture written for our edification, instruction, and comfort. There is never any doubt in this word that the LORD is greater than Jonah's troubles, and in this sense his troubles are already overcome as soon as Jonah turns back to the LORD in prayer, looking away from his troubles to the God from whom he has hitherto spent the whole story fleeing. So now, at the very beginning of his turning or conversion, he can confidently summarize the whole story of his redemption in advance.

The summary is in fact rather bland, even a cliché. All of us who pray the psalms have said this kind of thing dozens of times before: for instance, "In my trouble I called to the LORD and he answered me" (Ps. 120:1); or, "I called upon the LORD in distress, and the LORD answered me" (118:5); or, "In the day of my trouble I will call upon you, for you will answer me" (86:7). Given the extraordinary trouble Jonah is in, the use of this cliché is just a little surprising. Perhaps it is meant to help us see something: that no trouble is extraordinary to God, none beyond his help. Jonah's disaster is just one more trouble that God can get people out of.

This has another implication in reverse: we whose troubles do not seem as deep as Jonah's need not hesitate to pray Jonah's psalm, as we pray many other psalms that call to the LORD out of troubles that are not exactly our own. Even in our shallowness we have license to pray from the depths: "Out of the depths have I called to you, O LORD; Lord, hear my voice!" (Ps. 130:1). For in prayer we put on Christ, who prayed all the psalms, and so with him we can take on all the troubles and afflictions depicted in them. Indeed, insofar as our troubles grow like Jonah's out of our sins, they may not be as shallow as we think. So in prayer we may put on Christ also in his identification with Jonah. We too can call upon the name of the LORD from our troubles, knowing that he has already answered. His grace goes before us.

So whether our troubles are deep or shallow, uttering familiar clichés about how God answers us when we call really is a sufficient form of prayer. There is no need for us to be original in our supplications. As we shall see, Jonah's psalm itself is often quite unoriginal, much of it a pastiche of the songs of Israel.

The real problem with Jonah's psalm is that it comes so late. While the sailors above him, having already found safety and redemption, celebrate the goodness of the LORD with sacrifices of thanksgiving, Jonah finally gets around to doing what the captain had urged him to do quite some time ago (1:6): he calls upon the name of the LORD. The sailors had obeyed the LORD before it was too late, before they suffered shipwreck, whereas Jonah does not pray until he has hit bottom. Indeed we often pray too late: asleep in spiritual laziness or afraid to face God, we delay our prayers until disaster has already overtaken us and death is no longer something to fear, but has arrived and become our dwelling place. Yet precisely then we discover it is never too late for prayer. We can pray from the valley of the shadow of death (Ps. 23:4), just as Jonah prays from the guts of the fish.

No doubt we are just like Jonah when we pray our belated prayers: the answer has already overtaken us precisely in that we are now praying. Already, unbeknownst to us but all around us and over us, there is worship, doxology, and praise, as people of all nations make their vows and sacrifices far above Jonah's head. And meanwhile, down in the belly of the beast something even more remarkable has happened than the happy ending of Jonah 1: Jonah too is finally calling upon the name of the LORD. Redemption has begun all around.

From the belly of Sheol I shouted,

For a third time, the book describes the deep place from which Jonah calls upon the LORD: from the guts of the fish (2:1), from his trouble (2:2), and now from the belly of Sheol. The first description is the literal level of the story; the second is the bland, abstract language of feeling (applying to all of us who are in trouble, no matter what our story); and the third is a vividly poetic description that reveals the true meaning of the trouble in which Jonah finds himself. The rest of Jonah's psalm operates at this truer, poetic level. It has nothing to say about the fish and little of relevance to say about the other literal details of Jonah's troubles, but much to say about what it is like to go down among the dead.

For Sheol of course is the Old Testament place of the dead, the deep place where all flesh goes, never to return. It should not be thought of as life after death, not even a life of punishment like the New Testament Gehenna or hell. Sheol is a place of death, not life after death. It is what death looks like before everything is changed by the resurrection of Jesus Christ, who descended into Sheol as its conqueror, taking captivity captive (Eph. 4:8), and became the firstfruits of all who sleep in death (1 Cor. 15:20). To be in Sheol is simply to be dead, beyond all help unless God can give life to what is dead. To be with Jonah at this point in his story is to be where only Jesus Christ can visit and save you.

That must be why Jonah prays as if all is well. Buried in the heart of the sea, he shouts from Sheol, where Jesus is to come and conquer. Jonah is baptized here, buried in a death that is not merely his own but Christ's, so that he may be raised to a new life that is not merely his own but the LORD's. Praying from the belly of Sheol means praying from within the waters of baptism, where we die with Christ—where the LORD, which is to say the Lord Jesus Christ—has already heard the prayer of the dead.

It is striking how often biblical prayer is like this, speaking from death and destruction as if this was already a thing of the past. That is how the psalm goes, for instance, which our Lord himself prays on the cross, "My God, my God, why have you forsaken me?" (Ps. 22:1), yet ending with a celebration of the LORD's salvation in which the Gentiles are called to give thanks to the LORD for delivering him: "They shall come and shall declare his righteousness unto a people yet unborn, that he has done this" (22:31). Forsaken on the cross, dying so as to be the firstfruits of resurrection, the Lord Jesus knows that he is the Savior of all nations and prays accordingly.

We should bear in mind therefore one more parallel: Jonah is the representative Israelite for the original audience of Jewish readers thinking about the meaning of their captivity in Babylon, which is their time in the belly of the beast. Jonah swallowed up in the heart of the sea represents Judah swallowed up in Babylon, descending into a kind of national death. Nations don't return from exile, any more than people return from the dead. Yet the Judeans in Babylon pray and sing psalms as if they were simply there to be disciplined by their loving father, not destroyed. It is indeed there that they become a people dedicated to obedience to the law of God. They emerge from the depths of exile a new and reborn people, as if baptized in Babylon. Their time in exile is the time of their salvation, transformation, and renewal.

So Jonah praying in the guts of the fish is to remind us of the people of Judah singing the songs of Zion by the waters of Babylon, where they remember the Jerusalem that is to come (Ps. 137:1). Their resurrection from exile is not only the foreshadowing but also the precondition of our Lord's resurrection from the dead. If they had not returned to the land of Israel there would be no Jews—and therefore no Lord Jesus, no resurrection, and no salvation for the Gentiles.

and you heard my voice.

A sudden shift: after the introductory sentence referring to the LORD in the third person, the psalm switches to the second person, speaking *to* the LORD rather than *about* him. This of course is more congenial to the discourse of prayer, which is addressed to God. Yet it is still past tense: Jonah speaks to the LORD as to one who has already heard what Jonah speaks, has already done what he is asking him to do.

Using another scriptural cliché, Jonah says the LORD heard his *voice*. That cannot literally be true, for there is no voice in the heart of the sea, among creatures that have no breath. Jonah must be praying in silence, as voiceless as the dead. It is perhaps the only silent prayer in the whole Bible. Yet it comes before the God of heaven, who not only beholds the depths but hears the voice of the voiceless.

This is comfort beyond words. All of us who shall at one time be as poor as dead can pray and be heard, no matter how helpless or dead we may be inside. Imagine being laid low by Huntington's chorea, the degenerative disease that struck Woody Guthrie, gradually taking all movement from his body, even from his mouth and tongue, until the singer had no voice left. Even such a one may pray to the LORD and be heard. We can never descend so far as to be out of reach of divine mercy.

2:3 You threw me into the deep,

Jonah now begins a second-person narrative, describing the actions of the one to whom he speaks. Therefore even as his prayer tells the story of his own life, our attention is drawn to the LORD's doings, not Jonah's. This is what makes the poetic narrative of Jonah 2 so fundamentally different from prose narrative of Jonah 1, although it covers many of the same events. In this second, deeper narrative we hear of Jonah not as doer but as sufferer. He does not appear as an agent in this story but as the one on whom the agent acts: that is why Jonah is the object, not the subject of the active verb in this sentence. For in every narrative of redemption, the redeemed appear primarily as grammatical objects of activity: "me" or "us," not "I" or "we," as for instance when we confess that "Christ died *for me*" or that "he was crucified also *for us* under Pontius Pilate."

The Jonah who appears in this narrative does not even retain enough agency to make the prayer a confession of sin. That would certainly require the word "I." But Jonah prays here not as one asking forgiveness, but as one who was once dead in his trespasses and sins (Eph. 2:1). The dead cannot ask for forgiveness, just as they cannot be healed and cannot save themselves. So the focus of this prayer is on things much larger than what Jonah has done or can do: on the power of the sea, death, and Sheol, as well as the will of the LORD to have mercy even upon the dead.

But there is no mercy without justice, so the first action in this story of redemption is the LORD throwing Jonah, who certainly is a sinner, into the depths of the sea. It is as if the part of the book of Jonah that concerns Jonah himself really gets started only when the sailors hurl him overboard. They are the hands of the LORD, his faithful servants. Before that point, the focus of the story was (though we may not have realized it at first) actually on the LORD's mercy to the sailors. But now in Jonah 2 it is about the LORD's mercy to Jonah. We are about to see what the LORD does with dead sinners.

But let us make no mistake. They are dead because God kills them. For the LORD is the one who throws Jonah into the sea. (The verb here is different from the one translated "hurl" in Jonah 1, but carries no appreciable difference in meaning.) Just as this does not mean the sailors didn't actually hurl Jonah overboard (for these are not rival explanations, but two perfectly compatible descriptions of the same action, like saying both "I tripped" and "I wasn't watching where I was going"), so also this is the deeper truth behind the important fact that sin is its own punishment, leading inherently to death. Sin is its own punishment precisely because the LORD made human beings to live in his sight, so that when they turn away from him they turn inevitably to death, as Jonah does in his descent in Jonah 1. This is the LORD's doing, who made us that way. It is his doing that sinners are indeed the cause of their own death, as Jonah is indeed the cause of his own sinking into Sheol. It's Jonah's fault, but that does not mean the LORD didn't put him there. This is good news, for the result is that in every trouble we may turn and pray to the one who brought us there, who can also bring us out. From whatever hell we sinners have made for ourselves, we may say to the LORD, "*You have laid me in the lowest pit, in darkness, in the deep*" (Ps. 88:6), and therefore we may have hope.

This means we begin by recognizing how deep our trouble is: it is our trouble with the LORD. Jonah's psalm signals this at the start by echoing the language of Israel's exodus and assigning to Jonah the place of the enemy that the LORD destroys. We hear this language when the Judean exiles return from Babylon and Nehemiah tells the founding story of Israel's identity as a nation using the same vocabulary as Jonah's psalm, in another second-person narrative addressed to the LORD: "You divided the sea before them, so that they went through the middle of the sea on the dry land; and their persecutors *you threw into the deep*, like a stone into the mighty waters" (Neh. 9:11). Nehemiah's vocabulary in turn echoes the original song celebrating the LORD's victory at the Red Sea, telling of Pharaoh's chariots and riders: "The depths have covered them; they sank into the deep like a stone" (Exod. 15:5). The opening verse of Jonah's psalm thus portrays Jonah in terms that Israel traditionally reserved for Pharaoh. It is as if we were standing that day at the Red Sea and saw Moses and his people thrown into the deep instead of Pharaoh and his armies.

For the returning exiles reading the book of Jonah, that must have been what it felt like at first to be taken to Babylon, reversing the direction of the exodus "out of the house of bondage" (Exod. 20:2). It felt like the lowest pit, the death of Israel.

into the heart of the sea,

The word for "heart" here is the same as the anatomical term for the organ in our chests and the psychological term for the power of understanding, but just like its English counterpart it can also mean the "middle" or center of something, especially if it is remote, inaccessible, and deep. The phrase "the heart of the sea" is found often in the Old Testament, where it can mean the open sea far from shore, as in "the way of a ship on the heart of the sea" (Prov. 30:19), but also the depths of the sea beneath. Hence in the passage about the ships of Tarshish (quoted in the comment on 1:3) the ships both sail on the heart of the sea (Ezek. 27:26) and sink into the heart of the sea (27:27).

Scripture is clear that the LORD is master even over the heart of the sea. By exercising this mastery he saves his people from Pharaoh's army, as all Israel sings in his praise:

> At the blast of your nostrils the waters piled up;
>   the floods stood up in a heap;
>   the deep congealed *in the heart of the sea.* . . .

> You blew with your wind, the sea covered them;
>> they sank like lead in the mighty waters. (Exod. 15:8, 10)

Picking up on this language, the psalms tell of the LORD defending Israel against the power of the sea, which can bring down the highest mountain—imagery for the tumult of invasion and the destruction of nations. God is a mighty fortress for Israel, saving them from the very heart of the sea:

> God is our refuge and strength,
>> a very present help in trouble.
> Therefore we will not fear,
>> though the earth give way
>> and *the mountains fall into the heart of the sea,*
> though its waters roar and foam
>> and the mountains quake with their surging. (Ps. 46:1–3)

This contrasts with the safety of the city of God:

> God is in the midst of her,
>> she shall not be moved;
> God will help her right early.
> *The nations rage, the kingdoms totter,*
>> he utters his voice, the earth melts. (Ps. 46:5–6)

The nations raging are like the waters roaring, and the kingdoms tottering are like the mountains falling into the heart of the sea, as imagery from other psalms confirms, describing how the God of Israel

> established the mountains,
>> being girded with might,
> and stills the roaring of the seas,
>> the roaring of the waves,
>> *the tumult of the peoples.* (Ps. 65:6–7)

So the floods and the waves are regularly images of the tumult of the peoples, the waves of invading armies come to swallow up Israel (see also Ps. 124:1–5). Jonah being thrown into the heart of the sea is therefore a reminder of Jerusalem, the city of God in Judah, *not* being protected from the tumult of the peoples, from the raging of the nations, like a mountain that is washed into the heart of the sea. This is Jonah's Babylonian exile.

and the flood surrounded me.

Here begins a series of images of being surrounded, overwhelmed, and entangled by the waters, which echoes a great deal of other biblical poetry about besieging armies, the power of Sheol, and the terror of divine wrath. It starts with Jonah on the surface and the waters flooding in all around him, like armies come to besiege a city. The verb "surround" is in fact often used of military forces besieging an enemy (Eccl. 9:14; 2 Kgs. 6:15; 8:21), as well as violent mobs attacking a house (Gen. 19:4; Judg. 19:22; 20:5), and hence also of Israel among hostile nations (Ps. 118:10–12). Still, as it is one thing to be surrounded by waters on every side but quite another to be swallowed up by them, so also the worst has not happened yet when a city is besieged but not captured.

All your waves and breakers have passed over me.

Now it gets worse. Using language lifted straight from Ps. 42:7, Jonah describes the water not just surrounding him but going up over his head. Worse yet, it is the LORD's own water, "*your* waves and breakers," so that the danger Jonah faces in these depths is the LORD himself, as the psalm says, "You have overwhelmed me with all your waves" (88:7). The power of water to engulf and destroy makes it a fit image for the terror of the fierce indignation of God:

> Your wrath has swept over me;
>   your dread assaults have destroyed me.
> All day long they surround me like a flood;
>   they have altogether engulfed me. (Ps. 88:16–17)

This does not mean that the flood of God's wrath is something other than the armies of Israel's enemies. Rather, in every enemy, in the depth of Sheol itself, the enemy that confronts us is our God. This is both inescapable terror and the ground of all comfort and salvation.

2:4 Then I said, 'I have been cast out from before your eyes,

The first act of Jonah described in his prayer, his second-person narrative, is itself an act of prayer. For the one aspect of human agency that prayer cannot forget is human speech. So Jonah speaks of his own speech: "Then I said . . . ." The only thing he has done in this narrative so far is to say what the LORD has done.

When the word "I" appears a second time in the sentence, it is the subject of a *passive* verb, which once again means that Jonah is not the doer but the done-to. Acknowledging the sovereignty of divine wrath, Jonah looks back at the path of his very active running away from God as if it were none other than the path of his being exiled from God. The whole time that Jonah was descending, fleeing from the face of the LORD in Jonah 1, God was in fact casting him out of his sight. Jonah's flight is the LORD's doing, the just punishment of Jonah's disobedience that casts him into exile, taking him further and further away from the land of the living.

In the same way, the people of Israel turning away from the LORD and falling into the worship of golden calves were eventually taken captive by the Assyrians as the LORD "cast them out from his face" (2 Kgs. 17:20). These are two descriptions of the same series of events, one from a human and one from a God's-eye point of view. The same double description applies to the Judeans, who turn from the LORD and are taken captive by the Babylonians, as Jeremiah warned them in the name of the LORD while standing at the very door of the temple: "And I will cast you out from my face, as I cast out all your kin, the seed of Ephraim" (Jer. 7:15). As we have seen, Jonah's descent is fundamentally the same as theirs, going down from Jerusalem and away from the face of the LORD in his holy place (see comment on 1:3).

yet I will look again to your holy temple.'

A drowning man about to sink for the last time beneath the waves takes one final look homeward and sees the place where all meaning, beauty, power, and glory have their habitation: "your holy temple" or, more literally, "the temple of your holiness"—which is to say the place where the LORD God is set apart as holy. Despite his unique unlikeness to all other things, God has chosen a place on earth, a holy habitation to which we may look in prayer.

As we have already noted (see comment on 1:3), the temple stands at the opposite end of the scale of holiness from Sheol and the heart of the sea. It is the center of sacred geography, in contrast to the outer darkness, the formless waste of chaos, disorder, and death where Jonah is now sinking down, thrown out like garbage, cast out like the scapegoat. Yet even here, he can look back at the place that gives meaning and definition to all other places, as all other places are "down" from the holy place.

For as Jonah has already borne witness (1:9), the LORD is the God of heaven, who made the sea and the dry land. He dwells between the cherubim, enthroned on high, and precisely for that reason he "beholds the depths," as the three Hebrew children sang in the furnace (Song of the Three Young Men 32). God does not dwell on earth; he is too big for that, and even the heaven of heavens cannot contain him (1 Kgs. 8:27). In this respect the temple is like the footstool of God who is enthroned above (1 Chr. 28:2); it is the place where, as it were, he rests his feet and therefore the best place on earth to come into his presence and worship (Ps. 99:5; 132:7). But there is no place on earth or even in the depths of the sea where he is absent. Precisely in his height he is present in all the depths. Uncontained even by the heaven of heavens, he is beyond the limitations of time and space and therefore present at all times and places, unlike all things that are dependent for their being on the world he has created.

"Look again" can also have the sense of "look back" or "keep looking." Despite his exile far from the face of the LORD, Jonah looks back to that from which he is exiled. That he can look toward the holy place even here in the trackless waste in the heart of the sea is the spatial correlate to the temporal fact that Jonah's prayer from the guts of the fish speaks of his redemption in the past tense, as if it has already happened. He can look to the LORD in the temple even in his absence from it, just as he can praise the LORD for a deliverance that is still distant from him in the future. For the temple is indeed the place of the future, where one faces the King of kings on his throne and awaits what he will do, expecting his justice, mercy, and redemption to come. Thus the temple represents not just the ordering and creative power at the beginning (as in the usual Near Eastern understanding, found for instance in the *Enuma Elish*) and the cyclical return of seasons (as in the sacred calendar of festivals in Jerusalem) but also, perhaps most fundamentally, the eschatological future, the justice and mercy we await in the face of the LORD.

It is all the more striking, then, that the Judeans in Babylon would have had to pray for mercy at a time when the temple of Jerusalem was in ruins. For them to pray toward the temple was to look to a holy place that was still future. So even the place of the LORD's holiness is remembered as something yet to come, like Jerusalem yet to be rebuilt, which is never forgotten by the exiles in Babylon (Ps. 137:6). This is perhaps why the temple has not been mentioned earlier in the book of Jonah, even though its unnamed presence defines all the movements of Jonah 1. What happens at this moment in Jonah's prayer is like the missing piece of a jigsaw puzzle dropping into place, so that we can begin to see the overall shape of the picture for the first time. It has a center we cannot see but toward which we may look again, like the hidden inner sanctum, the holy of holies in a temple yet to be rebuilt.

Such is the powerless power of prayer, utterly dependent on what is not yet, the promises of God still to be fulfilled. Christians pray similarly in the body of Christ, which is the temple destroyed and rebuilt (John 2:19–22) but now no longer visibly present among us. We await his coming, while in the meantime our life is not apparent even to ourselves but is hidden in Christ who sits at God's right hand and will surely come again in glory (Col. 3:1–4). For us to pray with Jonah is to look again to that heavenly temple, where Christ makes intercession for us before the Father. To him we lift our voices like sheep calling to their shepherd, even as we walk in the valley of the shadow of death (Ps. 23:4), about to be overwhelmed by waters that will actually kill us.

2:5 The waters encompassed me, up to my soul.

Now we come to the major narrative peculiarity of Jonah 2. After Jonah looks to the place of the LORD's presence, he is not rescued but descends further. He takes one last look toward the temple, then sinks under the waves and begins to drown. This after all is the usual way of prayer: we come before the face of God to make our petition, and then it is some time before we see his answer. So for instance in Ps. 73 the psalmist, oppressed by the triumph of the wicked, comes to the temple and sees the justice that *will be* done to them, understanding the end that is not yet (73:17). Jonah's psalm brings this anticipatory character of prayer to our attention very pointedly: you look to the LORD for rescue and redemption, and it comes. But first you die.

The waters come up to Jonah's soul because the word for "soul" (*nephesh*) is also the word for "life" and even "neck." As with the Hebrew word for "heart," the physical, biological, and psychological meanings of the term are inseparable here: as the waters rise up to Jonah's *neck*, they extinguish his *life* and swallow up his *soul* in the depths of Sheol. It is all one and the same happening.

The poetic imagery here is powerful but not new. It is the sort of thing from which the psalmist is always asking to be saved:

> Save me, O God,
> for the waters have come up to my soul.
> I sink in deep mire
> where there is no place to stand.
> I have come into depth of waters
> where the flood sweeps over me. (Ps. 69:1–2)

The depths surrounded me;

This is the same verb as when the flood surrounded Jonah in 2:3, but now the waters are not just all around him but above and below him, swallowing him up and taking him captive. He is no longer like a besieged city but like a people taken into exile.

In biblical poetry, engulfing waters very frequently are meant to be transparent metaphors for deadly enemies, as we saw in Ps. 124:1–5 (see comment on 1:17) and as we can also see a little later in the psalm just quoted:

> Deliver me from sinking in the mire;
> let me be delivered from my enemies
> and from the depth of waters.
> Let not the flood sweep over me,
> nor the deep swallow me up,
> nor the pit close its mouth over me. (Ps. 69:14–15)

The crucial point to note about this parallel language is that what this psalm asks to be delivered from, Jonah's psalm depicts as having taken place. Jonah is not delivered from the worst that could happen. His redemption comes on the other side of the worst, so that we may know that there is no worst from which the LORD cannot deliver us.

reeds were wrapped around my head.

This is a crown fit for a drowning man, tangled up in some sort of seaweed that binds him. The picture resembles another commonplace of the psalms:

> The cords of death encompassed me;
> the torrents of perdition assailed me.

> The cords of Sheol surrounded me;
>   the snares of death came before me. (Ps. 18:4–5)

The same imagery occurs in virtually the same words in Ps. 116:3 and 2 Sam. 22:5–6. This is familiar poetry!

Yet Jonah's diction is unusual and reminds us of a very specific body of water. "The Sea of Reeds" is the literal rendering of the name usually translated "Red Sea" in the biblical narrative of Israel's redemption from Egypt. The Hebrew word for "reed" is Egyptian in origin and used also in Exodus to refer to the reeds along the bank of the Nile where the baby Moses floated safely in his ark (Exod. 2:3, 5). Jonah is passing through his sea of reeds, but something is terribly wrong: he is not floating safe above it like little Moses or walking dry-shod through it like the people of Israel being brought out of Egypt; he is drowning like Pharaoh's soldiers, while the Gentiles above him in the boat from which he is thrown are celebrating the salvation of the LORD. The chosen one dies while the others live. But as we have seen, this is the very logic of redemption (see comment on 1:7), which is why Jesus identifies with Jonah, the chosen one who descends to Sheol so that people of all nations might live.

Even as Jonah descends to the very bottom, redemption is under way and all is well. So he continues in his song of praise.

2:6 To the bases of the mountains I went down;

Now Jonah gets to the bottom. Jonah 2:6 completes the theme of Jonah's descent from Jonah 1, using the same verb as in 1:3 and 1:5. But here he goes much further down. The poetry asks us to imagine Jonah *beneath* the bottom of the mountains. This is possible to imagine because ancient Israel pictured the earth as built on top of a measureless ocean, "founded on the seas" (Ps. 24:2) when the LORD "spread out the earth above the waters" (136:6). Just as there are waters above the blue dome of heaven, from which the rain descends, so there are waters at the bottom of the earth, from which the springs of water rise up (104:10–13). Hence when the LORD wished to obliterate the earth with a flood in the days of Noah, "all the fountains of the great deep burst forth, and the windows of the heavens were opened" (Gen. 7:11), drowning the earth with water from below and water from above. And when he wanted to renew the face of the earth, he put the waters back in their place, and "the fountains of the deep and the windows of the heavens were closed" (8:2).

Jonah has descended into these deepest of all waters, beneath whatever pillars are at the subterranean bases of the mountains. He enters "the waters under the earth" (Exod. 20:4) at the opposite end of creation from "the waters above the firmament" (Gen. 1:7) over the blue dome of heaven. He is as far beneath the surface of the earth as the heavens are above it, as far from the land of this mortal life as it is possible to get and even farther from the life of heaven and the throne of God.

And just as he gets down to this chamber of unfathomable depth, the door slams shut behind him.

the earth with its bars was about me forever.

The "bars" are moveable crossbeams on a door, like a bolt that is shot to keep a gate shut fast (Exod. 36:31–33). This is how Jonah's poetry pictures Sheol: the waters beneath the bottom of the mountains where he will nevermore know the breath of life. The psalm invites us to imagine this experience.

One of the cruelest torments ever devised is the water torture. There are many versions; the one used by the CIA is called "water-boarding." But the basic idea is the same: water is run up the victims' nose and mouth continually, so they cannot breathe. This induces a physiological process of drowning. Those subjected to it say it feels like dying. Imagine an experience that, if it had a voice, would say something like this: Here I am, I have come to a place where my last breath is behind me, on the other side of a door locked against me forever. Evidently death by crucifixion is like this also, only more prolonged: the victim can get little gulps of air, but less and less, as by a slow process of suffocation the power to draw breath is gradually crushed out by the weight of his own body hanging from the cross.

In such a place, what hope would feel like is permission to breathe. To have this permission taken from you forever is to be past hope, as Jonah once was. But he is praying now as someone looking *back* on a hopelessness that is behind him. His words give us a picture of it, so we can recognize ourselves when we are in such a place.

The Jews' name for this place is Babylon: a place where, as a people, it seemed impossible to breathe. This too can be imagined. Consider what it was like for the remnant of a Native American people, say, an unremembered tribe in New England that lingered on until the end of eighteenth century, a dozen or more old people on the fringes of a vigorously growing colonial town like Boston or New Haven. You feel already like an extinct people. You may have children, but they are not members of your people: they don't speak your language or understand the culture in which you were raised. You are the last to know how to live, breathe, and speak as one of this already-dead people. Forevermore there will be no one born to give voice to your native tongue, celebrate your festivals, or honor your gods. If known at all, the tongue you now speak will be studied as a dead language, and the culture that gave meaning to your life will be represented by objects in a museum display case. The living wisdom, skill, strength, and beauty of your people is already lost beyond recovery. You have no longer any leader, chieftain, or king, and your gods have failed you and fled, unable to save you from the power of the foreigners around you.

That is one way of imagining what it must have been like to be one of the many little nations swallowed up in the depths of exile in Babylon, past all hope and with no future as a people. Judah surely felt like this for a time, unable to live, speak, or breathe as the people of Israel—the people chosen by the God whose name is the LORD, who seemed for a time to be gone, wholly absent, or never to have been at all. Even so, Israel could pray:

> I say to God, my rock,
>   "Why have you forgotten me?
>   Why do I go mourning because of the oppression of the enemy?"
> Like a deadly wound in my body
>   my enemies taunt me,
> while they say to me continually,
>   "Where is your God?" (Ps. 42:9–10)

The book of Jonah looks *back* on this experience, inviting us to reflect on what it means.

We have perhaps come upon the fundamental reason why Jonah's psalm is in the past tense. What it asks us to imagine would be unbearable in the present. The Bible has a place for such unbearable poetry, but it belongs in the book of Job or the Lamentations of Jeremiah, not the comedy of Jonah.

But you brought my life up from the pit, O LORD, my God,

Now we come to the turning point of the narrative. From the beginning of the book of Jonah we have been reading a story of unbroken descent, which has taken Jonah as far away from the face of the LORD as it is possible to get. Yet precisely here the LORD reverses the whole direction and movement of Jonah's story by bringing him back upward. The arm of the LORD is not too short for this (Isa. 59:1). There is no place where he does not know his own. As he tells Jeremiah: "'Am I a God nearby,' says the LORD, 'and not a God far off? Who can hide in secret places so that I cannot see them?' says the LORD. 'Do I not fill heaven and earth?'" (Jer. 23:23–24). And as the great biblical confession of divine omnipresence puts it:

> Where shall I go from your Spirit?
>   Where shall I flee from your face?
> If I ascend to heaven, you are there!
>   If I make my bed in Sheol, you are there!
> If I take the wings of the morning
>   and *dwell in the uttermost parts of the sea*,
> even there your hand shall lead me,
>   and your right hand shall hold me. (Ps. 139:7–10)

Jonah's story has this turning point because, as Jonah here confesses for the first time in the book, the LORD is "my God." Even being swallowed up by a beast at the bottom of the sea is different if the LORD is your God. Everything in the story so far leads up to this confession, and everything else in the story follows from it.

What the LORD actually does here conforms to another biblical cliché, in which all Israel is once again meant to recognize herself:

> O LORD, you have brought up my soul from Sheol,
>   restored me to life from among those gone down to the pit. (Ps. 30:3)

Jonah's story is a dramatization of a psalmic commonplace: "You have delivered my soul from the lowest Sheol" (Ps. 86:13). So of course is Jesus's story, as Peter and Paul both insist in their first recorded sermons (Acts 2:27; 13:35), quoting another version of the commonplace:

> For you will not leave my soul in Sheol,
>   nor let your holy one see the pit. (Ps. 16:10)

Because the children of Israel belong to the LORD, they cannot ultimately belong to Sheol. This is the fundamental ground of Israel's refusal to believe in its own death.

2:7 when my soul was fainting within me.

The faint soul is at the end of its strength. The imagery here depends on the fact that word "soul" (*nephesh*) also means "neck" or "throat," the part of ourselves that takes in food and drink to revive us in our weariness. Souls grow faint like a man who has made a long journey with nothing to eat or drink. Hence the soul can literally be thirsty, as we see in the proverb "as cold waters to a thirsty soul, so is good news from a far country" (Prov. 25:25), or hungry, as we see in this vivid comparison in Isaiah:

> It shall be like when a hungry man dreams he is eating,
>   but he wakes up and his soul is empty;
> or when a thirsty man dreams he is drinking,
>   but he wakes up weak, his soul still desiring. (Isa. 29:8)

Jonah's soul, sunk to the bottom under the bases of the mountains and in the belly of Sheol, has gone too far with nothing to sustain it. But again, this is precisely when the LORD reaches him: after all his resources have run out, all his strength is gone, and he is all the way down at the bottom of the place from which none can return. You can't be any weaker than the dead.

The LORD I remembered,

Biblical remembrance means a calling to mind, which can apply not just to what is past but also to what is present or even what is future, as the exiles in Babylon remember Zion, calling to mind the once-and-future home of the temple of their God. But the remembrance in this verse is particularly striking, in that the object of the verb is present but the subject is not. The LORD is there, but Jonah is gone.

This is signaled by the word order, which is as unusual in the Hebrew as in the English. The sentence puts the object of remembrance first, because the act of remembrance does nothing. It is not as if Jonah decides to remember the LORD and this saves him. Jonah is among the dead, who have no strength for acts of piety and remembrance—these are all behind him. But the LORD's arm is not too short for this, either.

and my prayer came into you in your holy temple.

There was once when Jonah looked to the temple of the LORD before he sank all the way down to the bottom (2:4), and that remembrance still lives before the LORD, his God, even when Jonah doesn't. For the LORD, the God of Abraham, Isaac, and Jacob, is not the God of the dead but of the living (Luke 20:38), which means that even when his people die, yet shall they live (John 11:25). So by the power of God, Jonah's last look toward the temple of the LORD comes before the LORD himself in the temple of his holiness, where all is well. So Jonah lives before his God even when he is dead.

This is why there is resurrection of the dead. Even when we are no more, our prayer, our faith, our remembrance comes before the LORD our God, who remembers us in his loving-kindness, hears our prayer and answers. And because he answers, there are those who hear the answer—like a dead man who hears the voice of Jesus calling him to come forth from the tomb (John 11:43–44). He is a corpse and a corpse cannot hear, but Lazarus hears because the Lord calls to him, and all to whom he calls in grace and power are given ears to hear. Thus in ourselves, in our flesh, even in our souls, we are dead because of trespasses and sins (Eph. 2:1)—but in his sight, when he remembers us in mercy as his covenant partners, his chosen and beloved, we live. We have permission to breathe and be.

Here Jonah's being recapitulates David's, as he tells it in his psalm of thanksgiving for deliverance from all his enemies:

> Waves of death encompassed me,
>   torrents of perdition assailed me,
> the cords of Sheol surrounded me,
>   the snares of death came before me.
> In my trouble I called upon the LORD,
>   to my God I cried for help.
> *From his temple* he heard my voice,
>   and my cry to him reached his ears. (2 Sam. 22:5–7)

Jonah is like David, whose voice came up before God in the temple, which had not yet been built, where nonetheless the LORD heard and brought him up from Sheol, out of the deep waters. In this also he is like the anointed Son of David, the Messiah, whose very body is the temple of God. For even while the temple of his body was unbuilt, for three days a ruin without life, his prayer on the cross came before the LORD, his God and Father, who brought him up from Sheol. He called himself forsaken (Mark 15:34), but that was only the beginning of the psalm he prayed on the cross, and the ending is a vow of praise for the LORD's deliverance (Ps. 22:20–31). The Lord's psalm on the cross has indeed a great deal in common with Jonah's psalm in the fish.

2:8 Those who pay heed to vanities of deceit

The human response to the divine redemption that is to come begins with attentiveness, paying heed: looking back to the temple (2:4) and remembering the LORD (2:7) who is "my God" (2:6). To pay heed to other gods is to give one's attention to what is not: to a deceptive emptiness or vanity—a word meaning literally "vapor" or "mist." The Hebrew term is the same one made famous in Eccl. 1:2, where it is reduplicated to intensify the effect: "vanity of vanities," meaning the most vaporous of vapors—such is this transitory human life in all its splendor. Here the phrase "vanities of deceit" emphasizes not only the transitoriness and insubstantiality of a vapor but also its illusoriness. We could imagine swamp gas or a will o' the wisp shining in the moonlight and misleading some poor fool into thinking he had seen a god or a demon or a fairy, someone to whom he might address words of hope and desire. Such are the idols of the nations.

To most modern readers this verse of Jonah's psalm will come as a jolt. Why does Jonah interrupt his narrative of deliverance to tell of those who are ignorant of the LORD who delivers him? This is the story of Jonah's own trouble, his calling from the depths of sin and death: why is he talking about someone else's sins? It is like when the pastoral idyll of Ps. 23 is interrupted by talk of the LORD spreading a table "in the face of my enemies" (23:5) or when the contrition of Ps. 51 concludes with talk of building the walls of Jerusalem and offering bulls on the altar (51:18–19). We find this kind of interruption frequently in the psalms, and this should tell us something: if we understand the psalms properly, we will see that these are not really interruptions at all.

The biblical psalms, including Jonah's, are the prayers of God's people. Most of them come from the mouth of David as the anointed one, the king who speaks for the whole people. His enemies are the enemies of God's people, and his redemption from Sheol is Israel's redemption from destruction. This is a fundamental assumption of the psalms, which explains why they observe no sharp distinction between "I" and "we," between the individual who speaks and the whole people who pray using his words. David (which is to say, the Son of David, his anointed successor as king) speaks for the whole people of God, and the whole people of God call to the LORD using the words of their king.

So of course they praise the LORD, their shepherd, for spreading a table for them in the face of their enemies. "Shepherd" is a transparent metaphor, even a cliché, signifying a king or ruler (in Ezek. 34 the LORD is Israel's shepherd, and in

1 Sam. 17:34–37 David speaks to Saul about how a shepherd protects his flock from wild beasts, implicitly like a king protecting his people from their enemies). The obvious and literal meaning of Ps. 23 therefore has nothing to do with shepherds and sheep and pastures, any more than the obvious and literal meaning of the phrase "the mouth of the river" has to do with mouths and teeth and tongues. "The LORD is my shepherd" means that the God of Israel is David's king and thus the true king of Israel, guarding and keeping his people and providing for them even during a siege when Jerusalem is surrounded by armies, thus "spreading a table for me in the face of my enemies" (23:5). This is no interruption in the flow of the psalm.

Likewise when Ps. 51, which appears to be an individual's prayer of repentance (using "I") concludes by asking the LORD to build the walls of Jerusalem so that bulls may be offered on his altar, this is not an unaccountable digression (and at the very end!) but the whole point of the psalm, which expresses the repentance of Judah and therefore looks forward to the restoration of the fullness of worship at Jerusalem and the temple. In the next verse, Jonah will conclude his psalm with the same kind of hope.

So also this apparent interruption in the flow of Jonah's psalm is not really an interruption. Jonah speaks as representative Israelite, like the Son of David who is the king of Judah, except that Jonah is from the northern kingdom of Israel. So his psalm must make clear: there is a difference between the northern kingdom and Judah. The Judeans return from exile, but the northern kingdom (Israel in the narrow sense, as discussed in the comment on 1:1) does not. This verse explains why there is this difference. It is a verse that belongs to Jonah's story because it explains why Jonah in the belly of the beast, representing Judah in Babylon, does not come to the same hopeless end as Israel in Assyria.

forsake their loving-kindness.

To forsake is to leave, like a man leaving father and mother to cleave to his wife (Gen. 2:24) or Ruth refusing to leave Naomi (Ruth 1:16) and leaving father and mother to be Naomi's support (2:11). Scripture frequently uses this word to warn against forsaking the LORD and serving other gods (e.g., Josh. 24:16; Judg. 2:12; Ezra 8:22). What one leaves behind in paying heed to idols is one's *hesed*, an extraordinarily rich word that has been translated "mercy," "steadfast love," and "loving-kindness" and also has strong overtones of covenant loyalty. A person in need and anxiety asks another to deal with him or her in *hesed* and *emeth*—loving-kindness and truth, or steadfast love and faithfulness (Gen. 21:23; 24:49; 47:29; cf. Exod. 34:6, discussed in the comment on 4:2). Precisely what one does not do in *hesed* is forsake someone. Human beings practice such steadfast love when they are like Ruth with Naomi (Ruth 1:8; 3:10) or Boaz with Ruth (3:10). More fundamentally, of course, it is the LORD who practices *hesed*, which is the mercy that endures forever (Ps. 118:1–4; 136), a loving-kindness that is as great toward those who fear him as heaven is high above the earth (103:11). Those who forsake their loving-kindness are thus those who neither practice *hesed* themselves nor benefit from the *hesed* of the Lord. They have lost any lasting hope of life.

This is why the northern kingdom, the ten tribes of Israel, are no more. Before Judah, they too went into captivity, swallowed up in the belly of the beast in Sheol, but their end was different, as Amos describes:

> Though they dig into Sheol,
>> from there shall my hand take them.
> Though they climb up to heaven,
>> from there I will bring them down.
> Though they hide themselves on the top of Carmel,
>> from there I will search out and take them.
> And though they hide from my sight *at the bottom of the sea*,
>> there I will command the serpent and it shall bite them.
> And though they go into captivity before their enemies,
>> there I will command the sword and it shall slay them.
> I will set my eyes upon them for evil and not for good. (Amos 9:2–4)

The imagery here resembles that of the great hymn of divine omnipresence, Ps. 139 (quoted in the comment on 2:6), but to the opposite effect. Here the Lord pursues his people to destroy them. For in turning to vanities one does not escape the Lord but rather flees from his gentleness, stumbles on his justice, and falls into his wrath (to borrow language from Augustine, *Confessions* 5.1.2). Jonah is the object of the same divine pursuit that Amos pictures here—taken by the Lord's hand from Sheol, bitten by the serpent of the deep, taken into captivity—except that in his case even the divine wrath is for good and not for evil. For Jonah's descent to the depths, like Judah's exile in Babylon, ends in the remembrance of the Lord; whereas the northern kingdom follows the idolatrous way of Jeroboam to the end, paying heed to vanities of deceit, forsaking their loving-kindness and therefore their life.

Of course, we might get the impression that Jonah thinks he somehow has better claim to the loving-kindness of the Lord than those who are less faithful than he. It is hard to imagine how he *could* think that, given everything we have read in this story and the whole nature of his prayer so far. But human folly is capable of thinking almost anything. So if this is our impression—and in case we are worried that the Bible might be endorsing such folly and self-righteousness—we can just read ahead to 4:2, where the loving-kindness of the Lord is precisely what Jonah finds most objectionable about his God. On any just reckoning, therefore, Jonah too must count as one of those who forsake their loving-kindness. There is no hope for him or for anyone else unless it is the Lord himself who does not forsake his loving-kindness. This verse should not mislead Jonah or us into forgetting the essential nature of all biblical prayer and of this prayer in particular: it is a call to the Lord out of misery and helplessness and a plea for undeserved mercy.

2:9 But I with a voice of thanksgiving will sacrifice to you;

Jonah switches to the future tense, promising to give thanks for a redemption that (let us not forget) has yet to take place. He does not yet have a voice for this, down in the depths of the sea (see comment on 2:2). Nonetheless his thanksgiving has already begun, since all along his psalm has been a sacrifice of thanksgiving and praise, a second-person narrative of the salvation of the LORD. The whole structure of Judean worship immediately after the exile must have been like this—a sacrifice of thanksgiving anticipating the full restoration of sacrificial worship in the temple that was to be rebuilt. It is as if the exile is not entirely over until the house of the LORD is restored in Jerusalem.

Jonah's use of the future tense here thus mimics the eucharistic structure of biblical eschatology as a whole. Eucharist is Greek for "thanksgiving," and when we give thanks for the salvation of the LORD we remember what is not yet consummated but is already present with us. Nowhere is this clearer than in the celebration of the Eucharist itself, when we remember the death of our Lord and Savior until he comes again. Hence the eucharistic acclamation: "Christ has died. Christ is risen. *Christ will come again.*" The body of Christ is the temple that was destroyed long ago but rebuilt in three days (John 2:19–21), which will be restored to us in visible glory on the last day, and which is already present among us in a hidden way, which is called in Greek a mystery or in the Western church a sacrament (see comment on 4:6).

Jonah, like us, remembers the salvation of the LORD his God until it comes in fullness. His prayer is itself a kind of firstfruits or down payment on his promise to offer a richer, fuller sacrifice in the future, presumably in the same temple where the voice of his supplication was heard. In speaking these words Jonah is making a vow, just as in many other psalms (see comment on 1:16), yet the vow itself is already an act of worship that begins to fulfill the vow, just as the celebration of the Eucharist is itself the beginning of the salvation for which the Eucharist gives thanks, a foretaste of the heavenly banquet.

I will pay what I have vowed.

To make this vow even in the guts of the fish is to put one's hope solely in the LORD, like penitent Judah promising that when the walls of Jerusalem are rebuilt "then bulls will be offered on your altar" (Ps. 51:19), a vow that could be paid only if the LORD rescues his own from the belly of the beast and rebuilds both Jerusalem and its temple.

And the book of Jonah adds an extra complication or two. Even after he has been redeemed from the belly of the beast, Jonah is not free simply to go home. He has been sent to Nineveh. Furthermore, even now while he is still in the depths there are Gentiles way above him offering sacrifices of thanksgiving and vowing vows (1:16). To fulfill his vow Jonah will have to join the Gentiles who are already worshiping the LORD his God, like the Judean exiles returning to the land of Israel to find "the people of the land" already worshiping in the name of the LORD (Ezra 4:1–4). There are evidently a number of twists and turns still to come in Jonah's story, as in Judah's. As always, our foretaste of the eschatological future does not mean that all our present problems are solved for us.

Salvation is the LORD's!"

The concluding words of Jonah's psalm are a shout of joy and love that is stronger than death. For it is a proclamation of the name of the LORD. Salvation is his in the sense of possession, even ownership: salvation belongs to the LORD (Ps. 3:8), for it belongs to him alone to save utterly from death and destruction. This is what everyone needs to know if they are to choose life (Deut. 30:19).

The Hebrew word for "salvation" comes from the same root as the name "Jesus," which is a variant of the name "Joshua," meaning "the LORD is salvation." What we have here is a fine pun, very much in the biblical style. Shouting even from the belly of Sheol that salvation is the LORD's, Jonah thereby proclaims the name of Jesus, Lord and Savior, and indeed anticipates the Christian confession that Jesus is the LORD. For to Jesus Christ alone is given the name above every name (Phil. 2:10–11), the name of the God of Israel, who swears by his own self that every knee shall bow and every tongue confess before him (Isa. 45:23), for he alone is the LORD—that is his name!—and he gives his glory to no other (42:8). Therefore Jesus cannot be Lord and Savior unless the holiest of all names, the name of the LORD, is his alone—unless, that is, this crucified man is none other than the LORD, the God of Israel, the creator of heaven and earth, just as the doctrine of the Trinity teaches together with the doctrine of the Incarnation. Confessing this, Jonah makes a rich down payment on his vow of worship, looking forward to the eschatological worship of the new Israel surrounded by a great multitude from every nation standing before the eternal throne and shouting: "Salvation belongs to our God, who sits on the throne, and to the Lamb" (Rev. 7:10).

But so far Jonah has made this confession only in the depth of the sea, where none but the LORD can hear him. That will not be sufficient. The burden of the rest of the book concerns whether he will confess that salvation is the LORD's even in Nineveh. It is time to find out. So Jonah's psalm comes to an end and the narrative resumes.

2:10 Then the LORD said to the fish,

The LORD says something, though we don't know what. This is the same verb used for ordinary saying throughout the book and throughout the Bible, introducing every kind of dialogue, divine and human. But the LORD's saying is unique, for what he says happens. He says "let there be light" and there is light (Gen. 1:3), for he commanded and all things were created (Ps. 148:5). Therefore when he speaks, his creation responds and obeys, from top to bottom, from stars in heaven to fish in the sea. All except his people. With them he still has a complicated story to get on with. So he says something to Jonah again in the next verse, getting things going all over again.

and it vomited Jonah out

You have to enjoy it—surely the most farcical moment in this comedy. Jonah's actual escape from the depths is a ridiculous anticlimax, not a dramatic rescue but a bit of indigestion. It is as if Jonah made the monster sick to its stomach. It would be nice if the belly of Sheol worked like that. And perhaps it does, thanks to the word of the LORD. Will we all laugh as we emerge from our graves on the last day? Will we be astounded as we blink and look around at ourselves? We thought death was so serious, but look at this silly mess! Time to clean up all the dirt and fish guts—yes, and let's get those grave clothes off Lazarus—it's all too funny looking for words!

But if that is how it is, then what is really important is not the mechanism by which death and hell are made to cough up the dead that is in them. The *how* of it is not what matters but the *why*: the word of the LORD is the power that defeats death, because God has promises to keep. The gates of hell cannot prevail against his covenant partner, his beloved, his chosen and anointed one. That is the why of it. Jonah is *God's* dove, to whom it belongs to live and not die, so *of course* he will give hell indigestion. When one greater than Jonah comes to the same place, he leads captivity captive (Eph. 4:8). Tradition has it that he comes forth leading all the LORD's ancient covenant partners out of their captivity in the depths of the earth: Abraham and Sarah, Moses and David, Adam and Eve, even Jonah himself. Sheol swallows our Lord but cannot keep him, for he descends not as a rebel fleeing from God but as the word of God in the flesh, as hell's conqueror not its victim.

Surely we can imagine everyone who waited for him in Abraham's bosom laughing with joy when they saw him. How could they take the darkness of death seriously when his light came among them? It is like that with Jonah in the belly of Sheol: it's just a little old sea monster, Leviathan, that the LORD made to play in the deep (Ps. 104:26)—nothing more, really, than a great big fish. Nothing serious, anyways.

on dry land.

At the end of this chapter of prayer from the depths, Jonah is back in his element, ready to walk again on the earth. The God of heaven is maker of the sea as well as the dry land (1:9) but the creature made in his image is really at home only in the one, not the other. So back we go to square one. After a foretaste of the power of resurrection we have to get on our own two feet, ready to start again. As the conclusion of Jonah's psalm hinted, there is work to do.

JONAH 3

The Repentance of Nineveh

Jonah Calls and Nineveh Believes (3:1–5)

3:1 And the word of the LORD came to Jonah a second time, saying,

It all starts again, just as before, with the very same words we read at the beginning except for the added phrase reminding us that it is the second time. The LORD is nothing if not persistent, always ready to begin again. But this time things should be different. For Jonah is not just starting over again; he has been given a new life out of the depths of Sheol, like Israel freed from exile in Babylon, like a man buried with Christ in baptism and raised to newness of life. The second half of the book of Jonah tells the story of one reborn from the dead.

So we go back to square one, yet expect a very different story. In the first half of the book of Jonah, the man of God runs away from God but ends up saving a whole boatload of Gentiles in spite of himself. In this half he will actually cooperate in carrying out his mission as a prophet. At least to some degree, his reborn will is in conformity with the word of the LORD.

3:2 "Arise, go to Nineveh, that great city, and call to her

So far the LORD's words to Jonah are almost the same as before (1:2). Just in case we wondered whether Jonah's escapades had done anything to change the LORD's intentions, we hear the same word that got the whole story going at the beginning.

Yet there is a slight difference, a clarification perhaps. Jonah is to call *to* Nineveh, not just call out *against* her. His voice is to go to these people and get into their ears rather than rising up over them to heaven. We are getting our first hint that Jonah's message to Nineveh is not to be all destruction, despite our first impressions.

the call that I speak to you."

Now, more explicitly than the first time, the LORD's commission makes clear the vocation of every prophet: to speak to others what the LORD has first spoken to him, making the word of the LORD public and audible and available for all. Yet strikingly, just as before, we are not told the content of the LORD's word to Nineveh, the specific words he would have Jonah say to them. Indeed, whenever we hear the LORD speak in this book, his word is addressed to the prophet—not to the other people, the Gentile sailors or the Ninevites. We never hear anything like, "Thus says the LORD to the city of Nineveh." And we never hear exactly what words the LORD tells Jonah to use in calling to Nineveh.

This may be a very significant omission. It is not how the story usually goes. One of the most characteristic features of ancient narratives—found not only in the Bible but in Homer and in ancient Near Eastern epics as well as in any number of folktales—is the repetition of the content of a message. First we hear for example what a god, king, master, or father says to a messenger, and then we hear what the messenger says when delivering the message, and then perhaps also how the message is repeated and understood (or not) by those who hear it. Sometimes the same words are repeated exactly, but in the Bible, which is extraordinarily subtle in its narrations, there is often some slight slippage in the message, and we are invited to wonder how it got there and what it means (e.g., Gen. 24:1–8, 35–41; 27:4, 7, 19, 31; 1 Sam. 15:3, 18; 1 Kgs. 12:10–11, 14; Jer. 26:6, 9). The most famous example is the LORD's prohibition of the tree of knowledge, spoken to Adam when he is the only human being in creation (Gen. 2:16–17), then repeated by Eve when the serpent asks her what God has said (3:1–3). She adds one clause to the prohibition ("neither shall you touch it"), and commentators have rightly wondered what to make of this. Has she misheard what Adam taught her? Has Adam not taught her right? Has one or both of them decided to "fence the Torah" by making the prohibition more stringent so as to make sure it is not violated? Is this done in a spirit of obedience? What is significant is that we are in no position to ask any such questions about Jonah's repetition of the LORD's message.

3:3 And Jonah arose

Again the same words as before (1:3) but this time to different effect. For now Jonah gets up and gets going in the direction the word of the LORD would have him go.

and walked to Nineveh according to the word of the LORD.

Once again the word of the LORD sets everything in motion (see comment on 1:1), but this time in the mode of obedience rather than flight. The will of Jonah is, for the first time in the book, actively conforming to the word of the LORD. At least for a little while we are seeing a new Jonah, the way we expect when one is converted to God and reborn. But we should also know—and unless we are complete fools, we Christian readers should know this from our own experience—that the reborn self still contains much of the old Adam who was to be drowned in baptism. The story of sin and redemption does not end with rebirth.

Now Nineveh was a city great before God,

The idiom "great before God" can simply mean "very big" or (as in the King James Version) "exceeding great." But it also suggests that Nineveh is somehow a big thing in God's eyes, something that matters a great deal to him. Perhaps that is why God himself keeps calling it "that great city" (1:2; 3:2; 4:11).

On the other hand, that the verb is past tense suggests that this greatness is now gone. If that is so then Israel too, taken into exile by the Assyrians, never to return, is already gone. We are reading the story of a moment of hope in the lives of two nations that are no more, a salvation offered and even received but subsequently rejected and lost. When we look beyond the bounds of the story we see tragedy—not comedy—looming. We will have to reckon with this before the end. The original readers of the story would surely have reckoned with it, too.

a three days' walk.

This makes for a mighty big city. Yet it is quite literally true of the great city of Nineveh or "greater Nineveh," as we might call it, which was an area encompassing four cities, including Nineveh proper and its environs. Genesis describes the whole area as built up by the mighty Nimrod after he had built up the cities in the plain of Shinar, the region of the Babylonian Empire: "From that land he went to Assyria, where he built Nineveh, Rehoboth Ir, Calah, and Resen, which is between Nineveh and Calah; that is the great city" (10:11–12).

But of course the reference to three days is also meant to remind us of the three days Jonah spent in the guts of the fish. We are not supposed to miss the parallel: for Jonah to walk into Nineveh, that great city, is like being swallowed up again by the monster in the depths of the sea and exiled from the land of the living. He cannot possibly be enjoying this mission. Perhaps we should also think of the three years that Samaria, the capital of Israel, was under siege before it fell (2 Kgs. 7:5), a shared experience of something like living death for the people of Israel before they were removed from the face of the earth forever, swallowed up by the Assyrian Empire. Yet above all we must of course remember the three days our Lord spent in death, being the sign of Jonah, making all these experiences look different because death itself is different after our Lord is swallowed up in it. Jonah has of yet no idea what waits for him at the other end of this walk.

3:4 And Jonah started to enter the city, one day's walk.

One day's walk is enough to get Jonah close to the heart of the city, in the middle of the metropolitan area of greater Nineveh, the greatest city in the greatest empire on earth. It parallels Elijah's one-day walk into the wilderness (1 Kgs.

19:4), where the prophet sits down to die under a juniper tree, asking the LORD to take his life. This city is like a wilderness where a prophet goes to die. Jonah will soon (4:3) be echoing Elijah's request, though not for Elijah's reasons.

And he called and said,

Jonah calls, as commanded. Once again he acts in conformity with the word of the LORD. And now we are finally going to get the content of the word that Jonah is to give to Nineveh. So far this has been just as hidden from us as the content of the word of the kingdom that plays such a role in Jesus's stories—for example, in the parable of the sower, where we never learn what is said in the word that affects different people so differently (Matt. 13:1–23). It turns out that, just as in the gospel parables where nothing quite makes sense until you recognize *who* is telling the story (esp. 13:17), here too the point of Jonah's message does not quite emerge until you see what it has to do with the messenger.

There are many ironies about the message we are about to hear. To begin with, it is a word of salvation that looks like a word of destruction. That clearly is in accordance with the LORD's intention, though not with Jonah's. Yet this discrepancy in intention between the LORD and his prophet is itself the source of more ironies: as we have seen, the text is not explicit about whether Jonah's words actually are the words the LORD gave him to speak. There is room to wonder whether, in the very content of the message, Jonah was trying to pull a fast one on the LORD—and whether what actually happened was that the LORD pulled a fast one on Jonah.

"Forty days

In the Bible the number forty indicates a time of trial or testing that leads to holiness, renewal, homecoming, and salvation. The waters of Noah's flood are upon the earth for forty days (Gen. 7:17), Moses is on the mountain with God for forty days (Exod. 24:18), and Ezekiel bears the iniquity of Judah for forty days (Ezek. 4:6). Most paradigmatic are Israel's forty years in the wilderness, which point forward to the forty days that Jesus was tempted in the wilderness after his baptism. Jonah has already had his baptism, plunged into the depths of the sea and brought back up to new life: could it be that these are *his* forty days of testing?

and Nineveh shall be overturned!"

The verb is the same used of the overthrow of Sodom and Gomorrah (Gen. 19:21, 25, 29). It becomes part of a biblical cliché used to describe wrath and destruction that is as bad as "when the LORD overthrew Sodom and Gomorrah." Strikingly, the cliché is applied to both Babylon (Isa. 13:19; Jer. 50:40) and Israel (Deut. 29:23; Lam. 4:6; Amos 4:11) and once to Edom, the nation that is closest kin to Israel, being descended from Esau, Israel's brother (Jer. 49:18). Evidently

Jonah finds comfort in it. If Nineveh's fate is like Sodom and Gomorrah's, he will be happy.

Yet even in this extraordinarily brief message, there are indications that things are not what they seem. To begin with, nothing is said about who will overturn Nineveh. There is no mention of the LORD or even of some generalized concept of a wrathful deity or indeed of any agent or cause of Nineveh's overturning. The message is terribly vague, in the fashion now made familiar by bureaucrats everywhere, who love using the passive voice to evade the issue of who is doing what to whom. (People of my generation may still remember the words of a high-level U.S. bureaucrat explaining how four nuns managed the trick of getting themselves massacred by a death squad working for our allies: in the course of the altercation, he explained, "shots were fired.") An active voice sentence would require Jonah to say *who* will overturn Nineveh. It is not characteristic of the God of the Bible to be evasive about this kind of issue. In that respect the wording of the message sounds more like Jonah's, as if it were meant to conceal something.

Above all, there is the ambiguity of the last word, which amounts to a kind of pun. To overturn can mean not only to overthrow and destroy but also to turn over, turn around, and turn one thing into another, as when Moses's staff turns into a snake (Exod. 7:15) or the waters of Egypt turn into blood (7:17) or when the prophet warns that the sun will be turned to darkness and the moon to blood (Joel 2:31). The turning can be for better or for worse: dancing and feasting turned into mourning (Lam. 5:15; Amos 8:10) or mourning and sorrow turned into joy and dancing (Esth. 9:22; Ps. 30:11; Jer. 31:13). Most strikingly, the LORD turns Balaam's curse against Israel into a blessing (Deut. 23:5; Neh. 13:2) and turns Saul into another man (1 Sam. 10:6), turning his heart into another heart (10:9).

Some such transformation or conversion, turning one thing into another, seems to be what the LORD has in mind, if these are indeed the exact words he has given Jonah to speak. So it may be that the LORD has fooled Jonah, giving him a message containing more good news than Jonah realizes. We need not suppose that the God of the Bible is above such fooling. Think of how he fools Pharaoh, leading him on at first and not revealing his own hand. At the start of negotiations he proposes just a brief trip—a mere three days (like Jonah's time in the fish!)—for his people to worship at some distance away from the Egyptians (Exod. 3:18), even though all along his intention is to rescue his people from slavery for good. He *plays* Pharaoh, as we say nowadays: he outwits and outmaneuvers him, luring him at last into a trap so as to win glory for his own name, to the end that the Egyptians and Pharaoh himself shall know, even by their defeat, "that I am the LORD" (7:5; cf. 8:10). One can imagine the ancient Israelites telling this story around their campfires and chuckling. It's not as if Pharaoh didn't deserve it.

Still, the irony of the story is even more satisfying if we suppose that Jonah himself, prophet posing as bureaucrat, supplies the evasive passive-voice term, so uncharacteristic of the LORD's very unevasive habits of speech, by altering the message the LORD has given him. We can almost hear the gracious and merciful God chuckling and saying to himself, "Okay, Jonah, have it your way. You want to say Nineveh will be overturned? Well then, I will make sure Nineveh is overturned for you! I will surely turn them upside down, convert them and turn them into something altogether new." Eventually, it seems, the LORD aims to turn the whole world upside down (Acts 17:6). Things keep getting better than Jonah wants them to be.

3:5 And the people of Nineveh believed God,

Nothing in the story so far has prepared us for the stunningly abrupt good news of 3:5. Yet this is the kind of good news the Bible often likes to give us, if for no other reason than to put to shame those of us who like to call ourselves believers and think of ourselves as God's own people. Thus when the LORD commissions the prophet Ezekiel to speak to his people, he adds: "You are not being sent to a people of strange speech and difficult language . . . whose words you cannot understand. Surely if I had sent you to *them*"—people like the Ninevites, we could say—"they would have listened to you. But the house of Israel is not willing to listen to you because they are not willing to listen to *me*" (3:5–7). Jesus himself had similar things to say about how the Gentile cities of Tyre and Sidon would have repented in sackcloth and ashes if he had done his great works among them, but the cities of his homeland do not wish to hear and believe (Matt. 11:21–22; Luke 10:13–14). And he explicitly holds up the repentance of the Ninevites to put to shame the unrepentant hearts of his own people, warning them that "one greater than Jonah is here" (Luke 11:32; Matt. 12:41). The faith and repentance of Nineveh is not so surprising when viewed in the context of the whole biblical message. It is just the sort of thing the biblical message anticipates. Yet in this particular story it comes about with no preparation, no explanation, falling out of the sky, as it were, or out of the very logic of biblical revelation. The only explanation for it is that it is just the kind of miracle of grace that the Bible is all about.

So the people of Nineveh believed God. It is hard to resist adding: "And it was counted to them for righteousness." This of course is spoken properly of Abraham (Rom. 4:3, quoting Gen. 15:6), but in the light of the gospel we see that Abraham is "the father of all who believe" (Rom. 4:11), which in this case must include the people of Nineveh. God can raise up children for Abraham even out of the stones (Matt. 3:9)—so why not out of Ninevites? All it takes is believing.

But such believing itself takes a miracle of grace far more astounding than the one that kept Jonah alive in the fish. Who could believe that Jonah's call would bring Nineveh to a belief like Abraham's? It is like believing that mere belief could move mountains, as our Lord says (Matt. 17:20). It would be like someone in Jesus's day believing that the Jews could overturn Rome. But history is even more astounding than the Bible, as the atheist Nietzsche reminds us, for by means of belief in Christ the Jews did in fact conquer Rome. It takes no faith at all to see this: all we have to do is consider to whom they bow down in Rome today, as Nietzsche sourly observes. A few centuries after the King of the Jews died on a Roman cross, the Roman people were bowing down and worshiping him as God in the flesh. In this peculiar and ironic way, as astounding as the overturning of Nineveh, "Rome has been defeated beyond all doubt" (*On the Genealogy of Morals* 1.16). Since mountains are a common biblical symbol of mighty kingdoms (e.g., Jer. 51:25; cf. the psalms quoted in the comment on 2:3), the faith of Rome and thus of the whole Western world fulfills this word of the Lord Jesus: believing in Christ did indeed move this mountain and overturn it. Since Nineveh eventually came to naught while Rome and its Western heritage still lives, we may even suspect that Rome's overturning is the true fulfillment of Jonah's prophecy (see comment on 4:11). One greater than Jonah is indeed here.

It is clearly not Jonah but the word of God that converts Nineveh. We hear of Jonah uttering one brief sentence, never even mentioning God, and that is the extent of his prophecy. Perhaps we can imagine him repeating himself. But what we are not invited to imagine is any kind of dialogue between him and the Ninevites comparable to the tense but fruitful conversation in Jonah 1, from which the sailors learned that the God they were dealing with was the LORD. The Ninevites apparently have no opportunity to question Jonah about who he is and what God he serves, and evidently he never tells them. We do not hear of Ninevites calling upon the name of the LORD like the sailors, and their belief is described using the generic term for "God" (*Elohim*) that any pagan could use. Jonah, we have to assume, never instructs them.

Everything happens as if Jonah's word is disseminated throughout Nineveh with all the anonymous power of rumor. Suddenly everybody seems to have heard: Nineveh is about to be overturned! And they all turn to each other and murmur, "What shall we do?" With the fear of God is the beginning of wisdom. Meanwhile Jonah apparently just slips away unnoticed (4:5). Nobody in Nineveh has anything to say to him, and perhaps no one even remembers who first uttered the message. It doesn't matter. It is God's message, and the Ninevites believe it and are justified before God.

and they called a fast

The same language is used for calling a solemn assembly in order to sanctify a fast in Israel (Joel 1:14; 2:15). The Ninevites are repenting the way Israel should. They do not even call upon their false gods, like the sailors in Jonah 1. We hear of no pagan priests and magicians, as in the narrative about Moses and Pharaoh in Exodus. The miracle of grace continues.

Fasting is the body's way of praying: you voluntarily empty yourself and make yourself miserable so that God may have mercy, as if your belly itself were crying: "See how empty I am! I have no strength and no helper! O you who are merciful, see how deep is my need and have mercy on me!"

But fasting is inarticulate, like the belly itself, knowing not the name of its God but feeling its own poverty and need. For the Ninevites, this is an advantage. Uninstructed about the God with whom they are dealing, they repent and worship in the most profound way available to people who do not know the name of the LORD.

and put on sackcloth

Sackcloth is an outward and visible form of bodily repentance. A belly repents by fasting, a heart repents by being broken and contrite (Ps. 51:17), a community repents by neglecting to eat and dress themselves properly. So the people of Nineveh lay aside everything that would make them comfortable and content with their lives, putting on destitution like a garment, as if to say: "We are beggars who have nothing—have mercy on us!"

It is a little like the people who put on burlap bags during the Depression because they owned nothing better. "Sackcloth" is quite literally the cloth from which sacks were made—if you can call it cloth at all. (The same word is used for the sacks used by Joseph's brothers in Gen. 42:25, 27, 35.) It was a coarse weave of goat or camel hair, good for making sacks but not really fit to clothe human beings. And of course that is the point. You can only imagine wearing this stuff if you are destitute. To put it on voluntarily is to say, visibly and unmistakably: "I am without resource, in utmost poverty." It is to approximate, by voluntary self-abasement, the desperate state of Jonah in the depths or the sailors at wit's end. It is the most concrete way possible for the Ninevites to show that they believe the word of warning they have heard and take it seriously. The danger that threatens them cannot be seen, but the sackcloth that can be seen on them shows that they know it is real. When Jonah began his day's walk into Nineveh, they did not look poor and afflicted, but he told them they were and they believed him, and now they look it.

There is hope in this self-abasement, a mute expectation that those who humble themselves will be forgiven and healed (2 Chr. 7:14), even justified and exalted as the Lord says (Luke 18:14) and exemplified in his own life (Phil. 2:8–9). But this means that those who normally exalted themselves will have to be humbled. Stunningly, that happens here too.

from the greatest to the least of them.

The "greatest" means the aristocracy, the great ones in the city (see 3:7), the high and mighty: they too fast and put on sackcloth to display their mortal destitution. This of course is not how an aristocracy ordinarily behaves. To join in Nineveh's repentance they are willing to put themselves at the same level as the poorest of the poor. They too are overturned. The miracle of grace continues, spreading human solidarity throughout this community of newborn believers. It will spread all the way to the king.

The King and God (3:6–10)

3:6 And the word reached the king of Nineveh,

It is not clear if "the word" here means Jonah's message or simply news of the fast called by the people of Nineveh. In any case, by this time the word is clearly not something coming directly from Jonah's mouth. There is no hint of Jonah being summoned before the king and having the kind of confrontation with him that Moses had with Pharaoh. This king is much better than Pharaoh, just as this prophet is much worse than Moses. Perhaps the king is actually better off without Jonah's interference.

In fact the king's response to the word is wonderful. A responsible man like the captain of the ship in Jonah 1, he cares for his people as a king should, but is even more insightful: with no storm blowing, no boat about to sink, just one brief and ambiguous message coming apparently from nowhere, he realizes the city is in great danger and something has to be done to save it. Evidently the people themselves are the ones who convince him. He learns that they have called a fast and put on sackcloth, and he follows suit, amplifying their efforts at penitence with a proclamation that makes it official policy for the whole city. It seems he is not above following his own people (how many kings are this wise?), jumping on the bandwagon when he sees it carrying them toward life, not death.

We do not know who this king is. We are not told his name, his lineage, his sins, his wars, or even his policy toward Israel. Elsewhere in Scripture the only individual king of Nineveh we hear of is Assyrian Emperor Sennacherib (705–681 BC), called by his minions "the great king, the king of Assyria" (2 Kgs. 18:19), who breaks off his siege of Jerusalem after sudden disaster and returns to Nineveh, where he is assassinated by his own sons in the temple of his god (19:35–37). Scripture remembers him as the proud king who boasted of being stronger than the gods of all other nations, including the LORD (19:10–13; cf. 18:34–36). His confrontation with Hezekiah, and especially the boasting of his henchman, the Rabshakeh, outside the walls of Jerusalem, is an important moment in biblical history, of such thematic interest that Scripture recounts it three times (2 Kgs. 18–19; 2 Chr. 32; Isa. 36–37). The book of Jonah tacitly invites us to compare him with this anonymous king of Nineveh and ask: Which one of these two behaves like a true king?

and he arose from his throne

Like Jonah (1:3; 3:3) the king of Nineveh arises to take action. But in contrast to Jonah, his action is a symbolic declaration of his own helplessness—something Jonah did not get around to recognizing until he was in deep water. The king's first act is to leave the majesty of his kingship behind him. He gets up off his seat, something the mighty don't ordinarily do unless they are knocked off (as Mary reminds us in the Magnificat in Luke 1:52). Normally, the king sits while all his inferiors stand in attendance around him and his petitioners kneel before him. To rise from his throne is to join them all, leaving behind the visible seat of his authority. But he does this precisely in order to exercise his authority for the good of his people. It is the first of a whole string of admirable actions, truly royal and worthy of imitation.

and took off his mantle and covered himself with sackcloth

The king divests himself of glory, though not of responsibility. He will be ruler only in repentance. And even in this he is meek enough to follow the lead of his own people, who have already called a fast and dressed themselves in sackcloth. Conforming to their faith, he removes all the visible splendor of royalty that protects his mortal body and replaces it with the same garb of abasement they all have on. His gesture of humility is therefore also a gesture of solidarity—one vulnerable human being joining the rest as they beg for mercy. This is a great king indeed. Only the one who wears a crown of thorns rules in greater humility.

Not that he is utterly without company. He joins a series of Israelite kings who humble themselves before the LORD and thereby delay the evil that the LORD speaks of bringing upon his people. In the southern kingdom, the key examples are Hezekiah (2 Chr. 32:26) and Josiah (2 Kgs. 22:19–20). In the northern kingdom it is Ahab, of all people, who tears his clothes, puts on sackcloth, and fasts when the prophet Elijah speaks of the evil the LORD will bring upon him (1 Kgs. 21:20–21, 27). The word of the LORD then comes to Elijah: "Because he has humbled himself before me"—a phrase that thus tells us the essential meaning of fasting and sackcloth—"I will not bring evil in his days" (21:28–29). The king of Nineveh is on the same track as Ahab here—and without a prophet like Elijah to speak the word of the LORD to him.

One might expect him to tear his clothing, as kings often do when faced with a terrible crisis (e.g., 2 Kgs. 5:7; 6:30; 19:1; 22:11). But evidently it is sufficient that he rends his heart and not his garments, just as the LORD commands the people of Israel (Joel 2:13). And there is perhaps another reason he leaves his garment whole. This is a garment to honor even in laying it aside. The word "mantle" here is not the usual one for a royal robe, but is the same word used for the mantle of the prophet Elijah, the garment that he wrapped around his face so he could hear the LORD without daring to look at him (1 Kgs. 19:13) and that is bestowed upon his successor Elisha (1 Kgs. 19:19; 2 Kgs. 2:13–14). In the context of biblical narrative, therefore, to remove the mantle without tearing it is to honor the office of prophecy while disowning all claim to be a prophet.

In other words, the king makes no pretense of speaking for God. In this he displays wisdom as well as humility: he knows what he does not know, and he is not wise in his own eyes. Unlike Elijah, he has not met the living God. He knows he has no recourse but to await what God will do.

and sat in ashes.

Though sackcloth and ashes often go together (Esth. 4:1, 3; Isa. 58:5; Matt. 11:21; Luke 10:13), sitting in ashes goes a bit further as a demonstration of repentance and humility than merely putting on sackcloth. By covering himself in sackcloth the king joins his people and identifies with them; by sitting in ashes he goes beyond what they have already done and amplifies it with an especially dramatic gesture: he who once sat on a throne now sits on the ground in ashes.

The gesture is like Job's (Job 2:8). Job, however, had experienced great loss and suffering, while the king of Nineveh has experienced nothing but an uncanny rumor of disaster coming upon his people. All the greater, then, is his spiritual perception, together with his love for Nineveh, which causes him to abase himself so dramatically before God. Like any good king, he identifies with his people and then some. Their disaster is his disaster; he suffers it with them and also for them. Every good ruler is at least a little bit like that good shepherd who lays down his life for his sheep.

3:7 And he cried and said in Nineveh,

The king issues a proclamation to be heralded throughout the city, but the verb makes it into a loud cry for mercy to heaven.

The king's proclamation is the central event in the chapter. He is a responsible man, like the captain of the ship in Jonah 1. Like the captain, it is he rather than the LORD himself who elicits from Jonah a confession of the name of the LORD (4:2); in an irony worthy of the eschatology of Paul, this Gentile provokes the unbelieving Israelite to jealousy and a confession of Israel's faith (Rom. 11:11–14). But unlike the captain, the king of Nineveh does not know he does this; he never hears the name of the LORD, indeed does not even seem to know about Jonah. What happens is that somehow (surely by the invisible work of grace) he figures out where he stands before the God of heaven: he is a ruler responsible for an evil people who will be destroyed together with him if he doesn't do something to change things. So he makes official the fast already proclaimed by his people, calling them to repent and urging them to hope for the mercy of God. He figures all this out without any help from Jonah, who by this time appears to have gone off in a sulk. He even recognizes his own lack of knowledge ("who knows?" in 3:9). He knows he is operating in the dark. But evidently he can recognize evil when he sees it, can even recognize when it is an evil for which he is responsible, and can be alarmed and afraid enough to take the right action.

by decree of the king and his great ones, saying,

The king has the proclamation authorized by the whole ruling class of Nineveh, its "great ones" or aristocracy, who are already participating in the fast called by the people (3:5). Once again the high are following the low, a very topsy-turvy thing to happen in the ancient Near East, which knows nothing of democracy. Even the process by which the Ninevites arrive at their particular forms of repentance is a kind of overturning of Nineveh's social order.

"Let human and livestock, herd and flock,

"Herd" means cattle, "flock" means sheep and goats; together they are the primary kinds of livestock, which along with human beings constitute the main form of wealth in an ancient Israelite household. The term for livestock is often translated "cattle," but that is too narrow, as the term includes both herd and flock; it is also often translated "beast," but that is too broad, as the term excludes beasts of the sea, birds of the air, and creeping things like reptiles and insects. The phrase rendered "human and livestock" is often translated with the resonant phrase "man and beast," but that also is too broad, suggesting the whole panoply of living things, whereas what we are concerned with here are basic elements of ancient economics.

Nowadays we are not used to thinking of living bodies as the basis of wealth, but this thought is fundamental to economics in its original form. In the Decalogue, for instance, the things that belong to your neighbor's house that you are not to covet include humans and livestock: wife, manservant and maidservant, but also ox and ass (Exod. 20:17). Economic prosperity and blessing mean that these belongings are fruitful and multiply. That is why, when Moses speaks of the LORD's blessing upon Israel, he specifies: "He will bless the fruit of your womb and the fruit of your land, your grain and wine and oil, the increase of your cattle and the offspring of your flock," and adds, "there shall not be male or female barren among you or your livestock" (Deut. 7:13–14; cf. 28:4, 11; 30:9). Economic wealth is thus the result of the first blessing of creation, when God blesses the living creatures including human beings and says, "Be fruitful and multiply . . . and fill the earth" (Gen. 1:22, 28). What fills the earth also fills the household with good things.

This is in fact the original meaning of the term "economics," which is Greek for household management. Ancient treatises entitled *Economics* are attributed to both Xenophon and Aristotle, and they are all about enhancing the wealth and prosperity of a household. That is why the discipline we now call economics was originally called "*political* economy," because it was concerned with the new theme announced in the title of Adam Smith's treatise: not the wealth of the household but the wealth *of nations*. We get an adumbration of that new theme when the king shows such concern for "humans and livestock," the basic elements of household wealth as Israelites understood them.

The king is concerned, because what admits of blessing and prosperity also admits of curse and destruction. The original readers of the book of Jonah would no doubt have regarded his concern as well founded. They would remember that a number of the plagues that the LORD sent against Egypt struck both humans and livestock: gnats (Exod. 8:17–18), boils (9:9–10), hail (9:19, 22, 25), and above all the final plague, which struck "all the firstborn in the land of Egypt, both human and livestock" (12:12; cf. 11:5; 12:29).

A deep inspiration prompts the king to include the livestock in Nineveh's acts of repentance, because they are included in Nineveh's prosperity. That inspiration is more explicit in the law of Moses, which declares that all Israel's firstborn, both human and livestock, are consecrated as holy to the LORD because, as the LORD says, "on the day that I struck down all the firstborn in the land of Egypt, I consecrated for my own all the firstborn in Israel, both human and livestock. They shall be mine" (Num. 3:13; cf. Exod. 13:11–16). The firstborn are "whatever is the first to open the womb among the people of Israel, both human and livestock" (13:2), which is to say they are the beginning of any future blessing of prosperity for Israel, any hope that flocks and herds, children and heirs, will be fruitful and multiply. The LORD claims them for his own, so that Israel may know that blessing and prosperity are his to give or take away. The proclamation of the king of Nineveh gropes toward this same understanding of the source of blessing.

not taste anything,

Taste, that primitive and inarticulate sense, so much less rational than sight and hearing (as Augustine pointed out in *On Order* 2.32), is nonetheless fundamental for our encounter with the goodness of the world. We put things in our mouth that keep us alive, and they taste good. If something tastes bad, we spit it out— it's rotten, poisonous, bad for us. So taste is a basic mode of the wisdom of the body, discerning good things from bad, life from death. To taste nothing is to lay aside this wisdom, making ourselves helpless and undiscerning and thus putting ourselves at the mercy of someone else who must judge for us what promotes our life. It is to give up the taste of good things that sustain us in being, because we seek a more fundamental ground of our being and we are afraid that by our manifold bad judgment we have made ourselves enemies of it. This is the body's participation in the fear of God which is the beginning of wisdom, for what we are afraid of is that the giver of all good things intends evil for us.

not feed or drink any water.

The verb "feed" is not the ordinary word for human eating. It is the word for what livestock do when they have good pasture; it can also mean "to shepherd" (as in "the LORD shepherds me"; Ps. 23:1). The word is used when flocks and herds are well taken care of. Just as the Ninevites afflict their own bodies by putting on sackcloth and fasting, they neglect their animals by giving them no pasture. All the living bodies that belong to a prosperous household are to be deprived of what makes for prosperity.

Living bodies are the basis of economics because bodily needs such as hunger and thirst are the basic form of economic demand. If we do not eat or drink we die, so food and water are things we just have to get, one way or another. (Modern Westerners who don't think of water as an economic issue should consider the growing crisis over the scarcity of uncontaminated water in the underdeveloped world, or put themselves for a moment in the place of an ancient herder looking for a well or an oasis to water the flock.)

In adding water to the fast that his people have already called, the king's proclamation gets drastic and radical. You can stretch out a fast for weeks, but without water you're dead in days. The king is leading Nineveh to renounce all the basic needs of the economy of living bodies: not only food and water but also clothing (since being dressed in sackcloth is as close to naked as you can get without indecency) and shelter (since the king sits in ashes, not by a warm hearth). Every blessing of prosperity, everything needed for a household to flourish, is to be given up so that the true source of blessing may have pity and give them what makes for life, not death.

3:8 Let human and livestock be covered with sackcloth

This is wonderful and bizarre, without precedent: the livestock are made not only to fast but to wear sackcloth! (In Judith 4:10 we read that the people of Israel put sackcloth on their livestock, but this passage was in fact inspired by the book of Jonah.) The sackcloth makes the animals' participation in Nineveh's repentance visible. The sight is comic, no question, but such comedy is only to be expected from a king trying to figure out how to appease the wrath of God without any help from the Law and the Prophets. He's improvising without a script.

Yet he's doing a pretty good job of it. The king's proclamation shows something of the magnitude of the wrath he fears: not an ordinary invasion, which would result in no harm to the cattle taken by enemies as spoils of war, but something more like the fire from heaven that overthrew Sodom and Gomorrah. Wrath on this scale is not so much punishment as cleansing; it gets rid of abominations by utterly destroying them, burning them clean off the earth and turning them into smoke. Perhaps the king also has some notion of Israel's sacred curse of *herem* (a king of Assyria uses the term in 2 Chr. 32:14), which includes the requirement: "Do not leave alive anything that breathes" (Deut. 20:16). When the armies of Israel attack a city under the curse of *herem*, they must slay human and livestock with the edge of the sword, then burn the whole city and all its spoil (13:15–16; cf. Judg. 20:48). Everything under the curse is sacred to the LORD in a peculiar and awful way: it is devoted to total destruction, nothing of it may be withheld or spared. This is a sacred duty not to be transgressed: saving the livestock of a city under *herem* and keeping it as spoils was a large part of the sin against the LORD that lost Saul his kingship (1 Sam. 15).

Dressing up the livestock in sackcloth is acknowledgment that they too will not be spared, because they belong to a city that is an abomination before God, devoted to total destruction. The king is right about the magnitude of the wrath to come, right to be terrified and rattled, right to be so unhinged by the seriousness of what he is facing that the effect is comic.

and let them call mightily to God;

Human and livestock are to call mightily, lifting up their voices "with strength" as the prophet says (Isa. 40:9). For they are calling to an unknown God and they do not know where he can be found, though no doubt they suspect he is the God of heaven (Jonah 1:9). Their call is a cry to heaven, counterbalancing the cry against them that has come up before the face of God (1:2; cf. Gen. 18:20). They call like Jonah from the depths (Jonah 2:2), but in their case from the depth of troubles they cannot see or feel but must simply believe in.

let them each turn from his evil way

The king of Nineveh unwittingly echoes the word of the LORD to the people of Judah, spoken repeatedly by the prophet Jeremiah, warning them to "turn, each one, from his evil way" (Jer. 18:11; cf. 25:5; 26:3; 35:15; 36:3). It was precisely because they did not heed such warnings that Israel was taken into exile in Assyria, as Scripture explains: "The LORD warned Israel and Judah through all his prophets and seers, 'Turn from your evil ways . . . .' but they would not listen but were stubborn like their fathers, who did not believe the LORD their God" (2 Kgs. 17:13–14). So when the Ninevites believe God (Jonah 3:5) and turn from their evil ways, they are rendering the obedience that the Israelites did not render to their God, as a result of which they were taken captive by the Assyrians, whose capital was Nineveh. The reversal is pointed and should not be missed: the people of Nineveh survived long enough to destroy the people of Israel because the people of Nineveh turned every one from his evil way, and the people of Israel did not.

and from the violence in their hands.

Hands are the bodily source of human power, the first of our tools for building as well as killing, the two great works of an expanding empire. For the people of Nineveh to turn from their evil ways, which are notoriously ways of violence and cruelty (Nah. 3:1–3), they must turn from the work of their hands, so that the only strength left to them is in the voice of their prayer, calling mightily to God. They must seek divine mercy rather than imperial power. How many great cities have done that?

3:9 Who knows? Perhaps God may turn and repent

What can the king of Nineveh do but hope that God—whichever God it is—will change his mind? Uninstructed, ignorant of the name of the LORD, this pagan ruler nonetheless gets it exactly right. His hope is like a groping in the dark, but he is unmistakably groping in the direction of the LORD, the God of Israel. For his hope is precisely that of the prophet Joel, who instructs Israel:

> Turn to the LORD your God,
>   for he is "gracious and merciful,
>   slow to anger and abounding in loving-kindness"
>   and "repents of the evil."
> *Who knows but he will turn and repent*
>   and leave a blessing behind him? (Joel 2:13–14)

This confession of the mercy and loving-kindness of the LORD is exactly what Jonah knows and isn't telling (Jonah 4:2). Joel quotes from Israel's fundamental confession of faith in the name of the LORD (Exod. 34:6), adding a quotation from the narrative context (32:11–14), in which the LORD, consistent with this confession of his name, responds to Moses's intercession for his sinful people by having mercy and repenting of the evil he spoke of doing to them.

Nineveh is following in Israel's footsteps without even a prophet to help them, but only a hopeful king—a king humbled, ignorant and wise, knowing he has access to no wisdom but that of humility and no hope but that of repentance. The words of this altogether extraordinary king are our sign that all is well with Nineveh.

and turn from his burning anger

The phrase is often translated "fierce anger," but the word for anger is also the word for nostrils, so that divine anger here is literally "the burning of his nostrils." We should picture someone snorting in fury, like Jesus at the tomb of Lazarus in John 11:38, where the Greek is a word used for the snorting of a warhorse—as if Jesus were going to battle, overcoming death his enemy. The burning of anger is a commonplace in many languages, and we shall hear more of it in Jonah 4.

Why picture a burning, snorting God? If sinners are to picture God at all, this is how they should do it: he is like a great king with fury burning in his face, about to pronounce sentence on a foul criminal who offends him. Such a picture might just be enough to get us turning from our evil ways and back to the way of life. Thus Augustine explains the purpose of anthropomorphic depictions of God in the Bible:

> The "anger" of God is not a disturbance of his mind; it is the judgment by which he imposes punishment on sin. . . . For unlike human beings, God does not regret or repent of anything he does; his view of absolutely everything is fixed, just as his foreknowledge is certain. But if the Bible did not use words like these it couldn't communicate so plainly to all the kinds of people it wants to reach—frightening the proud, stirring up the lazy, encouraging those who seek, and feeding those who understand. It couldn't do any of this, if it did not first bend down as it were and descend to those who are cast down. (*City of God* 15.25)

Like nearly all the church fathers, Augustine is convinced that God is impassible, free from the fickle changes of anger and other passions that turn the mind to and fro. The literal truth is that God has eternal and unchanging knowledge of all things in the universe and all events in its history—and knows what to do about them all long before they happen. Using a philosophical language congenial to Augustine, we could say: insofar as he is Justice itself, the eternal God judges and punishes sin, allowing no evildoer to live for long. But those less philosophical than Augustine must use their imagination. So the king of Nineveh rightly imagines God as a furious king burning with wrath and about to destroy him and his people.

and we won't perish."

The king's speech comes to the same hopeful conclusion as the captain's in 1:6. The end of our prayer and penitence, our calling to God in our troubles as well as our fasting, sackcloth, and ashes, is that we may not perish but live. This good motive cannot always be taken for granted, as we shall see (4:3). There are even theologians who think it is not disinterested enough, as if the desire not to perish contains some element of selfishness that makes our motives impure. But the God who commands his beloved to choose life, not death (Deut. 30:19; cf. Ezek. 18:31–32), knows nothing of this false purity of motive.

We ought to seek our own good, for this will lead us to God. Hence the very word "prayer" means begging. We beg for mercy so that we may not perish. After that follows the offering of thanksgiving and praise, as we have seen (Jonah 1:16). Though the praise of God indeed goes deeper than prayer, since it is the purpose of creation and the heart of the life that never ends, nonetheless we must first learn to beg for mercy from out of our troubles (2:2). The desire not to perish schools us in the love of God.

3:10 And God saw what they did,

The narrative picks up the language of the proclamation and continues to speak of "God" (*Elohim*). This is still the LORD, the God of Israel, but he is described in terms available to the pagan king of Nineveh, as if to confirm that in his affliction and distress for his people he has spoken rightly of the LORD, as Job did (Job 42:7). Indeed at this point we jump straight from the king's proclamation to a God's-eye view, and the latter confirms the former. The narrative here is telescoped: we don't stop to hear what the Ninevites do in response to the king's proclamation but suddenly are up in heaven with God looking down on the earth. The omniscient narrator moves us straight from human anxiety and hope to divine vision and good pleasure. We see what God sees, and it is good.

how they turned from their evil way,

The evil that came before the face of the LORD at the beginning of the book (1:2) is no longer there. What God sees instead are the Ninevites doing exactly what the king's proclamation said they should do. Divine vision here confirms human good intentions, seeing that they have been carried out. This is not a common occurrence in the Bible. Things are going astonishingly well here.

This does not mean that all will be well in the end. We have the heartbreaking biblical example of good king Josiah, "who *turned to* the LORD with all his heart, with all his soul and with all his might" and yet "the LORD *did not turn* from the burning of his great anger," with the result that Judah goes into exile (2 Kgs. 23:25–26). Because it is a matter of the LORD having mercy on whom he will have mercy (Rom. 9:15)—and this mercy is surely undeserved, a gift that no king can earn except the true Messiah himself—there is no guarantee that the turning of a king and his people will be met by the turning of the LORD. And yet where there is turning and repentance, there is good reason to hope. For the LORD delights in mercy, and his having mercy on whom he will have mercy belongs to his very name (Exod. 33:19; see comment on 4:2).

and God repented of the evil he spoke of doing to them,

Turn and turn about: the people of the city turn from their evil way, and God turns from the evil he spoke of doing to them. Between them all evil disappears like a mirage with no one to turn and see it.

Of course, the evil from which God turns is not moral evil or wickedness like Nineveh's (for his eyes are too clean even to contemplate such a thing; Hab. 1:13) but the bad things he had justly threatened to bring about in Nineveh. We need to get used to the fact that English is unusual in having two terms, "evil" and "bad," where most languages, including Hebrew, get by with one. Hence whenever we hear in translation of some "evil" we must ask whether this means moral evil or simply some other kind of badness, something gone wrong, some disaster or destruction, perhaps even bad things that are morally good because they are a form of justice—the bad things that bad people deserve to have happen to them because they are justly punished. Scripture speaks frequently of the LORD "bringing evil" in this sense upon evildoers (e.g., 1 Kgs. 9:9; 14:10; 21:21; Jer. 6:19; 11:11; 19:3; 23:12; 32:42), though often the shock of this language is mitigated by translating it as "bringing disaster." But the word is the standard catchall term for evil, the same one used here and throughout the book of Jonah.

The turning of God from the evil he spoke of doing is described as "repentance," the same word used for human repentance of sin, which is also a turning from bad things. The word suggests both regret and change of mind and is used often of God, who repents that he made humans on the earth and then resolves to kill most of the human race (Gen. 6:6), repents of making Saul king and then resolves to depose him (1 Sam. 15:11), and repents of bringing bad things upon his people and resolves not to do it (Amos 7:3, 6). The latter is the sense of the startling phrase "repent of the evil." The LORD does no evil or injustice, but in his justice he does punish, bringing disaster and other well-deserved evil upon wicked people, cities, and nations, so that the prophets can say, "Does evil befall a city unless the LORD has done it?" (3:6), and "I make peace and create evil; I the LORD do all these things" (Isa. 45:7).

For the LORD to "repent of the evil" is therefore to have mercy where he has threatened to execute justice. In the book of Jeremiah, where the phrase occurs rather frequently (18:8; 26:3, 13, 19; 42:10) the point is explained this way: the LORD says, "If at any time I declare concerning a nation or a kingdom, that I will pluck up and break down and destroy it, and if that nation, concerning which I have spoken, turns from its evil, *I will repent of the evil* that I intended to do to it" (18:7–8). The same kind of point is made in less startling language in the book of Ezekiel, where the LORD says, "Though I say to the wicked, 'You shall surely die,' yet if he turns from his sin and does what is lawful and right . . . he shall surely live, not die" (33:14–15). The explanation for this apparent change of mind is the unchanging character of God: "'As I live,' says the LORD God, 'I take no pleasure in the death of the wicked, but that the wicked turn from his way and live'" (33:11).

Explained this way, it is not so surprising to hear that the LORD "repents of the evil." The deep theological question is whether this repentance is an actual change of mind. This is an important question in the metaphysics of divine eternity: shall we think of God as beyond time and change, immutable and impassible, never overtaken by passions and never changing his mind, as argued by "classical theists" like Augustine (and most of the church fathers and medieval and Reformation theologians), or shall we take the biblical narrative of divine repentance more literally, as recent "open theists" do?

You might think the very fact that there is a narrative in which God takes part counts against the classical theist view, which places God somehow outside the changing events of time. Of course, classical theists argue that many features of the biblical narrative about God are not to be taken literally, such as God's strong hand (Exod. 13:3, 9, 14, 16) or his burning at the nostrils (Jonah 3:9) or his sitting on a throne in heaven (Ps. 11:4). The crucial test of their view is whether some incoherence or absurdity arises from taking the narrative literally at this point—and whether it is an incoherence that points nonetheless in a particular metaphysical direction. For instance, the biblical picture of God present locally in heaven, taken literally, does not cohere with the biblical conviction that God is present everywhere. But the details of the picture point beyond a local presence that would confine God to one place. He sits in heaven, but has his footstool on earth (Isa. 66:1; Matt. 5:35; Acts 7:49) at the temple (1 Chr. 28:2; Ps. 99:5; 132:7). Moreover, the beams of his chambers are laid on the waters (104:3), which is to say he sits in a throne room built on top of the waters that are above the heavens. This is as close to saying "outside space" as an ancient Near Eastern picture can get. Hence it is quite in keeping with the general direction of this imagery when Solomon at the dedication of the temple says, "Heaven and the heaven of heavens cannot contain you" (1 Kgs. 8:27). And if God is outside space, uncontained by any location, then (as classical theist metaphysics tell us) the only place he can be present is everywhere, all at once. The very logic of the picture, in its incoherence, points to omnipresence.

A similar incoherence in the narrative of the book of Jonah points toward a God outside time, which means he is present to all times at once. For on the one hand, God threatened to destroy Nineveh and then did not do it, which seems to be aptly described by saying he changed his mind. But on the other hand, as we have seen, it seems impossible to regard the conversion of Nineveh as anything but the LORD's doing, a miracle of divine grace. It is as if he did for Nineveh what he promises to do for Israel, giving them a new heart and a new spirit to obey his will (Ezek. 36:26–27). We can hardly imagine him deciding to do this at the last minute: it must have been what he intended for Nineveh all along. Just what you'd expect!—as Jonah himself complains afterward (4:2). From this perspective within the narrative itself, the repentance of the LORD does not look like a change of mind but a carrying out of God's will from long before, and indeed an expression of his unchanging character. Though for us his mercies are "new every morning" (Lam. 3:23), they do not catch the LORD himself by surprise, as if he had not known before that he would save Nineveh through Jonah or spare his people through the intercession of Moses. Clearly he had been planning all along to "repent of the evil." So the phrase does not refer to an unexpected change of mind but to a successful carrying out of his intention.

The classical theist metaphysics of an unchanging eternal plan carried out through dramatic changes in time does indeed seem to fit the particular shape of this story, both its inner incoherence and its inherent direction. While this hardly settles the issue, it does look to me like the classical theist interpretation is more plausible than literalism as a reading of this particular narrative.

"What then is the point of expressing such a metaphysics in the form of narrative?" an open theist could reasonably ask. In general, the narrative is about the changes that take place as temporal creatures come to know the eternal God. In particular, the biblical narratives of divine threat and repentance have something to teach us about the workings of divine mercy. Mercy is always compassion upon the miserable, but the deepest mercy is bestowed upon the miserable who are evildoers deserving their misery. The narrative sequence in which God says he will bring evil upon us evildoers and then repents of the evil casts light upon the depth of divine mercy by showing us the depth of evil, sin, and misery from which he rescues us. By leading us to anticipate the terror of what the LORD might do, the narrative shows us the glory of what he does do. Were it not for this sequence we might think that the reason the LORD has mercy is because he is not the kind of God who would ever take vengeance on the wicked. Such a god would be an indulgent fantasy, giving us a picture of mercy without justice—which is to say, a concept of mercy that is not really mercy at all but only a failure to uphold what is right and to vindicate the oppressed. To undermine that fantasy, the word of God undertakes the strange project of telling a *story* about unchanging divine mercy.

and did it not.

This is why we require a God's-eye view at this point in the story: it is a narrative of what God decided *not* to do. For that we need a prophet or an omniscient narrator who can let us in on God's thoughts.

Nineveh, evidently, has neither. Jonah does not tell them that the LORD has had mercy upon them and repented of the evil he spoke of doing to them. Jonah's vow to proclaim that "salvation is the LORD's" (2:9) goes so far unfulfilled, as if hidden in the depth of the sea. The loving-kindness of the LORD toward Nineveh is revealed not to the people of Nineveh but only to the people of Israel, who get to read the book. What the point of this revelation is, we must now inquire as we

turn to Jonah 4. Meanwhile we leave the Ninevites behind, still fasting and praying, having no idea whether they will live or die, and wondering: "Who knows?"
Of course the truth is that all is well with them now, but we do not learn if they
are ever told this. For that part of the story takes us beyond the book of Jonah to
choices that lie still in the future.

JONAH 4

The Repentance of the LORD

Jonah Contends with the LORD (4:1–4)

4:1 And it was grievous to Jonah, a great evil,

Strikingly, Jonah knows all about the repentance of the LORD, though we are not told how. Despite his malfeasance he remains a true prophet, present at the counsels of the LORD, as if he were one of the angels around the throne of God like courtiers around the throne of a great king, who are the first to hear his decisions. It is all the more striking that Jonah knows of this while he is actually still present in Nineveh, in a kind of exile far from the holy city and the temple.

At this point two words that recur throughout the text come together for the first and only time in the story: "great" and "evil." They come together precisely in the person of Jonah, in his perception of the mercy of God and the blessing of the Gentiles, a great good that is evil in his sight. What is the evil he sees? On the one hand the enemies of Israel are converted and saved—thus fulfilling Israel's identity, election, and calling as a blessing to all nations. On the other hand Jonah himself is made to look like a false prophet—as the word that the LORD gave him to speak succeeds in bringing mercy where it threatened destruction. Unexpectedly, it is blessing and success all around, both Israel and prophecy accomplishing what they were always meant to accomplish, and it grieves Jonah like a great evil. How the LORD deals with this grieving, this great evil in Jonah's eyes, is the story of the rest of the book.

How can Jonah be so grieved at all this good news? At the core of it is his feeling that he has been set up, made to look like a fool. And in all fairness to Jonah, he has been. He thought he knew what he was saying when he called to Nineveh and said, "Forty days and Nineveh shall be overturned!" using the verb for the overthrow of

Sodom and Gomorrah that can also—unfortunately for Jonah—mean conversion and being turned into something new (see comment on 3:4). By virtue of this double meaning—what amounts really to a pun—the LORD fooled his own prophet, keeping his plans to himself until he revealed what now appears to have been his intention all along, which was to repent of the evil he spoke of doing to Nineveh. Now Jonah realizes that he got it wrong, that God had always planned to operate quite independently of him, as if his thoughts were not Jonah's thoughts, and it grieves Jonah to the core. It is a great evil to him that the LORD repents of the evil.

His is the wrath of a theologian whose theology does not pan out. Jonah had been convinced he had the word of God interpreted accurately and precisely (not to say narrowly and restrictively) and all to his satisfaction, but then God turns around and undermines Jonah's whole theological project by fulfilling his word in an astonishingly unexpected way, as if its meaning were far broader and happier than anything Jonah had conceived. And he gets away with it by taking advantage of something as cheap as a pun! Every theologian and exegete should be able to sympathize with Jonah here. Mysteries and obscurities, textual corruption and historical context are one thing. Those are respectable problems that any scholar can handle. But a pun! That's just cheating. And as a result of that sneaky little swindle, God gets to be far more merciful than Jonah's theology would allow him to be. The things God will do to get away with being God. . . .

We should mention, in all fairness to God, that it does not seem that Jonah has been made to look like a false prophet or a fool to anyone but himself. He is still in Nineveh at this point, but the Ninevites seem not to be paying any attention to him. In one of the many intriguing gaps in the narrative, we have no idea what the Ninevites think of him or whether they notice him at all. As we have seen, the most likely story is that his call to Nineveh spread with all the anonymous power of rumor, not attached to his name or person at all (see comment on 3:5). So even if he were to proclaim to them that God had changed his mind, Jonah need not identify himself as the one whose prophecy has been overturned.

Still, the prospect of making such a proclamation must have been deeply unappealing to him, and what he does instead, as we read further, is leave the city and wait to see what happens to it, evidently hoping that Nineveh will be destroyed after all. We ought not forget that in the long run he does get his wish, and Nineveh is no more. Huge questions about the purposes of God loom here.

and he was angry.

The word "angry" corresponds to the word for "burning" in the phrase "burning anger" (3:9). It would not be wrong to translate "he burned with anger" or "he was all burned up." The English idiom matches the Hebrew, both indicating the same physiological signs of anger: a flushed face and a hot flash of fury rising up from within, like a fire when it is kindled or a match when it flares white hot. The same idiom can describe the wrath of the LORD that is kindled by the sight of evil and burns as he punishes it (Num. 11:1; Deut. 6:15; Isa. 64:5; Lam. 5:22).

This is why the wrath from which the king of Nineveh hopes God will turn is described literally as a burning of the nostrils in Jonah 3:9.

But this time it is Jonah who is burning mad at God. His wrath burns hot enough that he is ready to sit in judgment over the judge of the universe, aggrieved like Job, who wished he could summon the LORD to court (Job 9:14–18; 23:3–7). But unlike Job, Jonah is quite confident that the LORD is merciful and gracious—that is precisely what has him all burned up.

4:2 And he prayed to the LORD and said,

Some prayer! It takes a sense of irony greater than usual even in the Bible to call this piece of hateful defiance a prayer. But this really is a comedy, and God is extraordinarily gentle with Jonah, if a little amused.

This is the point in the second half of the story that corresponds to Jonah's time at the bottom of the sea in the first half. He prays while he is still in Nineveh, just as he prayed while still in the belly of the beast in Jonah 2. Yet as he calls upon the name of the LORD for only the second time in the story, we see him in quite different circumstances from the first time. Back then he was plunged into the depths of a watery Sheol, yet celebrating the LORD's salvation (2:9); now he is high and dry, even getting comfortable (4:5–6), but the LORD's salvation is precisely what he complains about. In both cases he prays from a kind of exile, far away from the presence of the LORD in the temple. But he is in deeper trouble now than then, because this prayer is not a psalm of praise for the salvation of the LORD but a complaint against it. He has become one of those who "forsake their loving-kindness" (2:8). Back then he was in the realm of the dead but longing for life; now he is alive and well but would rather die.

"Please, LORD!

"Please" is "I pray thee" or "I beseech thee" in the older translations, as when the sailors first address Jonah (1:8) or pray to the LORD (1:14). Here the politeness quickly wears thin, and the updated translation aptly evokes the more ironic uses of the word "please" with which we are now familiar: "Oh *please*! Do you have any idea what you're doing?" or "Please! Tell me you're not serious!"

Wasn't this what I said when I was in my own country?

Jonah claims he knew it all along. This of course is how many people talk when they have been caught flatfooted, made a fool of, and don't want to admit it. So we needn't take what Jonah says at face value.

Jonah tells the LORD that he said all of this back at the beginning. If so, we didn't hear it. The omniscient narrator told us nothing about it. Of course it's not beyond the biblical narrator to save up some surprises for later (see comment on 1:10); in fact that's a typical trick of biblical narration. But another typical trick is to leave all sorts of gaps in the telling of the story that ought to get us thinking,[1] and surely one thing we ought to be thinking about is whether the reason we never heard of Jonah saying this back in his own country is that he didn't. The biblical narrator is reliable (if indirect and tricky), but Jonah is not.

One possible indication of Jonah's unreliability is that once again (see comment on 1:9), he avoids naming his own country—contributing to the phenomenon, so striking once you notice it, that the name "Israel" is never mentioned in the book of Jonah. The first thing Jonah does in this story is get up and get out of there, and for the rest of the time he is in a kind of exile, physically and spiritually—both feet and tongue far from his native Israel. It is hard to tell exactly where his heart is, except that it is turned against the LORD. That much our omniscient narrator makes abundantly clear.

That is why I fled to Tarshish before.

Jonah interprets his own motives in a way that brings us back to the opening of the book with a start. Is *this* really what was going on back then? Suddenly we feel the need to go back and reread, to see if we can reinterpret Jonah's past the way he insists the LORD must. In this way the book invites us to reread it even before we are finished, to check and recheck what we have been thinking about the meaning of Jonah's story. It is important to see that the narrative leaves this task of interpretation and reevaluation up to us. The narrator gives us no confirmation of the truth of what Jonah says here. So we have to decide what Jonah's word is actually worth.

Where to begin? Certainly the hatred, the frustrated desire for Nineveh's destruction, is believable. But can we really give up our initial impression that Jonah was running away because he was afraid (1:3)? That seems to be taking Jonah a bit too seriously. He hardly had the prescience to realize that it was the LORD's intention to have mercy on Nineveh all along. That the LORD would protect Israel by destroying the Ninevites was certainly a hope he could have harbored in his heart, but that the LORD instead would protect Israel by converting the Ninevites is a stupendous miracle, astonishing and unprecedented, for which nothing could have prepared him. To suppose that from the very beginning Jonah understood the ways of the LORD so deeply is to give him too much credit. His hatred is believable but not his claim to wisdom. The best way to interpret Jonah's story about his own motivations, his self-interpretation, is to call it a lie.

This means that Jonah is lying to God. It wouldn't be the first time someone has tried this, but still it's crazy. He must be beside himself with fury. If you are bent on justifying yourself in the heat of anger, you can make up anything that sounds good, any argument you think might carry the day—who cares if it's true, so long as it furnishes you with a weapon against your enemy? So Jonah madly

---

1. See Meir Sternberg, *Poetics of Biblical Narrative* (Bloomington: Indiana University Press, 1985).

justifies himself by boasting of being tougher and more merciless than God, when all he is, really, is more cowardly.

The wrath of God is bad, but thank God that human wrath is only human. Otherwise we would all perish, beginning with God. For at this point it is God who really burns Jonah up—it is God whom he would pervert and overturn if he could. It is almost enough to make you rethink the question of Jonah's cowardice. Here is a man with the courage to attack God for being merciful. Perhaps Jonah's calling as a prophet has sunk in at last, and he is finally ready to step wholeheartedly into the role. For one accusation you can't make against the prophets of Israel is that they lack chutzpah. They were always willing to complain and even to accuse God, and here is one willing to go so far as to lie to God, accuse him, and justify himself, all at the same time.

Only God's beloved could get away with this. But so it is: as we noticed in the comment of the very first verse, Jonah is the LORD's dove, his fair one, the apple of his eye. The LORD's patience with his beloved knows no bounds.

For I know

Though he has no special insight into the deep purposes of the LORD (as is so often the case, the ultimate meaning of the prophet's own prophecy is obscure even to himself, like a courtier in the very presence of the king being given a message to bear that he does not quite understand), Jonah does know what all Israel knows: the name of the LORD which the Gentiles do not know, but which the LORD will make known to them by the abundance of his mercy to Israel: "'I will vindicate the holiness of my great name . . . and the nations will know that I am the LORD,' says the LORD God" (Ezek. 36:23). This vindication, this making the name of the LORD holy even among the nations, has begun already with the sailors worshiping the LORD at the end of the first half of the book of Jonah. But the second half of the book does not get that far. We never hear of the Ninevites coming to know the name of the LORD, and it is clear that Jonah does not want them to know the LORD, for that would mean knowing his loving-kindness for themselves.

you are 'a gracious and merciful God, slow to anger and abounding in loving-kindness,'

At issue in Jonah's contention against the LORD is not just the fate of Nineveh but the identity of God. Jonah brings his anger into focus using Israel's most fundamental confession of the name of the LORD, given in the LORD's own proclamation of his name before Moses:

> And the LORD passed before him and proclaimed,
> "The LORD, the LORD, *a merciful and gracious God,*
>   *slow to anger and abounding in loving-kindness and truth,*
> keeping loving-kindness for thousands,
>   forgiving iniquity and transgression and sin,

but who will by no means clear the guilty,
visiting the iniquity of the fathers upon the children
and the children's children to the third and fourth generation." (Exod.
34:6–7)

To proclaim the name of the LORD is to announce mercy but not to forget justice. The two-sidedness of the proclamation does not propose a neat formula for balancing mercy and justice but rather leaves this up to the judgment of the LORD, whose justice and mercy can both be trusted. When Christians pray, "Thy will be done, on earth as it is in heaven," we should be aware that it is *this* God whom we are asking to accomplish his will.

Of course it is clear from the proclamation itself as well as its narrative setting that the judgment and will of the LORD incline toward mercy. When the LORD announces that he will proclaim his name, making all his goodness to pass before Moses, he adds, "And I will be gracious to whom I will be gracious and will show mercy to whom I will show mercy" (Exod. 33:19). He does not add: "And I will withhold grace and mercy from whom I will withhold grace and mercy," for that would be missing the point.

Moses gets the point. When the people of Israel rebel in the desert, he intercedes for them by quoting this proclamation of the name as a promise of mercy, then urges the LORD to "forgive the iniquity of this people according to the greatness of your loving-kindness" (Num. 14:17–19). Likewise, Nehemiah quotes from the proclamation to explain why the LORD did not destroy his stiff-necked people long ago (Neh. 9:17–31). And the many psalms that quote from it also emphasize the greatness of the LORD's loving-kindness, often and gladly repeating the confession that the LORD is "gracious and merciful" (Ps. 86:15; 103:8; 111:4; 145:8).

But it is possible also to emphasize justice and wrath, especially when thinking of Nineveh. The prophet Nahum is the most prominent example. As we have already seen (see comment on 1:2), the book of Nahum praises the goodness of the LORD by celebrating his wrath against the great and wicked city that oppresses his people. Hence it is with gladness that the book of Nahum opens by speaking of the wrath of God, quoting from the more formidable part of the proclamation of the name:

The LORD is a jealous God, and avenging,
the LORD is avenging and wrathful.
The LORD takes vengeance on his enemies
and keeps wrath for his foes.
The LORD "is slow to anger" and of great might,
and the LORD "will by no means clear the guilty." (Nah. 1:2–3)

Even here we have both sides: the LORD is slow to anger but does not let the guilty get off with impunity. Yet the direction is not toward a mercy that remembers justice, but rather toward a justice that is slow to anger but once kindled will not forbear to take vengeance, for the good of all who have suffered from the cruelty of that "city of blood" (3:1).

Jonah would like to preach the same glad tidings of wrath as Nahum, but under the circumstances he can't. Nahum, prophesying a century or more after Jonah, does get the last word on Nineveh, as the LORD indeed destroys it forever (for the dates and their significance, see comment on 1:1). But Jonah is faced with a Nineveh that lives, at least for a while, under the mercy and abundant loving-kindness of the LORD, still slow to anger. Hence his relation to the proclamation of the name is unique among the prophets: he quotes the part about a gracious and merciful God because he wants to complain about it.

Other elements of the proclamation of the name also reflect badly on Jonah. The LORD is "slow to anger," unlike Jonah, who is burning in fury and would be quick to destroy if he could. And above all, the LORD is "abounding in loving-kindness"—that wonderful word *hesed* that we encountered in Jonah's psalm (2:8) when he looks askance at those who pay heed to vain idols and therefore forsake their *hesed*, their covenant loyalty, mercy, and steadfast love. Here, astonishingly, Jonah pays heed not to vanities but to the LORD himself, yet he does worse than forsake his loving-kindness—he hates it. He hates the fact that the LORD abounds in a loving-kindness that extends far beyond the bounds of his covenant with Israel. He would, if he could, prevent this loving-kindness of the LORD from abounding so much. He would, if he could, prevent the LORD from being who he is.

And in this he sets himself, finally, against the truth of the LORD, his *emeth*, a word so often paired with *hesed* in descriptions of who the LORD is that the phrase becomes a cliché in the psalms, familiar from the King James Version as "mercy and truth" (Ps. 25:10; 40:10–11; 85:10; 89:14; 115:1) and alluded to in the wonderful couplet:

> Your loving-kindness is higher than the heavens,
> your truth reaches to the clouds. (Ps. 57:10 = 108:4)

Jonah is protesting against the LORD's truth, accusing him in effect of being true to who he is, complaining that his name is true: "I AM WHO I AM" (Exod. 3:14).

Significantly, Jonah cuts short his quotation of the proclamation of the name, leaving out the term *emeth* ("truth"), which follows immediately after the abounding *hesed* ("loving-kindness"). Perhaps he means to imply that the LORD has not been true to his word: through Jonah he spoke a word of evil against Nineveh, and he has not kept it. But as we have already seen, he has in fact kept it to the letter, due to the punning ambiguity of Jonah's preaching (see comment on 3:4). Jonah has not been made a false prophet, though he has perhaps been made a fool. If so, it is his own doing, a result of his forsaking the loving-kindness of the LORD in order to pursue his own malice and mercilessness. It is a good thing, quite in keeping with the truth of the God who proclaims himself gracious and merciful, slow to anger and abounding in loving-kindness, that those who are eager to see destruction often find they have made fools of themselves. There is nothing for such fools to do but turn from their evil way, as the people of Nineveh have already done (3:10). Jonah needs to catch up with them—these overturned Gentiles.

and you 'repent of the evil.'

Like the prophet Joel (see comment on 3:9), Jonah adds to his quotation of Israel's confession of the name of the LORD a quotation from the narrative context in which it is situated: the story is of how the LORD, in response to Moses's intercession, repents of the evil he spoke of bringing on his people Israel for their worshiping of the golden calf (Exod. 32:11–14). Both quotations express the hope toward which the king of Nineveh is groping in his sackcloth and ashes: that perhaps God will repent (for he repents of the evil!) and turn from his burning anger (for he is slow to anger!). "Who knows?" says the king. Well, now it is clear that this rhetorical question has an answer: the prophet Jonah knows, but he's not telling. He obviously has no intention of letting the Ninevites hear the proclamation of the name of the LORD or know that "salvation is the LORD's" (Jonah 2:9). He joins in Israel's great confession of the name of the LORD only to use it as an indictment against the God of Israel for abounding too much in loving-kindness and repenting of evil.

We must be clear where Jonah gets it wrong. It's not as if we should never desire justice or even celebrate the wrath of God as Nahum does (see comment on 1:2). It is good news when the oppressor is toppled, the terrorist is caught, and the torturer enjoys no impunity. The arrival of justice is heartening for the afflicted. The LORD does indeed "take vengeance on his enemies" (Nah. 1:2) because he is the enemy of all the destroyers of the earth, and he destroys them (Rev. 11:18; cf. Jer. 51:25). The great danger is that instead of rejoicing at the vindication of the afflicted, we self-righteously identify ourselves as the afflicted and the victimized, taking pity on ourselves and not on others, so that in our imagination the LORD becomes a weapon in our campaign to destroy our enemies, an instrument for our own vengefulness rather than the judge of the whole earth.

This is why the wrathful and avenging God is free to "repent of the evil." He is judge of the whole earth and does not abide by the imagination of our hearts. There is nothing more characteristic of the burning anger of the LORD than his turning away from it, for this is precisely the wrath of one "slow to anger and abounding in loving-kindness." His aim is always to overturn the evil that destroys his creation, and he can accomplish this justly by destroying the evildoer, but yet more justly and gloriously by turning the evil heart into something new. He repents of the evil, therefore, in order to "overcome evil with good" (Rom. 12:21), defeating evil in the abundance of his mercy—doing more, not less than justice.

The repentance of the LORD, as the prophet confesses it in connection with the proclamation of the name, means that the God of Israel is inclined to save his enemies rather than destroy them. This has particular consequences for Israel, his people, whose enemies are his enemies. There is a two-sidedness in Israel's calling and election that accords with the two-sidedness of the proclamation of the name. Israel is to be a blessing for all nations, but there is also a curse for the one who curses them, as we can see when the LORD first calls their father Abraham:

> I will bless them who bless you,
>   and him who despises you I will curse.
> And in you all the families of the earth will be blessed. (Gen. 12:3)

So Pharaoh, who despises Israel, brings curses upon himself and Egypt in the ten plagues. Likewise the people of Edom who rejoiced at "the violence against your brother Jacob" (Obad. 10) is no more, fulfilling the prophecy, "Jacob have I loved and Esau have I hated" (Mal. 1:2–3). For "Esau" here means Edom, the people descended from Esau, just as "Jacob," as so often in Scripture, means the people of Israel descended from Jacob.

Thus the blessing of Israel as the chosen people does not mean that others are not blessed, but on the contrary that all the families of the earth find their blessing in Israel—just what you would expect if the LORD God of Israel really is gracious and merciful, slow to anger and abounding in loving-kindness. He does vindicate and protect Israel from anyone who would be a curse for them, as Balaam discovers (Num. 24:9). But the purpose of this vindication, indeed of all God's ways with his chosen people, is not cursing but blessing for all nations. Even with Israel's enemies the LORD is inclined toward mercy, ever ready to repent of the evil he has spoken against them, for otherwise Israel's election would be in vain. It would defeat God's purpose if Israel were a blessing only to themselves.

And God's purpose is not defeated. Israel will indeed be a blessing to the Gentiles, and therefore the LORD does indeed repent of the evil he speaks against them. As we noted earlier (see comment on 3:10), the repentance of the LORD need not be conceived as a changing of his mind but rather as the fulfillment of his intention to save even the wicked, which brings about a new and surprising relation between him and his enemies—surprising to us, but not to him. For there is nothing more characteristic of the eternal will of God than this repentance, as we can see in the most fundamental divine intention of all, that which is (to use Karl Barth's apt phrase) "the eternal beginning of all the ways and works of God."[2] This of course is the election of Jesus Christ, the chosen one who is a blessing for all others, the beloved and only begotten Son who is the mystery of God's will hidden before the foundation of the earth and now revealed in these last days. We could say: Jesus Christ is the LORD eternally repenting of the evil he spoke of doing to evildoers, the Jew who is the absolute fulfillment of Israel's election to be a blessing for all nations.

2. Karl Barth, *Church Dogmatics* (trans. Geoffrey W. Bromiley et al.; Edinburgh: Clark, 1957), II/1.94.

The issue now is whether the prophet Jonah can live with this repentance of the LORD. At first it appears not.

4:3 And now, LORD, please take my soul away from me,

To be opposed to the repentance of the LORD is to be opposed to the very heart of the creator of the universe. Where can you go from here? Only toward nonexistence, as far away from the universe itself as you can. Unable to gain the world at the price of his soul (Matt. 16:26), Jonah would rather lose both world and soul forever. But that aim too is inevitably frustrated, for even when you die it is the LORD who takes your life, your soul or *nephesh*. In order to escape the LORD, his loving-kindness and his world, Jonah must keep on beseeching the LORD. In a fine irony, Jonah must once again say "please," like the sailors anxious about his soul in 1:14. Those Gentiles, fearful and wise and very far from accusing the LORD, took better care of Jonah's soul than Jonah did.

A yet deeper irony is the way that Jonah's request echoes that of his predecessor Elijah, the prophet of the northern kingdom of Israel who fled for his life (literally "went for his *nephesh*"; 1 Kgs. 19:3) to escape the wrath of Queen Jezebel, who swore to avenge the death of her prophets of Baal, saying: "So let the gods do to me and more, if I do not make your soul [*nephesh*] like the soul of one of them by this time tomorrow" (19:2). He goes a day's walk into the desert (like Jonah going a day's walk into the great city of Nineveh in Jonah 3:4) and sits down under a juniper tree, where he is ready to give up, asking the LORD to do what Jezebel threatens to do: "It is enough: now, O LORD, take away my soul, for I am not better than my fathers" (1 Kgs. 19:4). His fathers are dead, so why should he live?—especially since all his work as a prophet seems to be in vain, and Jezebel appears to have won. But this is a son of Israel and a prophet of Israel, and he is dealing with the God of Israel, who is not the God of the dead but of the living. Indeed, more spectacularly than any son of Adam, Elijah escapes death, for the LORD eventually takes him up alive, body and soul, into heaven in a chariot of fire (2 Kgs. 2:11). Perhaps this should be understood as a kind of delayed and ironic response to Elijah's request for the LORD to take his soul, in that wonderful mode of biblical irony, so abundant in the book of Jonah, in which God is free to do much better than asked.

At any rate, Jonah makes the same request, and he cannot be unaware of who made it before him. He is playing at being Elijah. We might think this is a mouse playing at being a lion, until we realize that he is a far more successful prophet than Elijah ever was. He does not merely escape an evil ruler but converts him along with his whole people. Elijah wants to die because his career as a prophet seems in vain; Jonah wants to die because his career as a prophet is an astounding success.

Of course Jonah doesn't see it like that, but it is still a bit of a puzzle what he does see. His mood is not despair but anger—so how does this mean he wants to die? At first glance he seems like a two-year-old throwing a tantrum because he didn't get his way, and that is certainly part of it. He wants death because he hates his career as a prophet, hates its very success, for it makes him look bad (as if he were a false prophet or at the very least a prophet who doesn't know what he's saying, like Balaam's ass) and it makes Nineveh look good, which was far from his intention. Everything he has achieved is a great evil in his sight, and he wants no more of it. Having been set up, he wants out of the game in the only way possible. His anger is saying: "No more of this! I've had it! I'm done playing along! I'm not going to be anybody's patsy any more, not even God's. Just kill me *now*."

for it is better for me to die than live."

Jonah concludes his longest speech in the narrative (aside from the psalm in Jonah 2) in a way reminiscent of the harrowing opening speech of Job, cursing the day of his birth and wishing he had never existed (Job 3). This of course is an affront to God, for it means that the Creator made some kind of mistake in giving him life and breath and being. One can sympathize with Job's complaint, because God seemed to be his enemy and his own existence seemed to be no good to himself. But Jonah seeks death so as not to have to see the *mercy* of God. His desire is the opposite of the hope not to perish, which motivates prayer in Jonah 1:6 and 3:9. Evidently he now wishes to go back down into the belly of Sheol from which the LORD rescued him in Jonah 2.

Jonah is not only the anti-Elijah, wanting to die not because his mission seems to have failed but because it has evidently succeeded. He is also the anti-Moses, quoting the proclamation of the name not to intercede but to complain. And he is the anti-Job, seeking death not because God is hard but because he is merciful. Finally, he is the anti-Abraham, arguing with God not in order to save the city that God has threatened to overthrow but to object to its salvation. Of all the figures in the Bible he is perhaps closest in spirit to Balaam, the comic prophet who keeps trying to curse but can only bless (Num. 23). But he is a Balaam who insists on getting his way, and therefore sees no way forward but death.

4:4 And the LORD said, "Is it good for you to be angry?"

The LORD does not answer Jonah's accusation against him. What could he say other than "I AM WHO I AM"? Still less does he comply with Jonah's request to die. He will be faithful and uphold both his own name and the being he has created. In response to Jonah's judgment, "It is better . . . ," he asks, "Is it good . . . ?" For he wants Jonah to consider the goodness of the LORD, beginning with the goodness of the life God gave him.

This is a new development in the story. Up to this point the LORD's speeches concerned Nineveh, the city that is "great before God" (3:3). Now he begins talking to Jonah about Jonah himself, because from now on it is Jonah's life that is at stake. In contrast to Jonah 2, where it was a foregone conclusion that the LORD would rescue Jonah's soul from the depths, here Jonah is truly in mortal danger. Back then, when Jonah called to the LORD from Sheol, you could say of him what Jesus said of Lazarus who was a few days from being laid in the tomb: this sickness is not unto death (John 11:4). But now we really do have the sickness unto death, the thing that made Jesus weep. For Lazarus's death was not a problem: Jesus saw it well ahead of time and already knew what he was going to do about it. But the unbelief of the Judeans—that was hard to see. Especially, it seems, he wept for Mary, who unlike her sister Martha does not confess faith in the power of Christ, the Son of God, to be the gift of resurrection and eternal life for her brother and for the whole world (contrast 11:25–27 with 11:32–35). The outcome of Jesus's battle with death was never in doubt. But his battle with unbelief, which is the central struggle of the whole gospel, the true battle between the light and the darkness that does not grasp it (John 1:5), still looks like it hangs in the balance.

So now the LORD is battling for Jonah's soul, that he may live, not die. And the question is not whether the LORD can give life, which is obvious, but whether Jonah can believe: whether he can ever rejoice in the LORD being the merciful and gracious God that he is. Can Jonah do what Nineveh has already done: believe God, repent, and live? The answer to that question is not obvious.

Jonah, at any rate, gives no answer that we know of at this point. Evidently he is willing to point out the LORD's faults but not to admit his own anger. He is not the first person to keep silence about his anger at God, nor the last. So he leaves the LORD's question hanging in the air unanswered. We will come back to it later in a new context (Jonah 4:9).

One thing the question already accomplishes, however, is to leave the word "good" echoing in our minds, a word which, in sharp contrast to the repeated use of the word "evil" throughout the text, has not made an appearance in the story before. The word hangs in the air together with the LORD's question, as if reminding us to wonder what's the good of all the LORD is doing in this story. What's he up to, really?

The Parable of the Gourd (4:5–11)

4:5 Then Jonah went out from the city

The last episode of the book begins with Jonah apparently ignoring the LORD's question—which, we should not fail to notice, is another way of not heeding the word of the LORD. It is not quite the same as the overtly disobedient flight at the beginning of the book, yet here too he turns his back on God, evidently without a word, and goes away from Nineveh. Later on he will actually be angry enough to talk back.

This aborted dialogue between Jonah and God takes place within Nineveh, where Jonah is still as it were in exile. Then he goes out from Nineveh—a move described using the same verb as the exodus in which Israel goes out from Egypt

(Exod. 12:41; 13:3–4; Ps. 114:1). But as in the book of Exodus, getting out from the place of exile does not solve all problems, and indeed raises some questions of faith and unbelief more sharply than before. Israel in exodus is not yet Israel in the promised land, and that gives them much reason for complaint, fear, and distrust. Jonah going out from Nineveh is in this respect a true Israelite.

and sat to the east of the city.

The language in Jonah 4:5 is resonant and suggestive. Jonah sits—in the seat of scoffers (Ps. 1:1)? He sits east of the city—like east of Eden, which is guarded by cherubim with a flaming sword (Gen. 3:24)? The image suggests that Jonah is still in exile, as all humanity is in exile from Eden, but also that he looks on Nineveh, of all places, as if it could once have been paradise. But instead of cherubim guarding the tree of life, Jonah sits east of the city hoping for its eternal death.

But further, if we imagine Jonah having a good view from some elevated location, we must also put him in more comic company—together with Balaam and his employer, who keep trying to find a good place high on a hill from which to survey the thriving host of Israel and curse it (Num. 22:41; 23:6, 13) but are repeatedly frustrated by the blessing of the LORD, which has no place for such a curse (22:12; 23:8, 11; 24:10). The LORD's people just keep flourishing, despite the best the prophet can do. So the prophet Jonah sits outside Nineveh and looks with exasperation at the survival of Nineveh, angry that the LORD is treating them as if they were his own people.

There he made himself a booth

The booth that Jonah makes is a *sukkah*, a word with quite definite associations. It is the word for the little outdoor shelters built during Sukkoth (the plural of *sukkah*), which is the festival of booths or what older translations call the feast of tabernacles. Along with Passover and Pentecost, Sukkoth is one of the three annual festivals of pilgrimage, when all Israel is to gather before the face of the LORD in Jerusalem (Deut. 16:16). Imagine the holy city decked out for celebration at festival time, populated by these temporary shelters in which all Israel lives outdoors for a week, each like a rustic little house outside the houses of the city, a reminder of the time when Israel dwelled in tents as the LORD brought her out of Egypt (Lev. 23:43) having no abiding city but under the protection of their God. The booths are made of wild branches and adorned with fruitful living plants, for this is a harvest festival, "when you make your ingathering from the threshing floor and the wine press" (Deut. 16:13). Jonah sitting in his *sukkah*, outside Nineveh rather than Jerusalem, recalls this happier image but in more burning colors, as he awaits the harvest of the word of the LORD which he has just preached.

Other associations of the festival cluster around Jonah's booth as well. Sukkoth is connected in a special way with the reading and teaching of the word of the LORD. We are told that after Moses wrote down the law, he commanded it to be read in solemn assembly every seven years during the festival of booths in the year of release from debts, "so that they may hear and learn to fear the LORD your God and to observe diligently all the words of this law, and so that their children, who have not known it, may hear and learn to fear the LORD your God, as long as you live in the land" (Deut. 31:12–13). Sukkoth thus becomes a special time of the renewal of the knowledge and obedience of the law of God, passed down from generation to generation in Israel. This connection with the law is especially prominent in the life of postexilic Judeans, because Sukkoth is the first festival that is properly celebrated according to the law after the return from Babylon (Neh. 8:13–18; cf. Ezra 3:4). So the festival of booths that Jonah's booth recalls is in effect a celebration of the reinstitution of the Torah as the law of Israel's life. It marks what we can call, in retrospect, the beginning of Judaism. As we know from the biblical narrative, this is a beginning fraught with dangers and crises. The book of Jonah belongs with Ezra, Nehemiah, Haggai, and Zechariah in the company of the many biblical meditations on the meaning of these dangers and crises.

One last association is eschatological. During the festival of booths Israel is commanded to welcome Gentiles, strangers, and foreigners within their gates, including servants (Deut. 16:14). In a worldwide extension of this hospitality, the last days will see the people of the nations that once gathered around Jerusalem to besiege it—all those who survive the wrath of God—gathering to celebrate the festival of booths, to rejoice in the LORD together with Israel (Zech. 14:16). Outside such celebration there will be nothing but drought and plague (14:17–19). Jonah, the son of Israel sitting alone, burning mad and quite inhospitable in his *sukkah* outside the great city of the Gentiles, is both a reversal and a reminder of this eschatological picture of the Gentiles escaping drought and plague to gather and celebrate the goodness of the LORD in the city of God together with Israel. Jonah, all on his own, would like to overturn and prevent this biblical eschatology.

and sat down under it in the shade

Shade means protection, an important image that is crucial to what comes next. The prophet Isaiah, for instance, speaks of the LORD as a "a refuge from the storm and a shade from the heat" (25:4), almost perfectly matching the two kinds of physical danger in the two halves of the book of Jonah. But we should also be aware of the metaphorical resonances of this imagery, as Isaiah continues:

> When the blast of the ruthless is like a winter storm
> and the noise of foreigners like heat in a dry place,
> you subdued the heat with the shade of the clouds,
> and the song of the ruthless was stilled. (Isa. 25:4–5)

No form of protection for Israel can long be separated from her need for protection against ruthless Gentile enemies, who do after all seek to destroy her.

The protection has to do especially with the safety and salvation of Jerusalem, which the *sukkah* represents. Amos speaks of a day when the LORD "will raise up the *sukkah* of David that is fallen and close up its breaches and will raise up his ruins and build it as in the days of old, that they may possess the remnant of Edom and all the nations who are called by my name" (9:11). The *sukkah* of David with its breaches repaired is clearly the city of David, Jerusalem, with the breaches in its walls repaired, its integrity restored, and ready to be the eschatological home of all nations.

Yet more startling is Isaiah's image of a *sukkah* on Mount Zion in Jerusalem, which will be "for a shade in the daytime from the heat and for a place of refuge and a shelter from the storm and rain" (4:6). For on that day the glory of the LORD will settle on Zion in "a cloud by day and smoke and the shining of a flaming fire by night " (4:5). This language connects the exodus narrative, where Israel begins its journey out of Egypt from a city named Sukkoth accompanied by a pillar of cloud by day and fire by night (Exod. 13:20–21; cf. 40:34–38), with the poetic imagery in which the LORD is described as a warrior in his pavilion of thunder-cloud (Ps. 18:11 and 2 Sam. 22:12; cf. Job 36:29—all using the word *sukkah*), which is a heavenly version of the pavilion (another meaning of *sukkah*) in which military commanders camp in the field (e.g., King Ben-hadad of Aram waiting out the siege of Samaria, drinking too much with his allies in their pavilions; 1 Kgs. 20:12–16). So the pillar of cloud and fire, Isaiah is saying, is the pavilion of divine splendor, the temporary encampment of the mighty LORD God of hosts, the commander of the armies of heaven, as he goes with his people to bring them out of their bondage in Egypt. And that pavilion, that *sukkah*, will one day rest on Mount Zion, becoming the divine protection of Jerusalem, on the day when "the Branch of the LORD shall be beautiful and glorious" (Isa. 4:2). The Branch of course is the messianic king, the Son of David—imagery for which will begin to appear in the next verse.

In bringing together all these associations of Jonah's *sukkah*—the law, Jerusalem, and the Son of David—we have evoked the hopes of the remnant of the people of Israel, the Judeans returning from exile to Jerusalem. It would be hard for the original readers of this story to miss the fact that the dialogue about to ensue between the LORD and Jonah is addressed to them and their situation.

until he should see what would become of the city.

Jonah probably intends to wait out the forty days he spoke of in his proclamation, forty days of trial and testing (3:4). But at this point Nineveh has passed the test and it is really Jonah who is put to the test by his own obstinacy and burning anger. He is fighting against the LORD, and if he wins, he dies. So while he waits to see what will become of the city, the LORD is about to take action concerning what will become of Jonah.

But in the meantime we can pause with Jonah and consider what becomes of the city. All is well for the moment: the Ninevites have turned from their evil ways and the LORD has turned away from his burning anger. But eventually both turn back to what was before, Nineveh to wickedness and the LORD to wrath. For in another century or so Nineveh is no more, as thoroughly destroyed as Sodom and Gomorrah, and with it the nation called Israel, the northern kingdom of ten tribes which was taken into exile in Assyria, also passes into oblivion. Wait long enough, and all is not well with the Ninevites or with Jonah's own people, whose future is terribly intertwined with theirs.

Could this possibly be the ultimate upshot of the book of Jonah: the destruction of Nineveh and of Israel, too? That cannot be the whole story, for it does not conform to the shape of God's will for his chosen people or for the nations they are to bless. The Judeans, the remnant of Israel returning from exile in Babylon and reading this story, must wonder how their relation with Babylon may unfold differently from Israel's relation with Nineveh. The LORD is about to show them by what he teaches Jonah.

4:6 And the LORD God prepared a gourd

The episode that now begins and takes up the rest of the book is a kind of enacted parable, not unusual in the lives of the prophets (they are especially common in Ezekiel: 4:1–17; 5:1–12; 12:1–16, 17–20; 24:15–27; 37:15–28; but see also Jer. 19 and Hos. 1–3). What is unusual is that the parable is not a dramatic gesture that the LORD commands the prophet to perform as a sign to his people, but a drama staged by the LORD himself. And it is the prophet who is both the main character in the drama and the audience that needs to get the message. But of course the whole book of Jonah is such a parable, staged by the LORD so that the prophet and the people of God whom he represents may get the message. Indeed, it is not too much to say that the whole history of Israel is such an enacted parable, staged by the LORD, and so ultimately is the history of the universe.

The parable contains the hidden meaning of the book of Jonah—what the church fathers called its mystery (the Greek term *mystērion* was used by the fathers to refer to any hidden meaning of spiritual significance). This turns out to be not so different from the mystery of Israel's very existence, which is the mystery at the heart of all existence. As we will see by the end, this parable is like some of the parables of our Lord Jesus, whose mystery takes on the peculiar character of a question about whether those who hear it will get the point of the mystery (see especially his comments on the mystery of the parable of the sower in Matt. 13:10–17).

In the telling of this little parable something startling and solemn happens right at the beginning. The two divine names, the generic term "God" that is known to all the nations, even Nineveh (Jonah 3:5, 9), and the name of the LORD, the God of Israel—both of which have been used separately with some frequency in previous verses—come together here for the first and only time in the text. Here the history of Israel and of the nations, the story of the Jews and of the Gentiles, intersect in the name of the one LORD who is—mostly unknown to them—God over them all.

What the LORD God does, to begin with, is prepare something—the same verb of providential governance used in 1:17. Only this time the LORD prepares a gourd instead of a fish. It makes a difference. For when the great fish swallows up Jonah in the depths this is an image of the Judeans swallowed up in exile, captive in the belly of a great empire far from their land. The fish, it turns out, is for Jonah's good, saving his life, as exile in Babylon is for Judah's good, preserving their identity and calling as God's chosen people. But it does not feel that way at the time. The gourd is different, because Jonah can feel its protection on his own body. Disobedient and contemptuous of the LORD as he is, he can recognize this as God's good gift because it palpably saves his skin.

The word for "gourd" is unusual, used nowhere else in the Bible, and there is disagreement among scholars about exactly what kind of plant this is. Some call it a castor-oil plant, others a gourd; both designations are misleading insofar as the names get us thinking about what the plant produces, when the story wants to focus our attention instead on how it grows and how it protects Jonah. What we need to know about this kind of plant, whatever it is, is that it grows quickly but is slender and delicate, more like a vine than a cedar, yet is leafy enough to give abundant shade. So the plant provides protection from sun and wind but is itself vulnerable to their power.

Yet more significantly, it has a distinctive place among the many plants used in the Bible as images of royal protection from enemies. The kingdom of Assyria, for instance, is compared to a mighty cedar offering protection to all the peoples under it, so that "all great nations dwelled under its shadow" (Ezek. 31:6). But more typical of Israel is the image of a tree cut down with only a stump left (Isa. 6:13) from which, unexpectedly, a shoot sprouts up offering hope of new life (11:1). This shoot is the rod of Jesse, which is to say the successor to King David, Jesse's son. The imagery means that the Davidic lineage is still alive despite the royal succession being interrupted, the kingship of Judah apparently severed and cut off.

There is reason to think that Jonah's gourd also represents the line of David, a matter of no small concern to the original readers of this book. For the Judeans returned from Babylon with no king, but they did have with them a Son of David, which is to say one who belonged to the royal lineage. This was Zerubbabel (Ezra 2:2; Neh. 7:7), the grandson of the last ruling king of Judea, Jehoiachin, also called Jeconiah (1 Chr. 3:18). Zerubbabel was appointed governor of Judah by the king of Persia (Hag. 1:1) and was one of the leading forces in the rebuilding of the temple in Jerusalem (Ezra 3:8; 4:2–3). The prophets Haggai and Zechariah are given words of encouragement for him, together with his comrade Joshua, the high priest, also called Jeshua (Hag. 1:12–14; Zech. 3–4; cf. Ezra 5:1–2). Within a few years of these words the new temple is completed (Ezra 6:13–14; cf. 4:24).

But Zerubbabel, the son of David, must also have been the object of other, half-spoken hopes. From his loins would come the future kings of Judah, the true anointed rulers of the remnant of Israel, deserving the title "Messiah." Under the Persian Empire Zerubbabel was merely a governor, but under the LORD he is the once-and-future king. The passages are a bit obscure, but it is probably he to whom the prophet Zechariah gives the strikingly Davidic title "my servant the Branch" (Zech. 3:8) and "the man whose name is Branch" (6:12), alluding to the messianic passage in Isaiah: "There shall come forth a rod from the stump of Jesse, and a Branch shall grow out of his roots" (11:1).

Quite explicitly, it is Zerubbabel to whom the LORD speaks the resonant words: "'Not by might or by power, but by my Spirit,' says the LORD of hosts" (Zech. 4:6). We must remember that "hosts" here means armies of angels, as the prophetic words continue: "Who are you, O great mountain? Before Zerubbabel you shall become a plain" (4:7). Like its more famous parallel in Isa. 40:4, the mountain laid low is an image of a mighty kingdom humbled. Haggai concludes with similar words of encouragement for Zerubbabel:

> Speak to Zerubbabel, governor of Judah, saying, "I am about to shake the heavens and the earth and to overturn the throne of kingdoms. I am about to destroy the strength of the kingdoms of the nations and overturn the chariots and their riders. . . . On that day, declares the LORD of hosts, I will take you, O Zerubbabel my servant, . . . and make you like a signet ring, for I have chosen you." (Hag. 2:21–23)

Zerubbabel is the chosen one for whom the LORD of hosts will overturn armies and kingdoms—the same verb for Nineveh being overturned in the word of Jonah (3:4). At the end of the book of Haggai we have the sense of all Israel waiting to see what will become of the kingdoms that still oppress them—as if holding their breath for the time when the Branch of the LORD will at last be made beautiful and glorious as promised (Isa. 4:2), and on Mount Zion there is a *sukkah* for shade and shelter for his people (4:5–6). They know what it is like to wait with Jonah outside Nineveh.

and made it come up over Jonah

The growth of the gourd contrasts with the construction of the booth, which Jonah built for himself. This contrast corresponds to two ways that things can come into being, which the Greeks called art and nature. Art is the work of human hands and nature is not. We can build, but we cannot cause to grow. We plant and water, but God alone gives the growth (1 Cor. 3:6). Likewise men may sow their seed, but the LORD alone opens the womb (Gen. 29:31; 30:22). So it is different with the lineage of David than it is with the walls of Jerusalem. The one is of human making, the other must be awaited from the hand of the LORD.

to be a shade upon his head,

Scholars have often been puzzled why Jonah needs the shade of the gourd as well as the booth, and the really bad readers among them even make conjectures about the various strata of the text's composition in order to explain the puzzle. But they're not using their imagination. Just picture a traditional *sukkah*, and you will see: it has no roof, and therefore provides incomplete protection from the sun. This is one reason it is adorned with fruits of the field, the *lulav*, during the festival of Sukkoth.

In terms of the meaning of the parable the LORD is enacting, the point is this: the walls of Jerusalem that the returning exiles rebuild are necessary for Israel's protection from her enemies, but she will not really dwell in safety until she has a king, which only God can provide. Like Israel herself, Messiah is the LORD's, "the planting of the LORD" (Isa. 61:3) and "the shoot that I have planted" (60:21).

Ultimately—as a matter of eschatology—the only sure, enduring protection and deliverance from evil is the LORD himself who, according to the book of Revelation, in the end builds his pavilion or pitches his tent (the Greek term could mean both) to dwell among his people forever:

> And he who sits on the throne will *pitch his tent* over them;
> they shall hunger no more and thirst no more,
> nor shall the sun strike them, nor any heat. (Rev. 7:15–16)

The same verb is used to describe the ultimate fulfillment of the new covenant:

> Behold! The tent of God is with human beings;
> he will *pitch his tent* with them
> and they will be his people,
> and God himself will be with them, and be their God. (Rev. 21:3; cf.
> Jer. 31:33)

Why is this dwelling described as a tent—as if it were more like a *sukkah*, a temporary pavilion, than a walled city? In part because of the tabernacle or tent of meeting by which God dwelt with his people Israel in their wanderings, and in part because what we are looking for in the fulfillment of all things is not one of the metaphysical attributes of God but a human body. John signals this in his great witness to the Incarnation: "The word became flesh and pitched his tent among us" (John 1:14). "Tent" (*skēnos* or *skēnōma*) is New Testament imagery for the human body in its mortality, waiting to be clothed with a heavenly dwelling (2 Cor. 5:1–2; cf. 2 Pet. 1:13–14). For the heavenly dwelling of God with human beings is not a place called heaven but the tent called the body of Christ, he who is true Messiah who lives forever. This is the mystery, the hidden meaning of the gourd that protects Jonah. It is what Zerubbabel and his ancestry, the whole lineage of David and his descendents, have been pointing toward from the beginning.

to deliver him from his evil.

The verb "deliver" is the same one used in the idiom "to deliver from the hand" of an enemy or oppressor (Gen. 32:11; 37:21; Judg. 6:9; 8:34; 1 Sam. 4:8; 7:3, 14; 12:10). It is not the same as the word for salvation in Jonah 2:9, but the concepts are closely related.

What the LORD does for Jonah here is of course what we pray for from our heavenly Father in the final petition of the Lord's Prayer: "Deliver us from evil." All salvation in heaven or on earth is deliverance from some evil or other. Hence John Paul II, asked to give a brief definition of salvation, responded: "To save means to liberate from evil."[3] His words could equally well have been translated "to deliver from evil," as they are derived from this final petition, which in Latin reads *Libera nos a malo* ("liberate us from evil").

So the gourd is Jonah's salvation. At a literal level, it delivers him from the heat of the sun. But the parable is pointing toward a much greater deliverance: the protection of the people of God from all her enemies, whether in the spirit or in the flesh. Ultimately the gourd signifies liberation from sin, death, and the devil, the salvation that is the LORD's alone, because it is wrought by none other than the Lord Jesus, the Son of David who is also the Son of God. It is a thing to celebrate with the whole heart.

And Jonah rejoiced in the gourd with great joy.

This is the first time in the story that Jonah is happy. If the mystery of the gourd is truly the hope of messianic salvation as I have suggested, then it is easy see why. For the people of Judah returning from exile the time of lamentation seemed to be past, when they had to witness the power of their enemies: "The anointed [i.e., Messiah] of the LORD was taken in their pits—he of whom we had said, 'Under his shade we shall live among the nations'" (Lam. 4:20). For the last reigning kings of Jerusalem were taken by besieging armies like animals caught in a trap (Ezek. 19:4, 8–9). But under Zerubbabel and his heirs, it must have seemed at least for a while that the Judeans could anticipate joy in place of lamentation, as if they were ready to sing: "I sat down under his shade with great delight, and his fruit was sweet to my taste" (Song 2:3).

So Jonah rejoices under the shade of the gourd with "great joy," a phrase reminding us of the sailors who feared a great fear of the LORD (Jonah 1:16) and perhaps even offsetting the "great evil" that he finds in Nineveh's salvation (4:1). But the joy is short-lived.

---

3. John Paul II, *Crossing the Threshold of Hope* (ed. Vittorio Messori; trans. Jenny McPhee and Martha McPhee; New York: Knopf, 1994), 69.

4:7 And God prepared a worm

Once again God prepares something, as he prepared the fish (1:17) and the gourd (4:6) and later will prepare the strong east wind (4:8). The repeated use of this verb of providential governance underlines the point that all the events of this story, even when they seem contrary to one another, are his doing. The LORD prepares both the gourd and the worm that smites it; he both gives and takes away (Job 1:21), he both kills and makes alive (Deut. 32:39; 1 Sam. 2:6). The whole parable of the gourd is of his telling, as is the book of Jonah, the history of Israel and the history of the world.

For a second time (see Jonah 3:5) the narrative shifts to the name *Elohim* ("God"), the common name known to all nations. For now the LORD acts precisely as the God of all nations, the ruler of the history of all peoples, disposing even of the kingship of Israel, the Davidic monarchy. And he can accomplish his purposes through one little worm, like a single assassin putting an end to a dynasty.

when the morning came up the next day,

Evidently we should imagine Jonah enjoying one day in the sun under the protection of the gourd, and then disaster striking early the next morning. So we can think of the worm, like the gourd, as a "son of the night" (4:10): it turns up overnight, coming suddenly out of nowhere to accomplish the LORD's purpose.

and it struck the gourd

The verb "struck" is the word for a military attack, which used to be translated with the grand old word "smite": a king smites the enemies surrounding him in war (2 Kgs. 8:21), the Israelites smite the Moabites (3:25) and their enemies' cities (3:19)—examples could be endlessly multiplied. But this is also the word for God smiting with a plague (Num. 11:33), with blindness (2 Kgs. 6:18), or with a curse (Mal. 4:6).

An attack has begun on Jonah. It strikes first at his pride and joy, the only thing he has going for him—the gourd that is his salvation and deliverance from evil.

and it withered.

The gourd withers before the sun rises (4:8), which means that it does not fall victim to the sun's great heat but is destroyed by that one little worm alone. No overwhelming power is needed to dispatch this frail plant. Perhaps the point is something like this: it great takes armies to overcome a kingdom, but a king can be slain by a lone assassin, a simple illness, or mere accident.

The verb means literally "to dry up," though it has a wide range of uses having to do with the loss of strength and hope. The strength of human flesh is like the grass that withers (Isa. 40:7–8; cf. Ps. 90:5–6), and on a cross it "dries up like a potshard" (22:15). So it is with all the rulers of the earth when the breath of the Lord blows on them:

> He brings princes to naught
>   and makes the rulers of the earth as nothing.
> No sooner are they planted,
>   no sooner are they sown,
>   no sooner do they take root in the ground,
> than he blows on them and they *wither*. (Isa. 40:23–24)

What withers away, eventually, is all purely human hope and glory, which helps explain why in one of its uses this verb means "to be ashamed." Everything we take pride in dies, and we wither and dry up with the shame of it. This will be important as we try to understand Jonah's emotional response to the withering of the gourd. The connection can be seen in a vivid passage from the prophet Joel, which uses the verb five times:

> The fields are destroyed, the ground mourns,
>   because the grain is destroyed.
> The wine *dries up*, the oil languishes.
> *Be ashamed*, farmers,
>   wail, vinedressers,
> for the wheat and the barley,
>   because the harvest of the field has perished.
> The vine *dries up*,
>   the fig tree languishes,
> pomegranate, palm, and apple,
>   all the trees of the field are *dried up*.
> And gladness *dries up* from the children of men. (Joel 1:10–12)

The farmers are ashamed, embarrassed, and confounded because their work has failed, and everything they had to glory in has withered. Something like that must have been the feeling of the people of Judah when the lineage of Zerubbabel dried up—and with it the prospect of a glorious restoration of the Davidic monarchy. Zerubbabel's descendents for several generations are listed in the genealogy of the exiles that returned from Babylon (1 Chr. 3:19–24), clearly in hope of things to come. But that is the last we hear of them in the Old Testament.

Hence in later years, as we learn in detail from Josephus, Israel remained without a Davidic king and was ruled instead by the priestly family of the Hasmoneans, a succession of high priests serving in the rebuilt temple (*Jewish Antiquities* 13–14).[4] When our Lord Jesus came, called in his native Aramaic "Jeshua," he was successor to both priest and king—both Jeshua son of Jehozadak and Zerubbabel son of

---

4. See H. H. Ben-Sasson (ed.), *A History of the Jewish People* (Cambridge: Harvard University Press, 1976), chap. 15.

Shealtiel, the two leaders of the returning exiles of Judah. In both roles Jesus was an intolerable challenge to the high priestly rulers of Jerusalem governing kingless under the Romans. He only heightened the challenge by riding into the Jerusalem like a triumphant king (in Matt. 21:1–10 Jesus enacts the triumphal procession of a conquering Davidic king, who rides into the city on a donkey as a sign of victory and peace as well as humility, as in Zech. 9:9–10) and then proceeding to clean out the temple and set it to rights, as if it were under his high priestly jurisdiction (Matt. 21:12–14).

The withering of Jonah's gourd, therefore, is no trivial matter. It concerns the lineage of David, which is the mystery at the heart of the book, because it is the mystery at the heart of the history of Israel and indeed of the whole world—the same mystery that Paul declares was hidden for ages and generations but is now manifested to his holy ones even among the Gentiles, which is Christ among us, the hope of glory (Col. 1:26–27). But Jonah, like the people of Israel whom he represents, lives in the age of hiddenness, when the messianic line seems entirely dried up like a dead stump. They live with the mystery undisclosed: what has become of the rod of Jesse, the Son of David, the Messiah who is to come? For Jonah is well aware, like the book's earliest readers, that until the LORD makes a horn to sprout for David (Ps. 132:17) Israel is unprotected, still not freed fully from its exile, even after it has returned from Babylon and rebuilt the temple.

4:8 And it came to pass that when the sun rose

The worm struck early in the morning (4:7), before the sun was over the horizon, and removed the protection of the gourd that had delivered Jonah from evil. Now comes the attack in full force. Yet there is an interruption. Something else comes on the scene before the sun strikes Jonah.

God prepared a strong east wind,

As he prepared the fish (1:17), the gourd (4:6), and the worm (4:7), so God now prepares an east wind. Here the verb contrasts with the verb in 1:4, where the LORD "hurls" a great wind, an image of outsized violence. This wind is not hurled but "prepared" or "appointed" (as the verb could also be translated) so as to emphasize the effortlessness of God's control over all the forces of the world. The great wind in Jonah 1 is described in violent terms because that is how the sailors experience it—as an act of divine violence. But the strong east wind here is not depicted in such violent terms, because we are to see it more from a God's-eye view, as part of the story this divine narrator is telling us through the events of world history.

Unlike the great wind in Jonah 1, which affects the sailors before Jonah even knows about it, this east wind will reach Jonah before it gets to Nineveh, to whose east he sits. This is important, because in the Bible the east wind is bad news. Israel is situated between the sea on the west and the desert on the east, so in the Bible the east wind is a scorcher, a force of destruction that dries things up. It brings famine (Gen. 41:6) and plague (Exod. 10:13), it breaks the ships of Tarshish (Ps. 48:7; Ezek. 27:26), and it is a means by which the LORD does battle (Isa. 27:8; Jer. 18:17). In this latter respect it is also what parts the sea for Israel to pass over, when the LORD does battle for Israel against Pharaoh and his host (Exod. 14:21). The east wind can be good for Israel when it is directed against its enemies, but here it is evidently directed against Jonah. We know nothing of its effect on Nineveh.

The book of Ezekiel includes two parables in which the east wind dries up Judah's royal posterity in Babylon, pictured as a vine flourishing by abundant waters. In Ezek. 17 the vine is the transplanted royal house and nobility of Israel, flourishing with many branches, which is to say, with many young scions fit to be heirs of the throne. But the king of Judah breaks covenant with the king of Babylon, violating his oath of loyalty by cultivating ties with Pharaoh, the king of Egypt. The upshot is that the vine will be plucked up and the east wind will blow and cause it to *wither* (17:10, using the same verb as Jonah 4:7). For the covenant with the king of Babylon was for the good of the king of Judah, keeping him humble like a vine low to the ground, and the LORD therefore makes this covenant his own: "Surely it is *my* oath that he despised, and my covenant that he broke" (Ezek. 17:19), with the result that "in Babylon he shall die" (17:16). Similarly, in Ezek. 19 the princes of Israel are like branches of a flourishing vine, this time growing tall and proud, with strong stems fit to become royal scepters. But this vine too is plucked up, and an east wind causes its fruit to wither (again the same verb) so that "there remains in it no strong stem, no ruler's scepter" (19:14).

In light of these parables what is remarkable is that any scion of Judah's royal house remained at all. Zerubbabel must indeed have seemed like a stem growing out of a stump, hope precious and unexpected on the other side of death and exile. And yet the language of the parable of the gourd suggests that the same thing happens to Zerubbabel and his posterity as was depicted in Ezekiel's parables: a strong east wind comes and they wither.

The language of the parable of the gourd suggests this, but does not quite say it. In fact, to be precise, it does not say at all what the east wind does. God prepares it and appoints it for its work, but we do not learn what its work is. Something peculiar, unaccountable, and uncanny is going on here.

"The wind blows where it wills," says our Lord (John 3:8), in a passage whose Greek is deeply ambiguous and could just as well be translated, "the Spirit [*pneuma*] breathes [*pnei*] where it wills." We have the same ambiguity here, where the key word is *ruach*, which is the common word for wind (e.g., the wind the LORD hurled on the sea in Jonah 1:4) but also the word for the Spirit or breath of the LORD. A strong wind of the LORD's inspiration is blowing Jonah's way, but it may have two quite different effects. On the one hand, when the Spirit of the LORD blows, all flesh dries up like grass (Isa. 40:7) and the Spirit of the LORD is the east wind that lays waste the northern kingdom (Hos. 13:15). On the other hand, the Spirit of the LORD is also the fundamental gift that makes someone a prophet (Num. 11:24–29; 2 Kgs. 2:9, 16; Ezek. 2:2; Joel 2:28–29; cf. Isa. 42:1; 61:1). So this may be our only hint at the role of the Holy Spirit in Jonah's story. It is as if the same divine power that inspires him as a prophet also scorches him and dries him up.

If you can't stand the heat get out of the kitchen, we say. But like the other prophets of Israel, Jonah never asked to be in the way of this heat, this strong east wind. That was the doing of the LORD, whose Spirit blows where it wills. But again, we must not forget that the text does not say what this *ruach*, this spirit or wind prepared by the LORD, actually does, except that it blows in Jonah's direction. What exactly it accomplishes is a mystery it keeps to itself.

and the sun struck Jonah's head

First the worm struck the gourd (4:7), now the sun strikes Jonah's unprotected head. All shade gone, the powers of destruction can do their worst, striking from above. The LORD, the God of Jonah, seems absent. For here is what is not presently happening:

> The LORD is your keeper.
>   The LORD is your shade on your right hand.
> The sun shall not smite you by day,
>   nor the moon by night. (Ps. 121:5–6)

Jonah still has his booth, as Judah still has Jerusalem. But the living protection of their God, made present and palpable in the living Son of David, is nowhere to be seen. That which had delivered them from evil has withered. So Jonah, who is already burning up with anger inside, is now burned and scorched on the outside too, as if he also were a vine drying up and withering.

and he fainted,

Jonah is about to lose consciousness and pass out, an experience already uncomfortably close to dying. A moment comes when he wonders: why fight it? Wouldn't it be good to die right now?

and he asked his soul to die

Back in Nineveh Jonah had asked the LORD to take his soul away (4:3); now he asks his soul to do it. Poor soul! Souls can't quite do that kind of thing, for God created them to live. For all its fragility there is this rock-bottom, ontological stubbornness about our life, that it cannot simply choose not to be, much as it might want to. You have to do something violent to get rid of it.

There was a certain amount of bravado and theatricality in Jonah's requesting the LORD to take his soul. It was an attempt to manipulate, like a young person saying, "I'll just *die* if you don't get me that new car." This time Jonah's request is more deadly and more serious because it is not said for effect. He speaks to no audience but his own soul, so we can have no doubt now that his desire for nonexistence is utterly sincere.

And yet in the deepest way, he is still pretending. He acts as if he were all alone in the world, as if he could talk purely to himself, with no one else to hear. This is a fiction that won't last long.

and said, "It is better for me to die than live."

We have been here before (4:3), but this time it looks more like despair than anger. A little more time under the hot sun and Jonah will die, and that's alright with him. As he and his hopes wither, he is like the people of Israel grumbling in the desert, hankering after the fleshpots of Egypt: "Would that we had died by the hand of the LORD in the land of Egypt, when we sat by the fleshpots and had bread to the full!" (Exod. 16:3). Or again, when they hear the dire report of the scouts sent to spy out the promised land, telling of the size and strength of the people who stand against them, they say: "Would that we had died in the Land of Egypt! Or would that we had died in this desert! Why is the LORD bringing us into this land, to fall by the sword?" (Num. 14:2–3). The feeling that death is better than life arises when Israel cannot see that what the LORD is doing with them is for their good, not their harm. They give up on life because they give up on the LORD. And were the LORD not there to hear, that would be the end of the story.

4:9 And God said to Jonah, "Is it good for you to be angry about the gourd?"

God knows what Jonah is saying to himself in his heart of hearts. So he interrupts Jonah's miserable soliloquy, beginning with the same words as before: "Is it good for you to be angry?" (4:4). Like Jonah, God seems to be repeating himself. But that's not quite it: God has deliberately staged this parable so that Jonah would come to this point and see his life in a new way. In fact, what God says here ought to take us a bit by surprise, because unlike the earlier episode, the narrator has not told us Jonah is angry (4:1) and indeed the natural way to describe his state of mind is despair, not anger (see comment on 4:8). God's intervention in effect suggests an unexpected, indeed somewhat puzzling, way to interpret Jonah's feelings. But this time Jonah emphatically agrees.

And he said, "It is good for me to be angry enough to die."

"Damned right I'm angry!" we might say. This is the only time Jonah ever answers the LORD in the story, and it is an outburst from the depth of his heart. He is admitting his anger for the first time and perhaps also discovering just how angry he is, now that he finally admits it. For he doesn't just observe his anger but endorses it and calls it good. That's how to open the floodgates of emotion: not just to notice your feelings but to agree with them, to tell yourself at last that you are right to feel this way. Of course Jonah's feelings are not right at all—as soon as he says it he must be aware of this—but now he has made them an explicit matter for conversation. So now God can talk with him about how he feels, like a friend who wants to help him understand himself (a kind of friendship that in a professionalized society we pay for under the name of "therapy").

In admitting his anger Jonah must inevitably connect it to the desire for death, which has been his express wish ever since Nineveh was saved. So we get this startling connection between anger and death: Jonah is "angry enough to die." On the face of it, it is a very odd connection to make: wouldn't most angry people rather kill than die? But Jonah is angry at God, so there is no one to kill but himself. If you find your situation intolerable because you can't stand another person, then you get angry; but if the other person is someone who does not go away—*cannot* go away, can only live not die—then the only way to resolve your intolerable situation is to get out of it yourself. Anger at God is inherently suicidal.

God himself has brought Jonah to the point of seeing this connection. "Angry enough to die" is indeed a perfect description of Jonah's emotional state earlier in the chapter, when he was so outraged at how God set him up for a fool that he wanted to quit, to give up on life itself in order to escape his shame (see comment on 4:1). Now we have a label for this emotional state, which God has just helped Jonah discover is also how he is feeling now. He is suicidal, wants to give up living, because he is angry. His admission of this is the last thing he says in the book, the fundamental problem that is addressed when God gets the last word.

The parable of the gourd offers the people of Judah this same label—"angry enough to die"—for the danger posed to them by their response to the withering of their messianic hopes. Like the farmer who sees his vines and crops wither (Joel 1:11; see comment on 4:7), Judah is ashamed, "covered with reproach and dishonor" as the psalmist puts it (Ps. 71:13), and burning with anger because of it. Her danger is to be so angry with the LORD that she is ready to give up on her covenant relationship with him, which could only be her death as the people of God, her extinction from among the nations and kingdoms of this world. It is a danger that has always threatened believers in times of disappointed hopes and especially (as suggested in the comment on 4:1) in times when our theological understanding is overturned: we thought we knew who God is, and it was for our glory. And when our glory turns to shame, we are angry enough to die.

That the withering of the messianic line really was a source of *shame* for Judah is clear from the great psalm of messianic complaint. Addressing the LORD as the God who made an everlasting covenant with David, Ps. 89 appeals repeatedly (89:1, 2, 24, 33, 49) to his loving-kindness (*hesed*) and faithfulness (*emunah*, closely related to his truth or *emeth*, which appears in the pairing "loving-kindness and truth" in the proclamation of the name of the LORD in Exod. 34:6; the pairing of *hesed* and *emunah* likewise becomes a kind of cliché in Ps. 36:5; 88:11; 92:2; 98:3;

100:5). The psalm sings of the LORD's reigning in heaven and on earth (89:5–13), then of his making a covenant with David to establish his lineage forever (89:2–3, 19–37). But then comes the bad news:

> But now you have cast off and rejected—
>> you are full of wrath against your Messiah.
> You have renounced the covenant with your servant.
>> You have defiled his crown in the dust. . . .
> You have cut short the days of his youth.
>> You have covered him with shame. (Ps. 89:38–39, 45)

This is the withering of the gourd. Now compare the psalmist's response to Jonah's:

> How long, O LORD? Will you hide yourself forever?
>> How long will your wrath consume like fire? (Ps. 89:46)

"How long?" is the classic cry of psalmic complaint (6:3; 13:1; 74:10; 79:5; 80:4; 90:13) but it is also a cry of hope, for it is the cry of one who has not given up waiting, which is the essence of hope (130:5–6). But it is hard waiting, and to hurry God along, the psalmist tries to rub his nose in the shame of it all:

> Remember, O LORD, how your servants are mocked,
>> how I bear in my heart the insults of all the many nations,
> with which your enemies mock, O LORD,
>> with which they mock the steps of your Messiah. (Ps. 89:50–51)

It is not so hard imagining someone praying this psalm, tasting the ignominy and reproach of it, who eventually gives up calling out "how long?"—gives up begging and pleading, hoping and praying for the coming of the Son of David, figuring that the LORD has abandoned his loving-kindness and faithfulness. That is someone who is angry enough to die.

After being rescued from a kind of national death in their Babylonian captivity, which was like being brought up from the depths of Sheol (see comment on 2:6), postexilic Jews had to face a yet more serious threat to their own existence: their anger, shame, and despair over the loss of the messianic line. The parable of the gourd and the book of Jonah as a whole is the LORD dealing with precisely this issue.

4:10 And the LORD said,

After three verses which speak generically of "God" (4:7–9), the narrator introduces the final speech of the book by returning to the name of the God of Israel. It is the LORD who will get the last word, just as he got the first. But instead of a command that sets everything going at the beginning of the story (1:1), this time the word of the LORD is a question that is left open for all of us to answer as the story continues beyond the text.

"You pitied the gourd,

Once again the LORD has something rather surprising to say about how Jonah feels. He wants Jonah to see that behind his desire for death is anger, and behind his anger is pity. At least that is how it is now that the LORD has made him a participant in the parable of the gourd. Before this, Jonah was quite pitiless, as we saw in the first part of Jonah 4. So the parable has changed the character of Jonah's feelings and especially of his anger.

In Hebrew, "pity" is about how one looks at things, for typically it is the eye that is said to pity. Indeed, typically the command is for the eye *not* to pity when just punishment must be carried out (Deut. 7:16; 13:8; 19:13, 21; 25:12). So when Jonah looks with pity on the gourd, that means he desires for it mercy, not justice. In this he is like Judah, which desires that the lineage of David flourish despite the manifold evil and injustice of David's descendants who ruled over the people of Judah and led them into sin and disobedience, thus bringing upon them the wrath of God and exile in Babylon. Nonetheless their eye pities the offspring of David and wishes for them to live, not die.

Unlike Jonah's merciless hatred toward Nineveh, this is an emotion the LORD can work with. Behind pity there is always some degree of love, a certain tenderness toward vulnerable things that grow and die. Above all, pity means a desire that something should not perish but live. However self-serving this pity is—and we have no reason to think Jonah's pity for the gourd is anything but self-serving—it is a desire that something other than Jonah himself should live, and that is a place to start. It is in fact the place where the LORD starts teaching Jonah how he—the LORD himself—feels about things.

for which you did not labor

The gourd was not the work of human hands. It was not even like a crop planted and watered by a farmer who then watches anxiously to see whether the investment of time and energy and labor will bear fruit. The farmer has reason to hope for a reward for labor expended and may rightly pray for God to establish the work of his hands (Ps. 90:17). But this gourd is not the work of Jonah's hands or the fruit of his labor. It was prepared by God alone and came to Jonah as sheer gift, as the LORD's covenant with the house of David came as sheer gift to the people of Israel. Jonah invested nothing in this, yet with all his heart he wants it to flourish.

nor did you make it grow great,

Every process, causal power, and strength in this world, whether natural or artificial, comes from the Creator, the first cause of all that is and all that happens. Even where one person plants and another waters, it is the LORD who gives the increase and makes it grow (1 Cor. 3:6). So King David himself testifies concerning his kingdom and its power and glory: "Yours is the kingdom, O LORD, . . . it is in your hand to make great" (1 Chr. 29:11–12). Thus it was the LORD's doing that the gourd grew great like Nineveh, "that great city" (Jonah 1:2), which was even "great before God" (3:2). Throughout this story it is the LORD who does great things, bringing about the great wind and the great storm on the sea (1:4) and also the sailors' great fear (1:10, 16) and Jonah's great joy (4:6). Yet none of these great things is great like the LORD who gives them being. None of them has a permanent lease on life.

which was a son of the night and perished as a son of the night;

The gourd sprang up overnight and was gone by the next morning, living only one day on the earth (see comment on 4:7). "Son of the night" is the same construction as "son of Israel" or "son of Canaan," which we typically translate "Israelite" or "Canaanite." We could call the gourd a "nightling." It emerged from the darkness and returned to it, for it was "made in secret, intricately woven in the depths of the earth" (Ps. 139:15). Like everything that comes into being on earth, it could not help but perish, returning whence it came. It thus arrived at the end which both the ship's captain and the king of Nineveh tried to steer their people away from, hoping that "we won't perish" (1:6; 3:9).

There is so much in this world to look upon with pity. None of the great things in which we rejoice and none of the strong things that comfort us have their greatness and strength from themselves, and therefore none of them can hang on to their own being forever. This is true even of heaven and earth, as the psalmist testifies in one of the most somber moments in Scripture:

> Of old you laid the foundations of the earth,
> and the heavens are the work of your hands.
> They shall perish, but you remain. (Ps. 102:25–26)

So all of us who will perish call out to the LORD for pity. Consider again what the psalm of messianic complaint has to say about our shame and our hope. We cry out "how long?" because we know we cannot wait forever:

> Remember how short my time is—
> for what vanity you have created all the children of men!
> What man can live and never see death?
> Who can deliver his soul from the power of Sheol? (Ps. 89:47–48)

And there you have it: we cannot state our deepest hopes without coming up against the boundary of death.

But as the book of Jonah has already shown us (see comment on 2:2 and 2:6), the LORD can do something about death and its boundary. Jonah is a sign to

Nineveh because his soul has already been delivered from the power of death once. The God who caused the nightling to grow great can bring it up out of any depth of darkness he pleases. For he has chosen the weak things of this world to shame the strong, and lowdown, despised things, even things that have no being, to nullify what is in being (1 Cor. 1:27–28). It all looks like foolishness, but it is in fact the wisdom of God, which we could call the metaphysics of Christ. For as believers in the LORD have understood ever since Abraham, the God who "calls into being what has no being" is also the one who gives life to the dead (Rom. 4:17). This is why Abraham can offer up his only begotten son, the promised one, and hope to receive him back from the dead (Heb. 11:17–19). Sheol, death, and nonbeing are really no obstacle for the God and Father of our Lord Jesus Christ, who is the firstfruits of them that sleep in death (1 Cor. 15:20).

Therefore Abraham's hope, like the promise of God on which it is based, does not fail. In consequence, the lineage of Zerubbabel, which disappears from the Old Testament (see comment on 4:7), does not disappear from the Bible altogether. The two New Testament genealogies of the Messiah, despite being different at every other point along the line going back from Jesus to David, have in common the name of Zerubbabel son of Shealtiel (Matt. 1:12; Luke 3:27). So Jesus, the Son of David, is the successor to Zerubbabel for which Israel hoped. Once again a rod grows from the stump of Jesse, which had seemed forever dead (Isa. 11:1; see comment on 4:6), and the LORD calls into being what has no being.

Thus unbeknownst to Jonah, God's pity for the gourd goes deeper than Jonah's. Through the lineage of Zerubbabel, he offers up his only begotten Son to become a son of the night and to perish as a son of the night, and then he gives life to the dead, bringing him up from a place deeper in the darkness of Sheol and nonbeing than even Jonah knew. The concluding question of the book of Jonah implicitly connects this deep and hidden divine pity, which is the great mystery of the parable of the gourd, to the overt pity for the Gentiles that Jonah finds to be such a great evil.

Finally, while we are dwelling on hidden things, we can note one more absence in the text to set beside the missing names of Israel, Judah, Jerusalem, and the Spirit of the LORD. No woman is ever mentioned in the book of Jonah. Of course there are women among the people of Nineveh and perhaps also among the people on the boat. But the only individuals we hear of besides Jonah are male rulers in a man's world: the captain of the boat and the king of Nineveh. So it goes when we deal with the history of great ones in the ancient world. Women tend to show up only when there is a problem, especially a problem about lineage and succession, as happens in the patriarchal narratives in Genesis whenever there is always a question of how Abraham or Isaac or Jacob will get heirs. They show up as the site of the problem of barrenness but also of its solution, the miraculous grace of the LORD who opens the womb and brings new life where none could have been expected. They do not show up in the book of Jonah because there is no solution in sight. Yet the solution is waiting, hidden, prepared by the LORD to be revealed and brought to light at the right time, when a virgin daughter of Israel shall become a mother, saying, "Behold the handmaid of the LORD" (Luke 1:38), and singing, "My soul does magnify the LORD" (1:46). The book of Jonah silently awaits this lowly voice.

4:11 and should I not pity

The book of Jonah ends with an extraordinary question—as if God were asking Jonah's permission: "Is it OK if I have pity? Do you mind if I am who I am, the gracious and merciful God, abounding in loving-kindness and truth, who repents of the evil?" Of course, it's a rhetorical question, suggesting rather pointedly the conclusion of a line of reasoning: "You pitied . . . should not I pity . . . ?" But it's still a *question*, addressed to Jonah and expecting an answer. It makes Jonah responsible for saying what God should do and who God should be.

And it's not at all clear that Jonah will give the right answer. For of course he knows how he ought to answer, just as we do, but that does not mean he will answer as he ought—just as, when God gives commandments, we know what we ought to do but that doesn't mean we will do it. But whether by command or question or—in other biblical texts—by threat or accusation, the LORD is always teaching us the way of life. What is extraordinary here is that he does so by asking us a question about *himself*, and leaving it for us to answer. The teacher is God, saying in effect: "Think carefully, now. Who do you think I should be?"

Of course God is not really asking our permission or Jonah's. He has already made up his mind from eternity. Just as he already, unbeknownst to Jonah, looks with pity on the gourd, representing the Son of David whom he intends to raise from the dead, so also he already looks with pity on Nineveh and all the Gentiles who will receive mercy through the Son of David, who is the mystery of the gourd, its hidden meaning. So the question posed to Jonah is really an invitation: "You pity the gourd, which is the Son of David, the Messiah—good! Now why not join me in pitying Nineveh, which is the whole world of ignorant Gentiles, for whom this same Messiah is to be a blessing, so that they also might not perish?" And perhaps the invitation can also be stated: "You endorsed your own anger, which leads you only to death; why not endorse instead my pity, which leads to life for all, based on the eternal life that (as you wish and hope) I intend to give to this gourd that has withered?"

The pity of God is thus the repentance of the LORD, by which he turns from the evil he speaks of doing to evildoers. This is the love of God that was in Christ Jesus from the beginning. So the pity of the LORD should not be thought of as an emotion that overtakes him all of a sudden and changes his mind. His love is not like our love, but better, eternal, triumphant, though it embraces great suffering over the course of time.

Even the word "pity" does not mean quite the same thing when it is said of the LORD as when it is said of Jonah. For the LORD's pity is effectual and accomplishes its purpose. Hence unlike 4:10, when the word appears in 4:11 it can be translated, as in the King James Version, "spare." The LORD's pity spares us from death and destruction; it is redemption and life from the dead. Yet our pity is, to the extent possible, to be like his—seeking that others may live rather than perish. Despite himself, Jonah was the instrument of the LORD's pity for Gentiles in Jonah 1. Now the LORD invites him to become a willing partner in his effectual pity, his sparing of the Gentiles.

Unbeknownst to himself, Jonah has already taken the first step by pitying the gourd, which gets him moving in the same direction as the LORD, who spares the gourd by raising it from the dead. For this is the mystery of the parable of the gourd: that this son of the night that perished as a son of the night is not only the Son of David but also the only begotten Son of God, eternally God from God, in whom is everlasting life for all nations. To pity him, therefore, hoping that he might not perish forever, is already to be on board with the deepest intention of God, his eternal repentance from the evil he speaks of doing to evildoers like us. In the end, it is impossible to hope for the Messiah without hoping for the redemption of the world.

Nineveh, that great city,

But pity *for Nineveh*? That is like pity for Babylon, as the original readers of this story would immediately have felt. The LORD's question is surely meant for them as well. They are very much in Jonah's position, having rejoiced on many occasions in prophecies of the destruction of Babylon—and lo and behold, Babylon was taken by the Persians with very little bloodshed and no ruin overtaking the city.[5] This is quite in contrast with what had been threatened in the books of the prophets: an overturning like that of Sodom and Gomorrah (Isa. 13:19; Jer. 50:40), making it into a heap of ruins without inhabitants (51:37), following massacres in which babies are dashed in pieces (Isa. 13:16; cf. Ps. 137:9). And that is just a sampling of the vitriol.

Can the God of the Bible really get away with repenting of the evil he spoke of doing *to Babylon*? As it turns out, he could and he did—and it was a blessing for his people, as Babylon and the region of Babylonia harbored a thriving Jewish community for well over a thousand years, including rabbinic academies (*yeshivoth*) that produced the Babylonian Talmud and that continued teaching long after the Islamic conquest, over centuries in which the *geonim*, the heads of the Babylonian academies, were the most important scholars in Judaism.[6]

We can ask the same question of the New Testament, where the tradition of violent prophecy against Babylon continues, and we will get an analogous answer.

---

5. For details, see T. Cuyler Young Jr., "The Early History of the Medes and the Persians and the Achaemenid Empire to the Death of Cambyses," in *The Cambridge Ancient History*, vol. 4: *Persia, Greece, and the Western Mediterranean, c. 525 to 479 B.C.* (ed. John Boardman et al.; 2nd ed.; Cambridge: Cambridge University Press, 1988), 36–41.

6. See H. H. Ben-Sasson (ed.), *A History of the Jewish People* (Cambridge: Harvard University Press, 1976), 373–83, 421–28.

Just as Jonah's prophecy against Nineveh was meant to remind the original readers of the many scriptural prophecies against Babylon, so the New Testament
prophecy against Babylon (Rev. 18) was meant to be understood by the original
readers as referring to the overturning of Rome. And look what happened! Even
an atheist can see it, as we have already called Nietzsche to witness (see comment
on 3:5): Rome was defeated by the Jews, becoming a people that worshiped the
King of the Jews as if he were God incarnate.

The New Testament prophecies of the overturning of Babylon/Rome thus came
true in an even more ironic way than Jonah's prophecy of the overturning of Nineveh/
Babylon. It is as if the gourd were not only brought back from its withered state, but
grew great enough to protect Nineveh itself in its shade. That is to say: the Messiah
has come to life even after his death, becoming known throughout the world so that
he is blessing, conversion, and salvation even for Rome, the city that the New Testament refers to under the code name "Babylon"—which is in turn the city referred
to under the code name "Nineveh" in the book of Jonah. The conversion of Rome
may indeed be the truest fulfillment of Jonah's prophecy so far. For of these three
great cities—Nineveh, Babylon, and Rome—only Rome still lives. Only there can
we see what had been adumbrated in the very first chapter of Jonah: a conversion of
the Gentiles that would mean not merely their temporary escape from destruction
but their coming to know the LORD God of Israel and worship in his name, which
is eternal life. As we ponder the various responses that have been given to the LORD's
question at the end of the book of Jonah, we must keep this irony in mind.

in which there are more than a hundred twenty thousand human beings

The LORD here calls the Ninevites by the name *adam*, which is the generic
word for human being (as in the phrase "humans and livestock" in 3:7–8) as well
as the name of the first human being that God created, from whom all of us are
descended. The word should remind Jonah of this deep natural kinship of all
humanity, which includes himself. Jonah must not forget that he is a son of Adam
arguing with God about the destruction of so many children of Adam.

The word also points to a fundamental motive of the LORD's pity: each one
of these one hundred twenty thousand is *adam*, the human being whom he has
made. Each one of them is the LORD's creation, and everything he does in this
book is aimed at vindicating his creation against the powers of death and destruction. Jonah is wrong to wish for death, even for himself, while both captain and
king are right to hope that the God who threatens them is in reality such that
"we won't perish" (1:6; 3:9).

who can't tell their right hand from their left—

More's the pity: Nineveh, that great city whose evil has come up before the
face of the LORD, is full of thousands of human beings who have no idea where

they're going, as clueless about where to turn as a child who can't tell right from left. The LORD gave the law to his people so that they might know the way of life and not turn from it "either to the right hand or to the left" (Deut. 5:32; 28:14). But the people of Nineveh don't know the way and therefore wander far from it, destroying all that is around them, including ultimately themselves.

It is the task of wisdom to tell right from left, discerning between good and evil (1 Kgs. 3:9; Heb. 5:14). And though the people of Nineveh do not know the way, they are now groping in the right direction, turning from their evil way and the violence in their hands (Jonah 3:8), and hoping that God—whoever he is—will turn and repent, so that they may not perish (3:9). Who can teach them wisdom and the way of life that they seek? Who can tell them that the God who threatened them is the LORD, the God of Israel, who repents of the evil? The hint at the end of the book is that Jonah should pity them as the LORD does and therefore that he should teach them the name of the LORD, who is gracious and merciful, slow to anger and abounding in steadfast love, so that they too, like the sailors at the end of Jonah 1, may know the name of the God of heaven who has pitied them so. A happy ending for this story would be all nations, even the Ninevites, offering him worship, thanksgiving, and praise.

Again, like so many other times in the book of Jonah, we do not hear Jonah's response. But the LORD is trying hard to get a rise out of him, as we can see at the very end.

and also abounding in livestock?"

End of story. Yes, we are supposed to laugh. We should not suppose the LORD is above making a joke. Nineveh is "abounding in livestock" just as the LORD is "abounding in loving-kindness" (4:2). Well, everybody has to abound in *something*. Nineveh is a great city, rich and prosperous, and this is its greatness. Its wealth means that there is a great deal for the LORD to pity. He saves both man and beast (Ps. 36:6).

For the LORD does pity the livestock, just as he pities the one hundred twenty thousand humans, all dressed up in sackcloth, participating in Nineveh's repentance and awaiting the word of God together. For just as the livestock too are subject to the plagues and destruction that his prophets announce against the wicked (see comments on 3:7 and 3:8), they also are beneficiaries of the blessing of the Sabbath established in his law, wherein he gives rest from labor not only to sons and daughters, to menservants and maidservants, but also to ox and ass and all the livestock belonging to the house (Deut. 5:14; cf. Exod. 20:10). The last words of the book of Jonah point toward this Sabbath rest for all, a time set apart and holy when human beings may look upon the livestock and every other creature that God has made and Adam named (Gen. 2:20) and laugh on behalf of the whole creation, which is finally freed from vanity (Rom. 8:20), delivered from evil and rejoicing in the praise of the LORD.

EPILOGUE

Jonah, Jacob, and the Older Brother

The Open Question

Students often ask what they are supposed to "get out of" a text, as if its message were something they could take home with them and later produce as the right answer on an exam. But the book of Jonah is not that kind of text. It teaches us in a more difficult way that changes who we are, which means it must frustrate our desire to "get something out of it." It does not give us answers to take home with us, because it is precisely our desire for easy answers that it must undermine (in a moment we shall see why the easy answers are positively deadly). Instead it concludes with a very hard question. Not that we always find it hard—we have gotten good at "getting something out of" our texts—but the fact is that if we find it easy we have not understood it. The aim of this conclusion, therefore, is not to get something out of the book of Jonah but to get a sense of why its concluding question should be so hard for us.

The question takes the form: "Should I not pity . . . ?" It is an open question, left unanswered at the end because it is meant for all of us who read the book, not just for Jonah. The answer we give will have everything to do with who we think we are and who we think Jonah is. Like all our reading of the Bible, it depends on the identifications we are willing to make with its various characters (see Introduction), which is to say, it is tied up with the kind of "who?" questions we face over and over again in the Bible: Who are we? Who is Jonah? Who is Israel? Who is Jesus? We give the wrong answer to these questions not because we have failed to learn some obvious lesson but because we do not believe the difficult thing the LORD has to teach us about who we are. Our unbelief (as suggested in the Excursus) is like failing to see what time it is, like not knowing the time of our visitation or recognizing who it is that has come to speak with us in this very text. Since we can be saved only by believing the one who speaks in this text, this is a matter of life and death.

It is the LORD who asks us, "Should I not pity . . . ?" To understand this book aright we need to see why the LORD's question is as difficult for us as for Jonah and why, like Jonah, our life depends on it. In this epilogue I will try bringing the question into focus by seeing how it arises out of the whole structure of the book of Jonah, how it is answered by our Lord Jesus, how the subsequent history of Christians and Jews makes this question just as difficult for Gentile Christians today as it ever was for Jonah. It is difficult because we are murderous like Jonah, and to see the shape of the difficulty it helps to look at what else the Bible has to say about our murderousness. Hence at the center of this discussion is our Lord's parable about the murderous older brother and its relation to the story of the murderous older brother Esau, and how this bears on the question of who is the true Israel. This will lead us to Paul's application of the theme of jealous brothers to the relation of Jews and Gentile Christians, which will bring us back to ourselves. The course of the discussion will be complex, involving shifting and ambiguous identifications of who we are. But I think these are merely intellectual complexities, which can be resolved easily enough with careful thought, leaving us with the really hard question still unanswered, waiting to change us. The complexity is there to block our escape from the real difficulty of the question.

Why It Can't Be Easy

We can begin to get at the difficulty by seeing what the easy answers are trying to protect. Consider how the same moralistic tradition that would teach us to avoid being like Jonah (see Introduction) also tries to turn the word of the LORD in the end into an easy question. It goes something like this: "Well, it's perfectly obvious that we, as Christians, do not want to behave the way Jonah does. We, as Christians, aim to love everybody and save them all. So *of course* we want God to pity those poor Ninevites. Jews, we know, are not like that, and that's the real problem addressed in the book of Jonah. What we, as Christians, have to do is convert Jews like Jonah and make them Christians, so that they too can become loving, caring people instead of intolerant, legalistic, and self-righteous. We really do have to work hard to keep from being anything like those self-righteous Jews. But we pray for their conversion in the final redemption, when there will be no more Jews, only Christians. That is what we, as Christians, are working for every day, which just goes to show how serious we are about showing God's love to everyone."

I caricature, but not by much. The slack phrase "we, as Christians" quite often does the deceptive work my caricature suggests. It makes Christian ethics a matter of maintaining Christians' self-image and self-esteem: what "we, as Christians" do—by definition, as it were—is whatever we are supposed to do to make us feel like we are being good Christians. And, it turns out, our being good Christians makes us feel like we are paragons of love toward everybody, even when we hate their very existence as a people and wish that there were no more of them. Jews have particularly good ears for this kind of hypocrisy, since for quite some time they have been listening to us and wondering when we will reconcile ourselves to the continued existence of the Jewish people.

And that gets us back to the LORD's open question. It is indeed a question addressed to Jonah the Jew, the prophet of Israel who in a kind of parable represents the people of Judea returning from their exile in a city they hated. The meaning of the question would have been bluntly obvious to these original Jewish readers: should not the LORD, the God of Israel, have pity on these Gentiles, who are not Judeans and do not observe the Jewish law? Should he not have had pity even on Nineveh, the city of Israel's exile, which means also on Babylon, the city of the Judean exile?

But the question does not die with the original readers. For now Gentile Christians have, by the grace of God in Christ Jesus, been brought into the covenant with Israel and therefore share the questions and difficulties of the Jews. Indeed, precisely because Christians have stepped into the place of the Jews, they must answer the difficult question originally addressed to the Jews about the Gentiles, but which now has the ring of a question addressed to Gentiles about the Jews. The meaning of the question is something like this: should not the God and Father of our Lord Jesus Christ have pity on the Jews, who *do* observe the Jewish law and are not Gentiles? Is it too much to ask of Gentile Christians that they tolerate the LORD having pity on his own people and desiring that they not perish but live—which means, that they continue to exist *as a people*, observing the law and covenant he has given them? Do you suppose Christians could stand it if God were in this particular way gracious and merciful, abounding in loving-kindness toward his own people?

It hardly needs to be said that the Christian track record on this question over the centuries is not good at all. We have insisted that *we*—not the Jews—are the people of God now, and the logic of this claim has made us murderous. As we shall see, the Bible has a great deal to say about our murderousness, if we have ears to hear. We can begin with the LORD's question to murderous Jonah.

The Meaning of the Question in Jonah

Consider, by way of reviewing the book of Jonah, exactly how we got to this difficult question. The word of the LORD began things by setting Jonah in motion, which means that Jonah was free to disobey, as human beings in general and God's people in particular are wont to do. Yet in all Jonah's actions, the LORD fulfilled his promise of making his people a blessing for all nations: using Jonah's disobedience for his own good purposes, bringing redemption and knowledge of the LORD to the people on the boat, throwing Jonah into the sea so that he might know the depth of the salvation of the LORD, and repenting of the evil he had spoken of doing to the people of Nineveh. In Jonah 1 he makes disobedient Jonah into a Christlike blessing for the sailors, a scapegoat who removes all uncleanness from them; in Jonah 2 he is the one who is already Jonah's salvation even in the belly of Sheol; and in Jonah 3 he makes Jonah's evasive and ambiguous proclamation into a miraculous means of grace to overturn Nineveh, turn it topsy-turvy and make it new. He thus takes an unwilling Jonah through a foretaste of Good Friday, Easter, and Pentecost: his giving up his own Son as the sign of Jonah for all nations, his overcoming the power of death, and his preaching of good news to the whole world by the word and Spirit of Christ.

Yet as things stand in Jonah 4 the LORD's work is not finished, for the overturning, conversion, and renewal of the Gentiles is not yet completed. Unlike the people on the boat, the people of Nineveh still do not know the LORD and are therefore in no position to offer him worship, thanksgiving, and praise, which is to say, to participate in eternal life together with his people Israel. So now the LORD as it were makes a proposal: why not let Jonah cooperate not only in the letter of the LORD's calling to the Gentiles but also in its spirit? Whereas in Jonah 3 a reborn Jonah, raised from death in the waters of the LORD's baptism, had gone so far as to obey the external demands of God's word, arising and going to Nineveh and calling to it as the LORD commanded him, now in Jonah 4 the LORD asks Jonah—*asks* him, mind you!—to share his heart, to join him in repenting from evil and taking pity on the Gentiles.

At the end of the story, it is not at all clear that Jonah has gotten that far. So the LORD applies a little pressure, a pressing question that grows out of the parable of the gourd. To feel the pressure, we need to get at the mystery of the parable, its hidden meaning, which would have been more obvious to the original Jewish readers than to us. The parable of the gourd links the LORD's pity for Nineveh (i.e., the Gentiles who destroy his people) with Jonah's pity for the gourd (i.e., the house and lineage of David, the Messiah). Pity means the love that desires evil people to live, not die. The Jews who were the first readers of the book of Jonah already knew that Nineveh was the evil city that destroyed Israel, very much like Babylon, which was the evil city that swallowed up Judah, and they already pitied the house of David, that lineage of mostly evil kings, desiring its restoration. Given how they already thought and felt about these evils, the open question for them was this: you want the house of David to live, not die—shall not the LORD your God, who has proclaimed to you that he is gracious and merciful and abounding in loving-kindness and who repents of the evil, want even the evil city of Babylon to live, not die?

Why would any Jew in his right mind want that? Go back to the literal level of the story for a moment and consider Nineveh rather than Babylon. Try this thought experiment: imagine that Jonah, despite his track record so far, actually acquiesced in the LORD's pity for Nineveh. What then would he have to do in response to this final question of the book? I think it is plain that he must go back to Nineveh and take the enormous risk of telling them who he is and who God is, beginning with "thus says the LORD, the God of Israel, to Nineveh" and hoping that they will hear and believe. He must aim for what the LORD has clearly been aiming for all along, that Nineveh would become like the boatload of Gentiles in Jonah 1, fearing a great fear of the LORD, offering sacrifices in his name, and making vows to him. It is hard to imagine: the bloody city that would become the capital of the Assyrian Empire worshiping in the name of the LORD, the God of Jonah and his people Israel. It is very hard to imagine and evidently it did not happen, for if it did we have to figure Nineveh would not have destroyed Israel. It is a stunning thought, but hard to avoid once you imagine literally the consequences of Jonah giving the right answer to the LORD's question: if Jonah had joined the LORD in desiring life for Nineveh, not death, then Israel too would have lived, not died.

This stunning consequence of a literal reading of the book of Jonah stems from a fundamental feature of the whole biblical narrative, which underlies what I have been calling the mystery of the parable: the identity of Israel is tied to its vocation to be a blessing for all nations. This is because in the Bible the elect are always chosen for the blessing of others (see Gen. 12:3). It would make no sense, in the logic of biblical redemption, for the chosen people to be chosen for their own glory and aggrandizement. The God who elects them is the LORD, who is gracious and merciful, slow to anger and abounding in loving-kindness, which means that those whom he elects serve his purpose of repenting from the evil he threatens to do to evildoers. Always, therefore, the identity and existence of the elect depend on the LORD's eternal purpose of blessing others. That is why the elect do not survive unless the LORD their God succeeds in blessing others, as the book of Jonah teaches. But, of course, the elect do survive, for the LORD always succeeds in his purpose, even when he has to use the disobedience of the elect to do so.

Consider again the mystery of the parable, as it presented itself to the book's original readers, Jews who have returned from Babylonian exile like Jonah disgorged from the belly of beast. Can it be that their life depends on the LORD pitying Babylon? Can it be also that they will need to have pity on the people of the land around them, who are like the sailors in Jonah 1, desiring to worship the LORD even though they do not know the Jewish law and are in no position to be good Jews? Most stunning of all, can it be that the future of the house of David, represented by that withered gourd, is linked somehow to the LORD's taking pity on Gentiles, people who are not good Jews—even Babylonians?

Our Lord's Answer

To bring this mystery fully into focus, consider how these questions originally looked to the greatest Jew of them all, Jesus our Lord, for whom—as for any Jew of the time—"Babylon" meant Rome. The open question for him was this: can he imagine himself as a Messiah, a King of the Jews, who does not overcome these new Babylonians but dies so that they might live? That question, I suggest, is the source of his agony in the garden of Gethsemane. It is not that he is afraid to suffer and die—he surely has enough courage for that—but that the cup he is asked to drink is the LORD's pity for Babylon, which is to say, a mercy and loving-kindness that spares even the Romans by doing nothing less than handing over to them the King of the Jews, the Son of David, together with all Israel's hopes for deliverance from the Roman Empire. Can Jesus stand to be *that* Messiah? We know his answer. He prays, "Not my will, but yours, be done" (Luke 22:42), and the Roman Empire is the beneficiary, together with all of Western civilization after it. His prayer at Gethsemane is the decisive answer to the LORD's open question at the end of the book of Jonah, and the salvation of the Gentiles is the result.

By the same token, the gourd withers but is not dead, for the LORD does pity it, too. This means that although Jesus is handed over to death, once again causing the messianic hopes of the Judeans to wither, the LORD does not allow his holy one to see corruption (Acts 2:27), and as a result the house of David now has one to sit on the throne forever: for this Son of David has triumphed even over death. Just as the LORD's question suggests, his pity for the gourd, his determination that Messiah shall not die but live, is tied to his pity for the Gentiles, for Nineveh and Babylon and Rome. And although neither Nineveh nor Babylon is still with us, Rome and its Western children have been blessed now for thousands of years by the mercy and loving-kindness of this same Messiah.

This then is what it costs to be the elect of God: the Jews give up their Messiah for the blessing of the Gentiles, for such is the decision of Messiah himself, the King of the Jews. On behalf of these great and evil cities—Nineveh, Babylon, Rome—and their many cousins around the Gentile world, Jesus Christ is the eternal repentance of the LORD, his turning away—from the very beginning—from the evil he intended to do to evildoers, so that the earth might be full of the knowledge of the LORD, as the waters cover the sea. And precisely in this divine pity for the Gentiles Jesus lives and reigns forever, as the King of the Jews raised from the dead. So the LORD does have pity on the withered messianic gourd, causing it to live not die, precisely so that he might have pity on the great, evil city of Nineveh and its many successors.

The Question Addressed to Gentile Christians

And where does this leave the Jews? That, I take it, is the meaning of the LORD's open question as addressed to Gentile Christians. We have joined the Jews in pitying the gourd, the house of David, earnestly desiring that it not perish but live forever. And we have indeed gotten our wish, for Jesus the Messiah is exalted to the right hand of God forever in glory and eternal life. And now should not the LORD pity his own people, the remnant of Israel, his beloved, his dove? Shall they not live forever, even as a people? *Can we live with that?* It may be that our own life depends on it, just as Jonah's did. For Paul makes clear that the church of Jesus Christ will fail of its eternal purpose if it is not a blessing to the Jews.

Two objections arise at this point from the heart of the Christian theological tradition. Aren't the Jews now unbelievers, failing to receive their own Messiah? And haven't they forfeited their place as the people of God, to be superceded by the community of those who believe in Jesus Christ? Indeed they are unbelievers: we could put them in the same category with ourselves and the apostle Peter, the Jew who denied Christ three times (Luke 22:54–62). But we must not neglect to follow that other Jew, the apostle Paul, who would rather lose Christ than lose the Jews (Rom. 9:3). So in answer to the second objection, Scripture gives us no room to think that God would ever abandon Israel his beloved, the apple of his eye (Deut. 32:10), whom he could no more forget than a mother forgets her suckling child (Isa. 49:15). They are his chosen people whom he called as his own and with whom he established an everlasting covenant (Gen. 17:7; Ps. 105:10), that they shall be his people and he shall be their God (Exod. 6:7; Lev. 26:12).

Therefore the LORD's question, "Should I not pity . . . ?" remains an urgent and difficult one for Christians to answer, and indeed the history of Christian answers to it make us look quite a bit worse than Jonah at the end. If we want to find an adequate answer to this still-open question, we need to turn again to the Lord Jesus.

The Jealous Brother

Consider a story told by our Lord himself, parallel in many ways to the book of Jonah and just as subtle and profound. When the prodigal son returns from the pigs to his father, his older brother stays away from the ensuing celebration because he is angry—angry enough to die, we might well say, for that is what will happen to him if he is not reconciled to his father. So, because this son too is his beloved, the father in his mercy leaves his house a second time and speaks to the prodigal's brother: "Child, you are always with me, and all that is mine is yours" (Luke 15:31). This is an affirmation of covenant loyalty, of loving-kindness and truth, just as we would expect from the God of Israel. But it is not the last word, for that concerns the younger brother whose salvation makes the older brother so jealous: "It is fitting to celebrate and rejoice, for this brother of yours was dead and is alive, was lost and is found" (15:32). To refuse this good news is not only unbelief in his father's word, it is to wish his brother had stayed dead—it shows a murderous heart. And just like the book of Jonah, the story concludes without telling us his response. It is in substance the same open question as the one that the LORD addresses to Jonah, and it has to be heard in much the same way.

It must not have been hard for those first hearing this story to see that the older brother represents the Jews, the people who kept covenant all those centuries, or at least thought they did ("lo, these many years I have served you and never transgressed your command," the older son protests in 15:29), and who are jealous that through Jesus the Gentiles who once were lost are now found—and not only found but celebrated. Moreover, for all the father's reaffirmation of his covenant, it is clear that the older son's life depends on joining the celebration, the eschatological banquet, and that to spurn it is eternal death. So now we have the easy answer to the meaning of the parable: it is about the Jews' intolerance of Gentiles, about how we as Christians are not supposed to be self-righteous like the Jews, and so forth. For Christians to give this answer is deadly, as any Jew will readily see, for it endorses our murderous jealousy and self-righteousness, our desire to proclaim ourselves the true children of God in place of Israel. It is part of the genius of the parable that it catches us at this: as soon as we think we have got the message about self-righteousness (applying the message, of course, to others) we have shown our self-righteousness. We fall for it every time.

The brother to be celebrated is the one who confesses, "I am not worthy to be called your son" (15:21). Our Lord's parable offers us no other alternative to murderous jealousy. *The one who does not desire his brother's death is the one who knows he has no claim to be his father's son.* For the one who believes he is the true and obedient son—who rejoices in being the true Israel, the chosen one—is the one who would rather see his brother dead. That means us—Gentile Christians, who have claimed to be the true Israel all these centuries, giving the wrong answer to the open question at the end of the book of Jonah because we do not want the LORD to have pity on carnal Israel. What we have missed is that the biblical doctrine of election is good news. It is good news for the Gentiles that we are not the chosen people but the Jews are, just as it is good news for each one of us that I am not the chosen one but the Jew Jesus Christ is. This is the gospel we do not believe, and as a result we murder our brothers.

Who Is Jacob?

One of the profound subtleties of our Lord's parable is the way it echoes a story of jealous brothers that was told long before. Originally the younger brother was not the Gentiles but Jacob (i.e., Israel), who went away to a far country because he was fleeing for his life, having stolen the blessing from his older brother Esau, who thus had every reason to be jealous and in fact sought to kill him (Gen. 27). Nonetheless it was the younger brother who was elect, the heir of the covenant (the position the older brother in Jesus's parable takes for granted as his own), and it is the younger brother who becomes the father of the chosen people, so that when Esau's descendents, the people of Edom, gloat over the suffering of the people of

Israel (i.e., Jacob) the LORD can go so far as to say, "Jacob have I loved and Esau have I hated" (Mal. 1:2–3; see the book of Obadiah for explanation).

The complexities really begin when we ask which one of the two brothers in Jesus's parable has the better claim to be walking in Jacob's shoes: the older brother, who has been with his father all this time—who never thought of stealing the blessing and complains in effect that his younger brother has usurped his birthright just like Jacob did—or the younger brother, the disobedient one who broke all ties to his father, who went away to a far country in disgrace, having once been lost but now found? Which shoe fits which foot? I think the point is that there is a trap waiting for us whichever shoes we step into (our Lord's parables are often like that). No matter what we do to lay claim to a favored identification for ourselves, we find that the parable leaves no room for us to gloat over our brother. The younger brother over whom the father rejoices is the disobedient one, who knows he is unworthy to be called his father's son, whereas the older brother to whom the birthright has always belonged is now also disobedient, wishing his father's son were dead. The situation of these two brothers reinforces a point often overlooked in the original story of Jacob and Esau, which is that no one ever legitimately gets to be the chosen people. The heir of the covenant is the one who has robbed his sibling, the disobedient one whom God loves and celebrates. *The only way to be the true Jacob is to be in the wrong.*

Gentile Christians have spent a great deal of energy over the centuries bolstering their claim to be the true Israel, which is to say the true Jacob, the elect whom God loves forever in contrast to carnal Israel. This is a claim that gets tangled up in all sorts of ironic ways with the story of Jacob and Esau, not to mention the parable of the prodigal son. It is as if we were Esau stealing the blessing back from Jacob and now trying to claim his name and birthright as well. But such a claim, if it is accepted, puts the church in the very unstable position of the older brother in our Lord's parable, the one who claims to have been obedient all those years (suspicious claim!) but who hates the fact that his brother is still alive. It puts us in the place of a son who is angry at his father for having pity on his brother— angry enough to die, as Jonah reminds us. For we have staked our identity, even our salvation as Christians, on the wicked proposition that Israel is a people that has no right to exist—as if Israel were Nineveh. If we are in *any* sense Jacob, which is to say, Israel, then we are surely also Jonah, the Israelite who urgently needs to hear the LORD's question: "Should I not pity . . . ?"

Paul's Answer

It remains then for us an open question: should not the LORD, the God of Israel, who is the God and Father of our Lord Jesus Christ, pity his own people, the children of Jacob according to the flesh, and desire them to live, not die? We ought to bear in mind the answer given by Paul the Jew: "I could wish I were myself anathema, cut off from Christ for my brothers, my kindred according to the flesh" (Rom. 9:3). Strange that Gentile Christians, benefiting so deeply from Paul's theology, have answered so differently.

But perhaps we have a new opportunity to get it right nowadays. There are in the world today no small number of Jews who call themselves messianic—believers in Jesus the Messiah who insist on maintaining their Jewish identity, worshiping in the name of the Lord Jesus while observing the Jewish law. Nobody much likes them, for their very existence is a challenge to nearly everybody's identity: Jews are not supposed to be Christians and "we, as Christians" are not supposed to be Jews. Yet there they are, whole congregations of them, claiming to be brethren to both Jew and Christian. They are an open invitation to Gentile Christians to consider the possibility that the apostle really was right to say that the dividing wall of hostility between Jew and Gentile was broken down precisely in the body of Christ (Eph. 2:14–16), in which Jews are not absorbed into a Gentile body (ceasing to be Jews by giving up the Jewish law) or Gentiles into a Jewish body (becoming Jews by accepting circumcision and observing the whole Jewish law), but Jew and Gentile are together one body, brethren living together in peace.

Consider how Paul foresees the turning point in the old story of jealous brothers. In the letter to the Romans he teaches that not only are the children of Abraham, Isaac, and Jacob to be a blessing to the Gentiles (that is theology as old as Gen. 12:3) but now also the reverse: the Gentiles by their belief in Jesus Christ are to make the Jews jealous and save them (Rom. 11:11, 26). This astonishing and subtle suggestion leads us once again to consider complex and unstable identities: Is Esau now to be a blessing to Jacob? Or are the fleshly descendents of Jacob, the people of Israel, now to steal back the blessing of the covenant from Esau, the Gentile Christians who stole it from them? Or—a third possibility—are Gentile Christians, used to claiming that they are the true Jacob, to learn at last to do what Jacob eventually did, insisting that Esau receive his blessing in return (Gen. 33:10–11)? For that's how the original story of jealous brothers concludes: Jacob who stole the blessing at the beginning sets out at the end to give a blessing in return. When at last he comes to meet Esau after many years spent in exile in a far country, Jacob sends ahead all the blessings of prosperity he has gained in that time as a present to his brother, who, he fears, is still an enemy who wants to kill him (32:13–21).

And in seeking to bless this enemy, Jacob finds his brother. The story of jealous brothers comes to its conclusion with Esau running to meet Jacob like the father running to meet his prodigal son (the parallel with Luke 15:20 is too striking to be accidental) and then the two of them embracing with kisses and tears, each glad the other is alive (Gen. 33:4). By the end of the story Esau has clearly learned the lesson that the father in Jesus's parable is trying to teach the older brother. For what Esau now desires is not Jacob's blessing but Jacob himself, and he rejoices that his brother who seemed as good as dead still lives—the younger brother who was lost but now is found. Thus Jacob returning the blessing he stole and Esau rejoicing that his brother is alive discover together that brothers do not have to be murderous.

Paul seems to anticipate some such ending to the story of Jews and Gentiles in the body of Christ. He does not tell us who is really Jacob and who is really Esau—perhaps because that is the wrong question. But he does make it clear that not only are the Jews a blessing to the Gentiles through the Jew Jesus, but also that the Gentiles through their faith in Jesus are to be a blessing to the Jews.

The Question Today

Alas, see how well that has worked out so far—how often Gentile Christians have been a curse rather than a blessing to the Jews! So far we do not seem to have done any better than Jonah at answering the open question at the end—and certainly much worse than Esau. But this grim reflection does get us back to our problem at the beginning: it shows us why this is a difficult question for us, too. That will be enough to be getting on with. It is wrestling with the question in all its difficulty that changes us.

We can make one more point about our present situation. In recent years the messianic Jewish congregations have done us the great favor of making the open question quite concrete. "Should I not pity . . . ?" says the LORD, which is to say: should not the God and Father of our Lord Jesus Christ desire for his chosen people to live, not die, in this particular way—as Jews who are still Jews even as they believe in the Jew Jesus? Perhaps it is true that like the Ninevites they hardly know how to tell right from left, for they face deep problems about how to be Torah-observant Jews as believers in Jesus in fellowship with Gentiles within the body of Christ. But if the LORD himself desires his people to live, not die—to continue to exist as a people even in the faith of Jesus Christ, the Son of David— then perhaps we who are Gentile Christians may be called upon to make some adjustments in our own way of life in order to be one body with these brothers of Jesus according to the flesh. It remains an open question.

"Should I not pity . . . ?" the LORD asks his people in conclusion, and only one of us has consistently given the right answer. (Paul gave the right answer too, but only after years of trying to stamp it out [Gal. 1:13].) More precisely, we could say that this one, Jesus Christ, is the right answer in person, as he is also the eternal repentance of the LORD in person. He is both the divine loving-kindness and the obedient human life of the elect in response to it. The rest of us, who are so murderously jealous and eager to be Jacob rather than Esau, would do better to class ourselves with ignorant pagan sailors and bloody Ninevites (who will otherwise surely rise up in the judgment and condemn us) as those who are unworthy to be called children of our Father—who must repent, be overturned, turn around, and go in a new direction, lest we perish. Yet if we read this story in faith we will inevitably find ourselves also with Jonah and Jesus in the depths of Sheol, where all perishing is overcome. It is as those who have already been rescued from the power of death that we face with Jonah the always open question, "Should I not pity ... ?"

Let us not mistake the nature of this difficult question. The LORD is not asking us to show what good Christians we are by being nice to people and trying to make them just like us. He is boldly, bizarrely, asking our permission to love our enemies (*we* have made them our enemies) so deeply that, by any measure we know how to use, these people whom we fear would undo our status as God's people look more like his beloved than we do. Can Jews rejoice that the LORD repents of the evil he threatened to do to Nineveh, to Babylon, to Rome? Can Christians rejoice that the Jews remain forever his chosen people, his dove, his fair one, the very apple of his eye? Can all of us on earth rejoice in such love from heaven? Our Father in heaven has himself issued the invitation: come, older brother, whoever you are who think you are *not* disobedient and resent the one who *is*—the prodigal who seems indeed to be more beloved than you are—come and join the celebration around the fatted calf. The rejoicing has already begun, and you too are invited.

SUBJECT INDEX

Abraham, 137, 157
adam, 160
Aeschylus, 69
Ahab, 114
Amittai, 30
Amos, 33
ancient Near Eastern mythology, 75, 106
anger
    of God, 120. *See also* wrath of God
    of Jonah, 128–29, 130, 152–53
anti-Semitism, 18
arise, 34, 41, 52
Aristotle, 68, 116
ashes, 114–15
Assyrian Empire, 31, 32–34, 74, 107, 142
Augustine, 71, 101, 117, 120, 123
Azazel, 56

Babylon, 35, 36, 76, 159
    Rome as, 160, 168
Babylonian exile, 32, 59, 88, 89, 91, 95, 101
Balaam, 137
baptism, 77, 105
Barth, Karl, 135
belief, 110
blessing, 116
blessing of the nations, 47, 135, 167
booth, 139–41
Branch, 141, 144
burning anger, 120, 128–29, 134, 141–42

call, against Nineveh, 37
captain, of the ship, 51–53, 54, 113, 115, 157, 160

cargo, 50, 65
casting lots, 55, 63
chance, 56
chaos, 75
cherubim, 139
Christendom, dissolution of, 51
Christians, attitudes toward Jews, 164–65, 170
church, identifies with Jonah, 51
city of God, 89
classical theism, 123–24
cleanliness, 70–71
clothing, 118
comedy, Jonah as, 17, 64, 72, 76, 96, 104
comfort, 20
commission, of Jonah, 27
consummation, 73
conversion, of Nineveh, 109–10
covenant loyalty, 100
cowardice, 40
creation, 48–49, 60
crucifixion, 95
cruelty, 119
crying out, 37, 49, 119
curse, 135

Damascus, 33
Dan, 42
Dante, 51
David, 98, 99–100, 143–44, 154. *See also* lineage
    of David
Davidic covenant, 154, 155
Day of Atonement, 56, 70
Day of the LORD, 49

death, 44, 83, 85, 87–88, 104, 156–57
deep, 74, 88, 104
deliverance, 146
descent, of Jonah, 44, 50, 52, 72, 75–76, 91, 94
digging, 67
discernment, 80, 161
disobedience, 39, 166
divine violence, 149
dove, 30
drowning, 95
dry land, 66–67, 104
dying, 95

east of the city, 139
east wind, 46, 149–51
eating, 117
Eber, 58
economics, 116–17
Eden, 139
Edom, 108, 135
Egyptians, 58–59
election, 56–57, 134–35
    and blessing of the nations, 167
Elijah, 31, 33, 34, 41, 114, 136, 137
Elisha, 31, 33, 34
emeth, 133, 153
empires, toppling of, 38
enemies, 99, 134
Enuma Elish, 92
Esau, 108, 135, 164, 170–73
eschatological banquet, 73, 79
eschatology, 83–84, 92, 102–3, 140, 145
ethics, as self-esteem, 164–65
ethnicity, 58
Eucharist, 102
evil, 37, 48, 55, 58, 122, 127
evil and adulterous generation, 79–81
exile, 32–33, 45, 64, 77, 86, 93. See also Babylonian
    exile
    of Jonah, 129, 139
Exodus, 29, 76, 94, 138–39, 141
experience, 29
Ezekiel, 44

face of the LORD, 37, 39–40 45–46, 47, 78, 90–92,
    96, 121
failure, and credibility of confession of faith, 64
faith, 110
famine, 150
fasting, 111, 113, 115, 117–18
fear
    of Jonah, 40, 130
    of sailors, 47–49, 62, 63

fear of the LORD, 52, 60, 61, 67, 72, 167
figural reading, 18
firstborn, 117
fish. See great fish
fleeing from the face of the LORD, 38–40, 46,
    62–63
flock, 116, 117
flood
    of Jonah, 47, 89–90, 93
    of Noah, 30, 46, 47, 72
fools, 29
footstool, 91, 123
foreigner, 59
forsake, 100
forty days, 108, 141

gaps, in narrative, 130
garbage, 70
gathering of the nations, 11, 73
Gath-hepher, 34
genealogies, of Messiah, 157
Gentile Christians, 165, 168–73
Gentiles, 20, 41
    compassion on, 47, 168
    prayer of, 67–68
    provoke Jews to jealousy, 59
    worship of God, 73–74, 102–3
God. See also LORD
    of all nations, 147
    control of lots, 63
    impassability of, 120, 123
    omnipresence, 96, 101
    omniscience, 39, 123
    outside time, 123
    pity of, 157, 158–59, 160, 166
    repentance of, 122–24
    sovereignty of, 74–75, 90
"God of heaven", 59–61, 63–64, 68–69, 91, 169
gourd, parable of, 21, 22, 46, 142–59, 166–67
grace, 53
gratitude, 73
great evil, 46, 127–28, 146
great fish, 46, 74–78, 104, 143
great joy, 146
greatness
    of the LORD, 46, 61, 63
    of Nineveh, 36, 46, 107, 161
great storm, 46–48, 63, 67
great wind, 46, 149
grieving, of Jonah, 127–28

Habiru, 58
Haggai, 143
Hasmoneans, 148
heart, 93
heart of the sea, 88–89, 91
heaven, 119, 123
Hebrew (term), 58–59
hell, 19, 88
herd, 116, 117
herem, 118
hesed, 100–101, 133, 153
Hezekiah, 113, 114
holiness, 91
holy of holies, 92
Holy Spirit, 30, 151
hope, 95, 100, 154, 156
Hoshea, 34
hosts, 144
house of David, 166, 168
human responsibility, 51, 52, 54
human wrath, 131
humility, 114

ichthus, 77
idolatry, 33
injustice, 37–38
innocent blood, 69
invocation, 53
Israel
    abandonment of, 21
    among the nations, 30, 45, 50
    as blessing for all nations, 135, 167
    captivity by Assyrians, 90–91, 100, 107
    helplessness of, 33
    as northern kingdom, 30–32
    pity for, 169–74
Israelite, 58
"Israelogical" reading of text, 19, 22

Jacob, 31, 135, 170–73
Jehoiachin, 143
Jeroboam I, 31, 33
Jeroboam II, 31, 33, 35
Jerusalem, 39, 41
Jesus Christ
    as eternal repentance of the LORD, 173
    humiliation of, 45
    identifies with Jonah, 40, 50, 72, 84
    as a Jew, 31
    in Old Testament, 19
    prayer at Gethsemane, 168
    prayer on the cross, 86

resurrection, 86
    sacrifice of, 70–71, 102
    as sign of Jonah, 17, 80
    as scapegoat, 56–57, 70
    triumphal entry, 32
Jews, 41
    as chosen people, 19
    in Babylonia, 159
    Christian attitudes toward, 164–65
    and Gentiles, 20, 73, 142
    as original readers of book, 32
Jezebel, 136
Job, 96, 115, 137
John Paul II, 146
Jonah (book)
    Christian reading of, 19
    as comedy, 17, 19, 64, 72, 76, 96, 104
    open-endedness of, 20
    as parable, 36
Jonah (prophet)
    calling on the name of the LORD, 85
    calms sea, 71
    confession of faith, 59, 63
    descent of, 44, 50, 52, 72, 75–76, 91, 94
    as false prophet, 127–28, 133, 137
    guilt of, 62, 63, 65, 66
    as LORD's dove, 104, 131
    name, 30
    points to Christ, 66, 80
    prayer of, 83–103
    prayer of complaint, 129–37
    as prophet, 54, 68, 69
    request to die, 137–38, 151–53, 155, 160
    swallowed up, 76–78
Joppa, 41, 42–43
Josephus, 148
Joshua (high priest), 143
Josiah, 114
joy, 146
Judah
    in Babylon, 35–36, 76, 86, 101
    as southern kingdom, 31–32
Julian of Norwich, 72
justice, 87, 132, 134
justification by faith, 70

kingdom of God, 32
king of Nineveh, 113–21, 157, 160
knowing God, 29

Lamentations, 96
laughing, 19

law of Moses, 32
Lazarus, 138
Leviathan, 74, 75, 76, 104
life, 68–69
lightening, of cargo, 50, 65
lineage of David, 21, 22, 144, 149, 154
livestock, 116–17, 118, 161
LORD, 28–29. *See also* God
  mercy on Jonah, 87
  presence, 39
  repenting of evil, 134–36
  sovereignty, 46
  vengeance on enemies, 134
Lord's Prayer, 146
love, for enemies, 174
loving-kindness, 46, 100–101, 120, 124, 133,
    134–35, 161, 171, 173

Mammon, 49–50
Medes, 35
Mediterranean Sea, 40–41, 42
Menahem, King, 33
mercy, 46, 87, 100, 120, 122, 132–33, 134
message, to Nineveh, 106–9
messenger, 35
Messiah, 99, 144, 149, 159
messianic Jews, 172, 173
miracles, 79–80
mission, 35
mist, 99
money, 43
moralism, 18, 164
Moses, 94, 113, 134, 137
mountains, 94
murderous heart, 169–71
mystery, of the gourd, 142, 149, 158

Nahum, 37–38, 132, 134
Naomi, 100
Nazareth, 34
Nebuchadnezzar, 76
neck, 93, 97
neighbors, 54–55
new covenant, 30
Nietzsche, Friedrich, 110–11
nightling, 156–57
Nineveh, 20, 31
  as capital of Assyria, 32, 35–36
  conversion of, 128, 130
  overturning of, 109–11
  pity for, 158, 159, 166–67
  repentance of, 81, 110–23

Noah, 30, 46, 47, 68, 72
northern kingdom, 30–33, 74, 100, 101, 142
northern prophets, 34

obedience, 106
O'Connor, Flannery, 83
older brother (parable of prodigal son), 164,
    169–71, 174
Old Testament, 17, 19, 80
open theism, 123–24
opulence, 44
overturning, 109, 112, 127–28

pagan, prayers of, 53
parable, Jonah as, 36
Paul, 41, 43, 59, 149, 172–73
peace, 30
Pekah, 34
Peter, 41, 42–43
Pharaoh, 94, 109, 113, 135
Pharisees, 79–80
Philistines, 42, 59
pillar of cloud and fire, 141
pit, 88, 96–97
pity, 155, 156, 157, 158–59, 160, 166
plagues, 116–17, 150
plant. *See* gourd
port cities, 42
poverty, 83, 112
power, 43–44
prayer, 52, 92, 121
pride, 147–48
prodigal son, parable of, 169–71, 174
profane, 43
promises of God, 92
prophets, 131
propitiation, 65–66, 69
prosperity, 116
protection, 140–41, 145
providence, 34, 143, 147
psalms, 99–100
pun, 128

Queen of the South, 79

Rahab, 75, 76
redemption, 66
Red Sea, 75, 88, 94
reeds, 94
religious pluralism, 49, 63
remembrance, 97–98
  of the LORD, 101

repentance, 67, 100, 112–15, 122
  of the LORD, 122–24, 134–36, 158
  of Nineveh, 110–23
resurrection, 52, 83, 98
  from exile, 86
reverence, 60
rod of Jesse, 143, 144, 149
Roman Empire, 168
Rome, 160
ruach, 150–51
Ruth, 100

Sabbath, 161
sackcloth, 112–14, 117–18, 161
sacred space, 41, 43
sacrifice, 70–71, 102
sailors, 46, 47, 73, 111
salvation, 61, 103
Samaria, 34, 35, 107
Saul of Tarsus, 41, 43
scapegoat, 56–57, 70, 166
sea, 41, 67, 74–75, 87–89
  calming of, 71–72
sea monsters, 74–76, 104
Sea of Reeds, 94
self-abasement, 112
self-esteem, 164–65
self-righteousness, 18–19, 53, 134, 164, 170
sending, 35
Sennacherib, 113
shade, 140–41, 144, 145
Shakespeare, William, 72
shame, 153–54, 156
Sheol, 85, 87–88, 90, 91, 95, 97, 104, 154, 157, 173
shepherd, 99–100, 117
ships, 43, 44
shoot, 143
Sidon, 41–42
sign of Jonah, 17, 21, 34, 78–81, 166
silence, of Jonah, 54, 86
sin, 87
sleep, 50–53
slow to anger, 131–33, 134–35
smite, 147
sociology of religion, 49
Sodom and Gomorrah, 37, 108–9, 118, 128, 142, 159
Solomon, 79, 80, 123
Son of David, 98, 100, 143, 149, 157, 158, 159, 168
Son of the night, 156, 159
soul, 68–69, 93, 97, 136, 151
southern kingdom, 31–32

Spirit of the LORD, 150–51
steadfast love, 100
storm, 46, 63
stump of Jesse, 143, 144, 149, 157
suffering, 19
suffocation, 95
sukkah. See booth
Sukkoth, 139–40, 145
sun, 151
supplication, 52
Syrophoenician woman, 42

tabernacle, 145
Tabitha, 42
Tarshish, 40–41, 43, 44
Tarsus, 41, 43
taste, 117
temple, 39, 91–92, 98, 99, 123
  rebuilding of, 92, 100, 102, 143
tent of meeting, 145
terror, 60
thanksgiving, of Jonah, 102
three days, 78, 107
throat, 97
Tiglath-pileser III, 35
Torah, 140
truth, 30
truth of the LORD, 133, 153
turning from evil ways, 119, 121–22
typology, 18
Tyre, 42, 44

unbelief, 40, 79–81, 138, 163, 169
uncleanness, 70–71, 166

vanity, 99, 101, 161
vapor, 99
vengefulness, 134
vigil, 52
vindication, of name of the LORD, 131
violence, 119
voice, of voiceless, 86
vows of sacrifice and praise, 73

wakefulness, and prayer, 52
water, 117–18
water torture, 95
watery chaos, 75
wealth, 43–44, 116
widow of Zarephath, 41
wilderness, 107–8
wind, 46, 150. *See also* east wind

wisdom, 60, 161
withering, 150
  of gourd, 147–49, 154
  of Jonah, 151
  of messianic line, 153–54
witness, 64
women, missing in book of Jonah, 157
word of the Lord, 27, 34, 65, 106
works righteousness, 53

worm, 46, 147, 149
wrath of God, 20, 65–66, 90, 118, 120, 131,
  132–33, 134, 140

Xenophon, 116

Zechariah, 143
Zerubbabel, 143–44, 145, 146, 148, 150, 157

SCRIPTURE INDEX

Acts

2:27 97, 168
3:25 40
7:49 123
9:36–43 42
10:9–16 42
10:28 42
13:35 97
17:6 110

Amos

3:6 122
4:11 108
6:14 33
7:3 122
7:6 122
7:9–11 33
8:10 109
9:2–4 101
9:11 141

1 Chronicles

3:18 143
3:19–24 148
12:22 53
28:2 91, 123
29:11–12 156

2 Chronicles

2:16 42
7:14 112
9:21 41

32 113
32:14 118
32:26 114
36:23 59

Colossians

1:26–27 149
3:1–4 92

1 Corinthians

1:27–28 157
3:6 144, 156
15:20 85, 157

2 Corinthians

5:1–2 145

Daniel

7 80

Deuteronomy

5:14 161
5:32 161
6:15 128
7:1–5 42
7:7 57, 70
7:7–9 56
7:13–14 116
7:16 155
13:8 155
13:15–16 118
16:13 139

16:14 140
16:16 139
19:13 155
19:21 155
23:5 109
25:12 155
28:4 116
28:11 116
28:14 161
29:23 108
30:9 116
30:19 103, 121
31:12–13 140
32:10 169
32:39 147

Ecclesiastes

9:14 90

Ephesians

2:1 87, 98
2:14–16 172
4:8 85, 104
5:15 52

Esther

4:1 114
9:22 109

Exodus

1:15–16 59
2:3 94

2:5 94
2:6–7 59
2:11–13 59
3:7 37
3:9 37
3:14 29, 133
3:15 28
3:18 59, 109
5:3 59, 78
6:7 169
7:5 109
7:15 109
7:16 59
7:17 109
8:10 109
8:17–18 116
9:9–10 116
9:19 116
9:22 116
9:25 116
10:3 59
10:13 150
11:5 116
12:12 116
12:29 116
12:41 139
13:2 117
13:3 123
13:3 4 139
13:9 123
13:11–16 117
13:14 123
13:16 123
13:20–21 141
14:21 150
15:5 88
15:8 88–89
15:10 89
16:3 152
20:2 88
20:4 94
20:10 161
20:16 55
20:17 116
24:18 108
32:11–14 120, 134
33:19 122, 132
34:6 100, 120, 153
34:6–7 46, 131–32
36:31–33 95
40:34–38 141

Ezekiel

2:2 151
4:1–17 142
4:6 108
5:1–12 142
12:1–16 142
12:17–20 142
16:49–50 37
17 150
18:31–32 121
19:4 146
19:8–9 146
19:14 150
24:15–27 142
27:25–27 44
27:26 88, 150
27:27 88
31:6 143
33:11 123
33:14–15 123
34 99
36:23 131
36:26–27 123
37:15–28 142

Ezra

1:2 59
2:2 143
3:4 140
3:7 42
3:8 143
4:1–4 74, 103
4:2–3 143
4:4 32
4:24 143
5:1–2 143
5:11–12 59
6:9–10 59
6:13–14 143
7:12 59
7:21 59
7:23 59
7:25 32
8:22 100

Galatians

1:13 173

Genesis

1:3 103
1:7 94

1:21 75
1:22 116
1:28 116
2:16–17 106
2:20 161
2:24 100
3:1–3 106
3:13 61
3:24 139
4:10 61
6:6 122
7:11 94
7:17 108
8:2 94
8:10–11 30
9:3–6 68
9:11 72
9:13–17 30
10:11–12 107
11:16–27 58
12:3 40, 57, 135, 167, 172
15:6 110
16:4 50
17:7 169
18–19 37
18:20 37, 119
18:21 37
19:4 90
19:13 37
19:21 108
19:25 108
19:29 108
21:23 100
22:18 40
24:1–8 106
24:35–41 106
24:49 100
27 170
27:4 106
27:7 106
27:19 106
27:31 106
28:14 40, 57
29:25 61
29:31 144
30:22 144
31:26 61
32:11 146
32:13–21 172
32:28 31
33:4 172
33:10–11 172

37:21 146
39:14 59
41:6 150
42:25 112
42:27 112
42:35 112
43:32 59
47:29 100

Habakkuk

1:13 122

Haggai

1:1 143
1:12–14 143
2:21–23 144

Hebrews

5:14 161
11:17–19 157
11:19 83

Hosea

1–3 142
8:8 76
13:15 150

Isaiah

2:12–17 44
4:2 141, 144
4:5 141
4:5–6 144
4:6 141
11:1 157
13:16 159
13:19 108, 159
19:24–25 36
24:18–10 48
25:4 140
25:4–5 140
25:6–8 73
27:8 150
29:8 97
36–37 113
40:7 150
40:7–8 147
40:9 118
40:22–23 60
40:23–24 148
42:1 151

42:8 28, 103
43:1–2 76
45:7 122
45:23 103
49:6 50
49:15 169
49:19 76
51:9–10 75
52:7 38
58:5 114
59:1 96
60:4–9 73
60:9 41
60:21 145
61:1 151
61:3 145
64:5 128
65:5 18
66:1 123
66:19–21 73

Jeremiah

6:19 122
7:15 91
11:11 122
18:7–8 122
18:8 122
18:11 119
18:17 150
19 142
19:3 122
23:12 122
23:23–24 96
23:24 52
25:5 119
26:3 119, 122
26:6 106
26:9 106
26:13 122
26:19 122
29:5–6 76
31:13 109
31:33 12, 145
32:42 122
35:15 119
36:3 119
42:10 122
49:18 108
50:40 108, 159
51:25 111, 134

51:34 76
51:37 159

Job

1:21 147
2:8 115
3 137
3:25–26 65
9:14–18 129
23:3–7 129
36:29 141
38:11 75
42:7 121

Joel

1:10–12 148
1:11 153
1:14 111
2:13 114
2:13–14 119
2:15 111
2:28–29 151
2:31 109

John

1:1 27
1:5 138
1:14 145
2:19–21 102
2:19–22 92
3:8 150
7:1 31
11:4 138
11:25 98
11:25–27 138
11:32–35 138
11:43–44v98
11:58 120
15:13 66
15:16 43

1 John

4:18 60

Jonah

1 87, 111, 113, 115, 159, 167
1:1 27–34, 154
1:1–2 17
1:2 34–38, 46, 55, 58, 105, 107,
    119, 121, 156

1:3 38–45, 94, 106, 113, 130
1:4 45–47, 67, 149, 150, 156
1:5 47–51, 53, 60, 65, 94
1:6 37, 51–54, 62, 63, 68, 84,
   121, 137, 156, 160
1:7 54–57, 58
1:7–8 66
1:8 57–58, 61, 129
1:9 53, 58–61, 69, 74, 91, 104,
   119
1:10 20, 58, 61–64, 65, 67, 72,
   156
1:11 64–65, 67
1:12 65–66, 67, 70
1:12–13 69
1:13 66–67
1:14 37, 67–70, 129, 136
1:15 57, 70–72
1:16 53, 61, 67, 72–74, 102,
   121, 146, 156
1:17 46, 74–78, 143, 147, 149
2 19, 45, 87, 137, 166
2:1 83, 85
2:2 37, 83–87, 119, 121
2:3 87–90, 93
2:4 90–92, 98, 99
2:5 76
2:6 94–97, 99
2:7 97–99
2:8 99–101, 129
2:9 102–103, 124, 129, 134
2:10 103–104
3 166
3:1 105
3:2 36, 37, 46, 105–106, 107,
   156
3:3 32, 36, 46, 78, 106–107,
   113, 137
3:4 36, 107–10, 136, 141, 144
3:5 56, 61, 70, 110–12, 115,
   119, 142, 147
3:5–7 110
3:6 112–15
3:7 46, 115–18
3:7–8 160
3:8 37, 66, 118–19, 161
3:9 54, 67, 70, 115, 119–21,
   123, 128, 129, 137, 142, 156,
   160, 161
3:10 121–25, 134
4:1 46, 127–29, 146, 152

4:2 40, 60, 101, 115, 120, 124,
   129–36, 161
4:3 108, 136–37, 151, 152
4:4 137–38, 152
4:5 111, 138–42
4:5–6 129
4:6 46, 147, 149, 156
4:7 46, 147–49, 150, 151
4:7–9 154
4:8 46, 147, 149–52
4:9 138
4:10 147, 154–58
4:11 36, 46, 47, 107, 158–61

Joshua
1:14 53
7:19 58
10:4 53
19:46 42
19:47–48 42
24:16 100

Judges
2:12 100
6:9 146
8:34 146
15:11 61
18 42
19:22 90
20:5 90
20:48 118

Judith
4:10 118

1 Kings
3:9 161
8:27 91, 123
8:27–40 39
8:60 28
9:3 39
9:9 122
9:26 42
10:22 43
11:26–12:19 31
12:10–11 106
12:14 106
12:25–33 33
14:10 122
16:31 50

17:8–24 41
17:9 34
18:34–36 113
19:2 136
19:3 136
19:4 108, 136
19:10–13 113
19:13 114
19:19 114
19:35–37 113
20:12–16 141
21:18 34
21:20–21 114
21:21 122
21:27 114
21:28–20 114
22:48 41

2 Kings
1:3 34
2:9 151
2:11 136
2:13–14 114
2:16v151
3:18 50
3:19 147
3:25 147
5:7 114
6:15 90
6:18 147
6:30 114
7:5 107
8:21 90, 147
14:23 33
14:25 33
14:25–27 30
14:26–27 33
14:28 33
15:8–15 33
15:17–22 34
15:29 34
17:3–4 34
17:5 34, 78
17:13–14 119
17:20 91
17:24–41 74
18–19 113
18:19 113
19:1 114
22:11 114
22:19–20 114

23:25–26 121
24:14 32

Lamentations

2:16 76
3:23 124
4:6 108
4:20 146
5:15 109
5:22 128

Leviticus

16:8 56
16:21–22 70
19:18 55
23:43 139
26:12 169

Luke

1:38 158
1:46 158
1:52 113
3:21–22 30
3:27 157
4:24–27 34
4:25–26 42
6:17 42
8:22–25 50
10:13 114
10:13–14 42, 110
10:29–37 74
11:29–32 79
11:32 42, 110
13:29 73
15:20 172
15:21 170
15:29 170
15:31 169
15:32 169
18:14 112
19:44 80
20:38 98
22:42 168
22:46 52
22:54–62 169

Malachi

1:2–3 135, 171
4:6 147

Mark

1:10–11 30
3:8 42
4:35–41 50
7:24–30 42
8:11–12 78, 79
14:38 52
15:34 99

Matthew

1:12 157
3:9 110
3:16–17 30
5:35 123
6:9 28
8:11 73
8:23–27 50
11:21 114
11:21–22 42, 110
12:38–42 79
12:41 42, 110
13:1–23 108
13:10–17 142
15:21–28 42
16:1–4 78, 79
16:17 41
16:26 68, 136
17:20 110
21:1–10 149
21:12–14 149
21:33–46 66
26:41 52
27:24 69

Nahum

1:2 134
1:2–3 132
1:7 38
1:15 38
3:1 37, 133
3:1–3 119
3:19 37

Nehemiah

1:4–5 59
2:20 59
7:7 143
8:13–18 140
9:11 88

Mark

9:17–31 132
9:31–32 64
13:2 109

Numbers

3:13 117
11:1 128
11:24–29 151
11:33 147
14:2–3 152
14:17–19 132
22:12 139
22:41 139
23 137
23:6 139
23:8 139
23:11 139
23:13 139
24:9 135
24:10 139

Obadiah

10 135

2 Peter

1:13–14 145

Philippians

2:8–9 112
2:9–11 28, 74
2:10–11 103

Proverbs

1:7 67
1:12 44
9:10 60, 67
25:25 97
30:19 88

Psalms

1:1 139
6:3 154
11:4 123
13:1 154
18:4–5 93–94
18:11 141
22:1 86
22:15 148
22:20–31 99
22:31 86

23:1 117
23:4 85, 92
23:5 99, 100
24:2 94
25:10 133
28:1 44
30:3 44, 97
30:11 109
33:6–8 60–61
36:5 153
36:6 161
40:10–11 133
42:7 90
42:9–10 96
46:1 53
46:1–3 89
46:5–6 89
48:7 150
51 100
51:17 112
51:18–19 99
51:19 102
57:10 133
65:6–7 89
66:13–16 73
69:1–2 93
69:14–15 93
71:13 153
73 92
73:17 92
74:10 154
74:13–14 75
79:5 154
80:4 154
85:10 133
86:7 84
86:13 97
88:4 44
88:6 88
88:7 90
88:11 153
88:16–17 90
89:1 153
89:2 153
89:2–3 154
89:5–13 154
89:14 133
89:19–37 154
89:24 153
89:33 153
89:38–39 154
89:45 154

89:46 154
89:47–48 156
89:49 153
89:50–51 154
90:5–6 147
90:13 154
90:17 155
92:2 153
95:3 37, 61
95:5 60, 69, 74
96:15 132
98:3 153
99:5 91, 123
100:5 154
102:25–26 156
103:8 132
103:11 100
104:3 123
104:10–13 94
104:24–26 74
104:26 104
105:10 169
107:23 41
107:23–27 48
108:4 133
111:4 132
114:1 139
115:1 133
116:3 94
116:12 73
116:17–19 73
118:1–4 100
118:5 84
118:10–12 90
120:1 84
121:5–6 151
124:1–5 77, 89
130:1 84
130:5–6 154
132:7 91, 123
132:17 149
136 100
136:6 94
137:1 86
137:6 92
137:9 159
139 101
139:2 39
139:3 51
139:7–10 96
139:15 156

143:7 44
145:3 46
145:8 132
145:8–9 46
148:5 74, 103
148:7 74

Revelation

7:10 103
7:15–16 145
11:18 134
18 160
18:2 36
18:16 36
18:17–19 45
20:13 83
21:1 30
21:3 145

Romans

4:3 110
4:11 110
4:17 157
8:20 161
9:3 169, 172
9:11–12 56
9:15 121
9:21 57
11:5 57
11:11 172
11:11–14 115
11:14 59
11:26 172
11:33 57
12:21 134

Ruth

1:8 100
1:16 100
2:11 100
3:10 100

1 Samuel

2:6 147
4:8 146
7:3 146
7:14 146
10:6 109
10:19–21 55
12:10 146

13:11 61
14:11 59
14:21 59
14:40–42 55
14:43 58
15 118
15:3 106
15:11 122
15:18 106
17:34–37 100
18:23 50
29:3 59

2 Samuel

10:11 53
22:5–6 94
22:5–7 98
22:12 141

Song of Songs

1:15 30
2:3 146
2:14 30

Zechariah

2:8 30
3–4 143
3:8 144
4:6 144
4:7 144
6:12 144
9:9–10 32, 149
11:1 144
14:16 73, 140
14:17–19 140

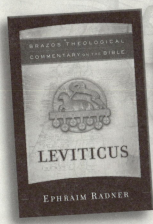

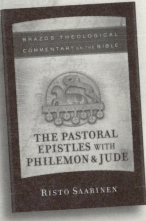